STUDIES IN LEGAL HISTORY

Published in association with the American Society for Legal History

Editor: Stanley N. Katz

Volumes in the Series

Frederic William Maitland: A Life *C. H. S. Fifoot*

Impeachment: The Constitutional Problems *Raoul Berger*

The Autobiographical Notes of Charles Evans Hughes
David J. Danelski and Joseph S. Tulchin, eds.

Prosecuting Crime in the Renaissance:
England, Germany, France *John H. Langbein*

Jefferson's Louisiana: Politics and the Clash of Legal Traditions
George Dargo

Americanization of the Common Law: The Impact of Legal Change on Massachusetts Society, 1760-1830
William E. Nelson

Jefferson's Louisiana:

Politics and the Clash of Legal Traditions

George Dargo

Harvard University Press
Cambridge, Massachusetts
1975

Library of Congress Catalog Card Number 74-25036
ISBN 0-674-47370-1
Printed in the United States of America

To my mother
and the memory of my father,
Nathan Dargo

. . . he also taught the people knowledge;
yea, he pondered, and sought out,
and set in order many proverbs.

Megillat Kohelet 12:9

Preface

In the study of history fruitful inquiry often stems from simple questions. During the preliminary research for this book I happened to tell a friend—a practicing New Orleans attorney—of my interest in the efforts to secure continental civil law as the foundation of the Louisiana legal system during the early years of American territorial rule. To my tentative questions as to why the civil law became established he responded with one of his own. "Why not?" he asked—a simple and understandable query but one which, I later concluded, was based upon faulty assumptions and insufficient historical information. His "why not?" presupposed that there were no viable alternatives to the civil law, that the overwhelming majority of the Louisiana population was committed to it, and, therefore, that it was as natural for Louisiana to be "civilian" in its legal orientation as for Virginia or New York to follow the English common law. In fact, the options were not foreclosed in advance. The final consolidation and permanent establishment of the civil law was not inevitable despite popular preferences. For powerful political and social forces were working to transform the legal institutions of Louisiana, and, but for the intrusion of unforeseen historical events, the life of the civil law in Lower Louisiana might very well have ended.

In short, in this book I argue that an important chapter in American legal history, in this case the redaction, in 1808, of the civil law digest—often referred to as Louisiana's first civil code—cannot be fully understood and appreciated if the historical analysis is confined to the legal parameters of the problem alone. Thus the reader will find that the first introductory chapter "locates" the problem by describing, in broad terms, what Louisiana and its people were like in the early nineteenth century and how its law differed with American law in some exemplary particulars. The next three chapters tell three separate but related stories. Chapter 2 is an analysis of the regime presided over by the man who governed in Lower Louisiana throughout the territorial period. Chapters 3 and 4 trace the impact of two major controversies that erupted in the years just prior to the adoption of the Louisiana digest. And then the last three chapters deal with the development of the conflict of legal traditions. The structure of the book rests upon the fundamental assumption that the partial resolution of this conflict cannot be fully comprehended unless it is viewed in its complete historical context.

This volume, then, is an answer to my lawyer-friend's question. Some of its chapters deal with matters that legal historians would prefer to leave to generalists, but I believe that they are part of the whole story. It is a book which straddles the frontiers of political, social, *and* legal history, for it attempts to make connections between legal problems and the kinds of issues which interest general historians. In these chapters I try to show how political developments outside the boundaries of legal controversy affected the outcome of that controversy, how the arguments surrounding the question of civil law versus common law reception were expressed and with what public perceptions and effects, and how competing elements in a dynamic process of cultural change interacted and eventually reached some kind of accommodation. Law, after all, comprehends all of man's experience, and legal history should reflect the multidimensional forces shaping its evolution.

This book has had an evolution of its own, and I welcome this opportunity to express my gratitude to those who have helped to shape it. It began as a doctoral dissertation at Columbia University, and I am especially indebted to professors James P. Shenton, Richard B. Morris, and Eric L. McKitrick who read, commented upon, and criticized my work. I am also deeply grateful to Professor Stanley N. Katz of the University of Chicago Law School, the editor of the Harvard Studies in Legal History, who patiently read the original manuscript and recommended numerous changes which together served to sharpen the focus of the book considerably. A number of other scholars have also generously given me the benefit of their knowledge and insight. Professor Robert A. Pascal of the Louisiana State University School of Law wrote detailed critiques of my work and was particularly helpful on technical matters. Nina N. Pugh, clerk of the Louisiana Court of Appeals, gave me the benefit of her judgments respecting a number of legal issues pertinent to chapters 4 and 7. Professor Lawrence M. Friedman of Stanford University Law School kindly gave me his reactions to points raised in the text plus his wisdom on the state of American law in this period of our history. Colleagues at The City College of New York offered a number of useful suggestions at a meeting of the History Department's faculty seminar. Naturally, responsibility for technical, factual, or interpretive errors which may remain is completely mine.

Many archivists and librarians gave unsparingly of their knowledge, time, and experience, but I wish to express special appreciation to Margaret Ruckert of the Louisiana Room of the New Orleans Public Library. She and her staff offered me every courtesy and complete access to the valuable sources in that repository and were extremely helpful in suggesting other places I might profitably visit.

My good friend, Dr. Isidore Budick, urged me to pursue this subject at a time when I most needed encouragement. Another close friend, Ms. Rhoda Chester, applied her fine sense of style to an early draft of this work. Mr. and Ms. René Lehmann of New Orleans extended their gracious hospitality during a hot summer in Louisiana and served as amiable guides to the batture, which I had to see for myself.

A grant from the Social Science Division of The City College of New York enabled me to bring my final draft to completion. Gladys Hartman retyped much of the manuscript in preparation for the printer. Aida DiPace Donald and Elizabeth Suttell of the editorial staff of Harvard University Press answered my every question and efficiently guided the book through the production process. Catherine Martin did a truly professional job of copyediting.

Finally, I am grateful to my wife Lois for her forbearance as well as for her advice on what sometimes must have seemed to be redrafts without end. Also, a word of thanks to Jessica and Stephen for leaving me enough typing paper to finish the job and who would be disappointed were they not to find their names in this book.

For permission to quote directly from manuscript sources I wish to express particular thanks to the following archives: Manuscript Department, William R. Perkins Library, Duke University (Durham, N. C.), for use of the Joseph Dubreuil de Villars Papers, the Ephraim Kirby Papers, and the John M. McCalla Papers; Department of Archives and Manuscripts, Louisiana State University (Baton Rouge), for use of the Nathaniel Evans Papers; Historical Society of Pennsylvania (Philadelphia), for use of the Gilpin Family Papers and the Simon Gratz Papers; New-York Historical Society (New York City), for use of the Robert R. Livingston Papers, the Albert Gallatin Papers, and the Van Duzer Miscellaneous Papers; Manuscripts and Archives Division, The New York Public Library, Astor, Lenox and Tilden Foundations, for use of the Peters Family Letters; Lorenzo State Historic Site, New York State Division for Historic Preservation (Cazenovia), for use of the Judge Strawbridge Diary; Church Historical Society

(Austin, Texas) for use of a letter to the Rev. John H. Hobart in the Protestant Episcopal Church Archives; Special Collections Division, Tulane University Library (New Orleans), for use of the Memoire of Bernard Marigny; and Alderman Library, University of Virginia (Charlottesville), for use of a letter in the Jefferson Papers.

In those few places where the original spelling in a quotation was inaccurate or unclear, I have simply made the correction without bracketing it. I have let stand all original capitalization and abbreviations.

Contents

Introduction

1. Jefferson's Louisiana: Land, People, Law 3

The Problems of Colonial Rule

2. William C. C. Claiborne and the Politics of Territorial Government 23
3. Burr's Conspiracy and the Orleans Territory 51
4. Edward Livingston and the New Orleans Batture 74

The Clash of Legal Traditions

5. Common Law vs. Civil Law: First Phase 105
6. Common Law vs. Civil Law: Second Phase 128
7. The Louisiana Civil Law Digest 154

Notes 177

Selected Sources 241

Index 253

Introduction

[1] *Jefferson's Louisiana: Land, People, Law*

For Jefferson's contemporaries, Lower Louisiana was a foreign country, a distant and forbidding land given to extremes of climate and topography and inhabited by an exotic people. A medical student, visiting in 1803, likened himself to Columbus discovering the New World, and, some years later, a more experienced observer could still write that the Louisiana country "even at this day, is less known than any other (inhabited by a civilized people) of the same extent on the globe."[1]

Many visitors came by sea, and their first impression may well have been one of overwhelming desolation as they entered the mouth of the Mississippi at the Balize, over one hundred miles southeast of New Orleans. The journey from the estuary to the city often consumed the better part of two weeks, and during the oppressively slow voyage upstream there was little to relieve the barren landscape of the deep delta.[2] "We entered the river in the afternoon," one early arrival reported. "As long as daylight would permit us a view nothing appeared but a dull uniform marsh covered with reeds . . . no cheering prospect to refresh the eye. All around is one dead level."[3] A French traveler described the mouth of the river as wearing "an aspect monotonous, sad and uninviting. A low and swampy shore, in many parts drowned by the river, uninhabited and uninhabitable where only a wild and misshapen vegetation subsists."[4] The first signs of civilization were visible along the river twenty-seven miles below the city, but they were "most wretched looking places . . . surrounded by boundless swamps [and] the . . . inhabitants breathe an air loaded with noxious exhalations."[5]

Not until the visitor reached the "English Turn" eighteen miles from New Orleans, where the meandering Mississippi described an almost complete circle, did more concentrated settlement begin. From here to distant Baton Rouge the lay of the land, and the unusual height of the river relative to it, forced riparian planters to shore up the banks as "levees" against seasonal overflows. To the traveler sailing to New Orleans for the first time, the levee added a peculiar dimension of unreality to his view. Only rooftops and treetops were visible from the boat deck for the water level was above the land.[6]

New Orleans at this time gave the appearance more of "a great straggling town than of a city." Surrounded by palisades in a partial state of decomposition, it stretched for one mile along the "eastern coast" of the Mississippi and penetrated a third of a mile inland. On its southwestern side a substantial suburb had grown up as the immigrant population from the United States had begun to spill over the town's original boundaries. Impressions of the bustling little metropolis varied. One visitor could scarcely imagine a more uninviting place, but another was enchanted with it.[7]

It partly depended on the season. The most delightful months were from late fall to early spring, but from June to early November the city was vulnerable to ravages of "fever." Smallpox, dysentery, and malaria were not uncommon, but yellow fever caused acute panic, probably because of its novelty. Indeed, the older residents accused the Americans of having brought it with them, and it was but small comfort to the Latin population that yellow fever seemed to strike the newcomers with greater frequency and virulence.[8] In addition, poor drainage, the lack of pavement, the pools of stagnant water at the bottom of the ditches near the city's dilapidated forts, the absence of proper sewage, and the irregular disposal of refuse and waste made the streets "a common sewer, a sink of nastiness, dirt and corruption" and fouled the warm summer breezes with stench.[9] Add to this the great swarms of mosquitos, and it is readily understandable why a northerner could conclude that "a summer residence in New Orleans must be extremely disagreeable."[10]

Just above New Orleans, however, the scene was markedly different. A nearly uninterrupted string of adjacent plantations lined both coasts of the river for many miles. From New Orleans to the Iberville River lay the wealthiest, the most comfortable, and the most densely populated area in all of Louisiana.[11] Here the pattern of cultivation was uniform because of the character of the local terrain. The land sloped downward from high riverbanks to low cypress swamps, so that cultivation was possible only in the narrow strip in between.

The French first established the standard size of a Mississippi land grant at eight arpents of riverfront width by forty arpents of depth, but there was no uniform plantation size by the time America took possession of the region.[12] For one thing, the French and Spanish maintained a system of forced heirship and partible inheritance, so that there was a tendency for riverfront lots to be subdivided into ever-narrowing strips. Moreover, the bends in the river altered the size of holdings on opposite banks.

Grantees on the convex side of a meander received more than the standard allotment, while those on the concave side got less. In order to encourage continuous settlement on both banks of the river, therefore, the Spanish permitted disadvantaged landowners to acquire multiple lots.[13] Along the other lowland waterways—the bayous Teche and Lafourche and the Vermillion River—the pattern of land cultivation and settlement resembled that which prevailed on the Mississippi.

Sugar cane was the staple of agricultural production in the lowland region below Pointe Coupée. Indigo had been the major crop of the eighteenth century, but successive crop failures in the early 1790's brought about a rapid change to sugar cultivation once a marketable variety was harvested successfully in 1795. By 1803 sugar plantations were concentrated along the main watercourses of the delta.[14] Above the Iberville cotton was rapidly replacing tobacco as a staple of the export trade. Fruits and vegetables plus a wide variety of other agricultural products were raised locally to serve domestic needs as well as for export. Fresh meat supplies came from the prairie districts west of Bayou Teche.[15]

Travel throughout the delta was mainly by water, and in spring communication from one place to another by any other means was virtually impossible. To some extent Louisiana's natural network of inland navigation was a great boon to settlement, since it meant that remote areas could maintain contact with the port at New Orleans. On the other hand, the principal rivers and bayous flowed on a roughly north-south axis, and consequently travel east and west could be quite roundabout and prolonged. Upstream journeys to distant settlements often took three to four weeks, while the downstream voyage, though much swifter, could be impeded by numerous navigational hazards.[16] Some land transportation did exist. Levees along the major rivers and bayous served also as roadways, the best example being the River Road along the Mississippi. Two other "highways" were the Old Spanish Trail, connecting Baton Rouge with the west, and the Nacogdoches-Natchitoches route, which went all the way to Natchez.[17]

While Natchitoches remained French in this period, other outlying settlements of Lower Louisiana attracted large numbers of Americans. The rich prairie soil, dry climate, mild winters, and good grazing lands of Opelousas and Atakapas offered excellent prospects for incoming Americans fearful of the delta's semitropical dampness, heat, disease, and general discomfort. Less well known and but sparsely inhabited were the lands along the Ouachita and Red rivers in the north and northwest. Here too the rich soil, the agricultural potential, the temperate climate, and the natural navigation system attracted immigrants from the United States.[18]

II

Thus, in spite of the unusual hazards to health, the vicissitudes of climate, and the isolation of the region, Lower Louisiana offered singular attractions for Americans. The amplitude of its space, the quality of its soil, and the pleasantness of its more remote reaches drew immigrants from the United States in ever-increasing numbers after the American takeover of all Louisiana late in 1803.

Indeed, Louisiana soon experienced a genuine population boom. Early in 1804, President Thomas Jefferson spoke of "the rage for going to that country," and the available statistics support his observation.[19] An official report indicated that the total population in 1803 was in the neighborhood of 43,000. Four years later, a local census put the figure at 53,000, and by 1810 the number had climbed to 76,000, an increase of over 75 percent in seven years. New Orleans itself passed through a minor population explosion. The number of inhabitants in the city proper rose from 8,000 to 17,000 in the 1803-1810 period.[20]

There were several reasons for this rapid growth. Undoubtedly immigration played a role. American settlers were the largest single group, but newcomers from the West Indies, and even some German redemptioners, also arrived between 1803 and 1806. In the spring and summer of 1809 some 5,700 mostly French-speaking refugees—whites, free blacks, and slaves—poured into the territory, the last major French migration to Lower Louisiana. In addition, slave smuggling continued throughout these years. It was difficult to patrol the coasts, and human contraband was brought into the territory via the bays, inlets, and bayous along the gulf.[21] Natural increase was another important cause of population growth. Family size was notoriously large. Some attributed the birth rate to the unusual properties in drinking water drawn from the Mississippi. A French traveler who interested himself in such matters stated it as fact "that women who in other parts of the world never breed, have become pregnant in a year after their arrival in Louisiana."[22] Whatever the cause of the high fertility, its effect was further to augment the growth rate.

The size of the population was in itself important. Lower Louisiana would be entitled to statehood once the total number of inhabitants passed 60,000 (which occurred within a few years of the Louisiana cession). But of even greater importance than the size of the population was its composition. The diversity of people of Lower Louisiana paralleled the diversity of its physical geography.

The racial distribution was almost equally divided between whites and blacks. In January 1807 there were about 26,000 whites, 4,000 free blacks, and 23,500 black slaves living in Lower Louisiana. In New Orleans itself, blacks constituted more than half of the city's total population. In some respects slaves who lived in New Orleans had greater opportunities than other southern bondsmen to move freely and work for hire. Urbanization made them much less deferential to whites and more defiant of the legal regulations of the French *Code Noir* which continued to govern their condition during the Spanish period. About one-third of the black population of the city in 1805 were "free people of color." Free blacks enjoyed a legal status and an economic position unparalleled in the American slave states at the time of the Louisiana acquisition and thereafter for a number of decades. They had full freedom to enter into business contracts and to own and transfer property, and they had full competence in civil litigation against whites and blacks alike. Even in criminal prosecutions free blacks could give evidence against whites.

Social distance separated all blacks from whites in some though not in all areas of public life. Whites worried about the possibilities of a "black revolt" similar to that which had occurred in Saint Domingue in the 1790's, especially since many black immigrants, slave and free, came from the West Indies. But the Spanish had also maintained some companies of free black militia, and the Americans soon discovered the advisability of allowing them to continue, though this was counter to general southern practice of denying arms and martial training to black people. Thus, while the free black population attempted to demonstrate loyalty to the American government, their special status in Louisiana law and society gave them an interest in preserving some elements of the established regime.[23]

The French-speaking community, by far the largest single group in the population, consisted of Creoles and recent immigrants (both white and black), Acadians, and natives of France. In the early nineteenth century the term "Creole" meant simply a native of Louisiana regardless of race, legal status, linguistic orientation, or national extraction. Thus Germans, English, Americans, Irish, "free people of color," and black slaves as well as the French and Spanish were entitled to the appellation "Creole" if they were born in the country. Obviously the Creoles were much too diverse to have real political or social impact as a cohesive group. The "ancients" or "old inhabitants" as they were loosely called, the natives of Latin derivation, did constitute an ethnic group with a real sense of identity and well-defined interests and goals. The "ancients" were French for the most part. They could be found on every income and occupational level and tended to be concentrated along the Mississippi at Pointe Coupée and in the city of New Orleans.[24]

The Acadians were the second-largest French-speaking group. They came to Louisiana in a steady stream from the 1760's through the 1790's, some by way of France. The Spanish encouraged their settlement in Louisiana because they were hardy, uncomplaining, and nonpolitical. The largest single group came in 1785: some sixteen hundred Acadians immigrated between May and December of that year. The Acadians settled in the parishes of St. James and Ascension midway between New Orleans and Baton Rouge, at Pointe Coupée, along the bayous Teche and Lafourche, on the Vermillion River, and at Avoyelles. The Acadians were poor but numerous, and during the territorial period they constituted a kind of peasant class, a source of mass support in the political effort to perpetuate French culture and French institutions in Louisiana when growing numbers of Americans threatened to transform the region's demographic composition and cultural character.[25]

The natives of France were the least numerous but the most influential of the French-speakers. A diverse assortment of refugees from Bourbon oppression, the French Revolution, and the black revolt on Santo Domingo, they contained within their ranks men of education and experience who quickly rose to positions of prominence in the French community. The old inhabitants of Louisiana resented their success but relied upon their talent and their leadership in the struggle against the common menace of Americanization.[26]

The two other major European groups were the Creoles of German descent and the Spanish settlers. Rhineland Germans were among the very first permanent settlers in Lower Louisiana. For a variety of reasons the French promoters of the Company of the West, which controlled Louisiana from 1717 to 1732, tried to recruit prospective settlers in countries neighboring France. They were most successful in Germany. Four thousand Germans are known to have reached the French port of Lorient in 1720, but the number that actually arrived in Louisiana by 1721 is disputed. Many of those who did moved up the Mississippi twenty-five miles above New Orleans to a section which came to be called the "German Coast." Although time and inter-marriage had, by 1800, dulled the echoes of the German language, to some extent the German imprint was still discernible northwest of the city in the complexion of the people, family names, and customs and manners. In New Orleans itself, German Creoles became butchers, mechanics, and members of the municipal guard.[27]

The Spanish community at Terre aux Boeufs began in 1788 when the Spanish Crown moved some fifteen hundred Canary Islanders to Louisiana in an effort to establish a popular base for Spanish rule. These *Isleños* settled along the underpopulated southern approach to New Orleans just below the English Turn. By 1810 they numbered under one thousand. The New Iberia settlement on the lower Teche consisted of mainland Spanish whose major influence was in introducing Spanish methods of cattle raising on the southwestern prairie.[28] Neither the Spanish nor the Germans had a separate political identity. After 1803 their ties to the French grew stronger once the threat of American acculturation became clear.

The English-speaking community also comprised a diversity of ethnic types. There were, to begin with, Scots, Irish, and English, many of whom had resided in the region for many years and occupied important positions in economic and political life. The Americans, themselves derived from many states and regions in the United States, settled nearly everywhere. Some came to New Orleans.[29] Others bought up some of the small farms along the Mississippi and turned them into sugar plantations. Still others went to the wide open areas beyond the established settlements. It was precisely in such areas—the western prairie district, the Red River, and Ouachita—that population climbed precipitously, at least in relative terms, in the territorial period.[30]

III

Despite the multiplicity of cultural types, however, ethnic conflict tended to be bipolar, with the "ancient inhabitants" and the "Anglo-Americans" at the extreme ends of the axis. To be sure, the split was not absolute. Individuals like Evan Jones sided with the "ancients" on particular issues, while well-known French settlers such as Julien Poydras of Pointe Coupée often defended the American regime. Some, following personal interest, could be found with one group or the other depending upon circumstances. Edward Livingston and Daniel Clark were the best examples of this type. In general, however, there was a significant cultural division. Almost every contemporary observer of Louisiana life in this period remarked it.[31]

Numerically, of course, the American population was outnumbered about seven to one at this time. But their potential for growth and their aggressive behavior bothered the local residents more than their numbers. English was now the language of government, and unlike the Spanish, who preserved much that was French, the new American officials showed every sign of being determined to transplant their institutions and culture into the territory. From the beginning, differences in life style were decided. For example, the French built "line settlements" along the rivers and bayous—that is, neat patterns of adjoining estates fronting the shoreline. The result was compactness and a strong sense of communal living. The Anglo-American settlement pattern was much more irregular and individualistic. Homes, barns, and storehouses were built haphazardly. Remoteness from one's neighbor was preferred. Boundary lines were irregular, and holdings varied greatly in size. In addition, American styles of architecture, of land clearing, stock raising, and fencing—even methods of grave design—were significantly different from those of French settlers. Consequently, Anglo-Americans and Latins found it irritating to live in the same areas. This helped to alienate one group from the other. Alienation and estrangement increased the likelihood of outright ethnic conflict.[32]

New Orleans reflected these divisions in microcosm. As a port city it was naturally more cosmopolitan than an ordinary town of equal size. It was, as one visitor put it, "a tower of Babel," particularly in the winter when trade was brisk and when the flatboats from the north and the ships from abroad were in.[33] Undoubtedly, the largest ethnic group were the French. Anglo-Americans constituted only about one-fourth of the total population of the city, but, despite their minority status, the Americans had the sense that they were the wave of the future and that their numbers would inevitably grow.[34] John Gurley, one of the new American land registrars, observed that "if the increase of American population should continue for three years to come to equal what it has been for the last nine months they must inevitably constitute a large majority."[35] Events did not verify this expectation, and in 1809 refugees from the West Indies added substantially to the French majority. For many more years than most Americans anticipated, or thought desirable, New Orleans remained a French city.[36]

Nevertheless, the Americans in New Orleans were highly visible. They concentrated in the Faubourg St. Mary, which quickly became one of the most important American communities on the Mississippi.[37] The "Yankees" were clannish and isolated. They viewed themselves as an English-speaking island in a

French sea, and like many islanders they tended to be defensive and suspicious. They were also somewhat bewildered. As one visitor reported while passing through the city in the spring of 1808, "Our Yankees feel not a little foolish upon their first arrival in this city, where the manners and amusements are so very different from their own."[38] Billiard parlors, dance halls, and the two French theaters were all open and thriving on Sundays. The Americans with their more staid Protestant habits were likely to be either offended or critical.[39]

For their part, Louisianians were not immune to fears and suspicions. Although many of the new immigrants from the north were men of substance, education, and experience, the French looked upon Americans as generally uncivilized. Their contacts with the American riverboat men had never been especially agreeable. The "Kaintucks," as they were called, disregarded harbor regulations, docked their boats wherever it suited them, unloaded their wares as they pleased, and generally made nuisances of themselves in town. The French were not likely to view the influx into their city of large numbers of the countrymen of such people with great enthusiasm. The identification of the Americans with the onset of yellow fever further heightened ethnic tensions.[40]

Thus New Orleans became the scene of a confrontation between two antagonistic groups. Ethnic conflict took shape at the very start of American rule in Louisiana. In the absence of organized political parties, ethnic identity supplied the most meaningful orientation to political life. The ethnic division in New Orleans and Louisiana, though not absolute or complete, was a basic problem of life and government there.[41]

IV

The *Kulturkampf* between the *ancienne population* and the Anglo-Americans for supremacy in Lower Louisiana manifested itself most sharply as a conflict of legal traditions.[42] For over three-quarters of a century Louisiana had lived under first the French and then the Spanish, whose laws were rooted in the Roman tradition. France and Spain were part of the legal "family" associated with European civil law, and Louisiana's Franco-Spanish population was determined to preserve that heritage.[43] At the same time, the new American population of Lower Louisiana was just as eager to continue to live under Anglo-American common law, which was prized because it was familiar and because it was thought to be the foundation of American liberty and political independence.[44]

Moreover, the United States government intended to transform the demographic composition, the culture, and the political orientation of Louisiana in order to bind it more closely to the still fragile union of American states. At a time when differences between Virginians and New Englanders were considered formidable, and when religious and racial distinctions as well as geographic size and state localism stood in the path of a strong American identity, the prospect that the United States could absorb a people whose laws and institutions were as foreign as those of the Louisianians seemed difficult if not impossible.[45] Thus the stage was set for a dramatic conflict between two legal traditions for supremacy in the remote southwest. And while this clash was emblematic of the larger confrontation of peoples and cultures, it was by no means purely symbolic. Real interests and fundamental principles of law were at stake. The differences between French and Spanish civil law on the one hand, and Anglo-American common law on the other, were numerous, important, and deep enough to cause Louisiana's settled population acute concern when the prospect of a wholesale legal transformation suddenly arose.

For example, marriage established a patrimonial relationship between spouses wholly different in civil law from what it was in common law. Both Spanish and French law recognized the *community property system*, and in Louisiana, in the absence of a prenuptial stipulation to the contrary, properties acquired by the spouses during marriage otherwise than by inheritance or donation belonged to the *community*. Although the husband retained control over "the community of gains," the marriage regime was essentially a contract between equal partners each of whom retained full ownership and management of his or her separate properties—that is, those not belonging to the community. When the regime was dissolved the community property was divided, with each spouse receiving half in full ownership.[46] In common law, on the other hand, marriage resulted in the merger of two persons into one. The wife was a *feme covert*, thoroughly subordinate to the will and authority of her husband. Most personal property belonging to the wife was vested in the husband. Rents and profits from her lands went to him. Marriage in common law meant, in effect, a surrender of the wife's legal personality, her civil capacity, and most if not all of her possessions for its duration. When widowed, the wife was only entitled to her dower, a one-third life interest in inheritable properties held by the husband during coverture, an inferior kind of insurance compared with the community property system wherein the wife received complete ownership of one-half of the community.[47]

Other rules affecting family relations exemplify the disparities between common law and civil law in the early nineteenth century. Children born out of wedlock could not be legitimated in English common law, but in civil law a marriage at any time subsequent to birth could make bastards legitimate. Here each system promoted a separate set of principles. The classic common law writers maintained that civilian rules governing legitimation were indecent because they struck at the sanctity of matrimony.[48] But civilians could argue that the rules permitting legitimation were derived from canon law, and that natural morality dictated that children should not be penalized for the indiscretions of their parents.[49] Whatever the relative weight of the moral arguments, however, the practical consquences of these different legal rules were clear. In common law an illegitimate son had no right of inheritance for, to paraphrase Blackstone, "the son of nobody can inherit nothing." But in civil law, bastards legitimated by marriage could inherit as if born during marriage. Even illegitimate children had rights. They inherited from their mother if she had no legitimate descendants, and from their father if he had no legitimate relatives or a surviving spouse; and if they did not inherit, they could always claim alimony from the heirs of their parents. Not until the nineteenth century was well advanced, in part because of the influence of Louisiana, did many American states begin to mitigate the rigors of the common law with respect to the rights of illegitimate children.[50]

The civil law as practiced in Louisiana always recognized the principle of *forced heirship*, which limited the testamentary freedom of a parent to a disposition of one-fifth of his property and narrowly circumscribed the legal grounds for disinheritance. Forced heirship was a pillar of family relationships. In contrast, the common law had long since established that a man's property was at his own disposal, and law courts could protect heirs from legal disinheritance only where the intent of the testator was open to doubt. In this respect, the common law's individualism and its tendency to locate decision-making power in the mature, reasoning adult stood out in sharp relief from the civil law which here, as elsewhere, upheld the family unit and the claims of family members when willful parental action might defeat them.[51]

Each system emphasized different concepts of order in the holding and disposition of property. The civil law worked to put property in the hands and under the control of the living. It promoted the commercialism of all property, including land, whereas the common law still adhered to notions born in the age of feudalism.[52] Thus, by the late eighteenth century, in civil law one acquired ownership and complete title to land, but in common law jurisdictions one still spoke of having an "interest" or an "estate" in real property. Despite the demise of the primogeniture rule and the development of free alienability, the fee-simple estate, partible descent, and the convergence of real and personal property,[53] many of the old but familiar concepts, terminologies, interests, and forms of action rooted in the classic English common law persisted.[54] To Louisianians long used to the far simpler *allodial* landholding system, the possible introduction of principles of law which smacked of the antiquated feudal doctrine of *tenures* was downright menacing.[55] Thus an admirer of Louisiana law would, in the 1820's, contrast its "simplicity, unity, precision and clearness" with the "intricacy, complexity, uncertainty, and indistinctness" of the law of real property which still prevailed in common law America.[56]

The whole thrust of the civil law was to identify the owner and the thing owned, whereas common law tended to keep them separate. By the end of the eighteenth century the modern civil law had revived the Roman concept of absolute *dominion* while the common law still wrestled with more fragmented notions of property—the relativity of title, the competing claims of present and future property holders, and the differences between legal and equitable ownership.[57] Although the American common law states, by the time of the revolution, had abandoned the entail as a method of blocking the free alienation of land, another device, the trust, was developing into a method for enabling the private individual to control the disposition of his property, both real and personal, long after his death.[58] In contrast, because it lacked a history of feudal landholding, Louisiana resisted impediments to free alienation. The Digest of 1808 would bar *fidei commissum* and *substitution*, rough civil law equivalents to common law devices that created "future interests."[59] The Digest required that transferees be alive at the time of an act of transfer, thus making dispositions in favor of the unborn impossible, and it provided no way in which the control of property might be denied its owner of full age and sound mind.[60]

In the law of obligations, too, civil law and common law showed marked divergences. According to the common law, in contracts not under seal, a valuable *consideration*, however small, had to be given in return for a promise. But the civil law had no exact equivalent to consideration. The closest thing to consideration in civil law was *cause*—the motive or purpose behind an agreement making the assumption of obligation credible and reasonable.[61]

In civil law, the buyer was protected by an *implied warranty* in a contract of sale—unlike common law where the seller's warranty had to be expressed or agreed upon. Should the seller's goods fail to possess qualities which the buyer had a right to presume and without which he would not have agreed to the purchase, then the buyer could bring an action for recission of the sale. In addition, the price paid had to approximate the value of the goods received at the time they were sold. If it did not, with some forms of property the seller could sue for *lesion* or the injury resulting from the nonreceipt of sufficient compensation.[62]

In common law, testamentary guardians were virtually free of judicial interference in their administration of the estate, but in the civil law the judge exercised continuous control over them. In the absence of a testamentary provision, "tutors" in Louisiana were appointed by a judge acting on the advice of a family council; in the common law states, guardians were completely under the appointment and control of the courts of chancery or probate.[63]

In Louisiana, in order to secure a pledge from the claims of the pledgor's creditors, a pledge agreement required an authenticated act stating the amount of the debt and the nature of the thing pledged, but in common law simple verbal agreements were usually sufficient. Moreover, in Louisiana the creditor could sell an unredeemed pledge only under a court decree, but, in common law, in the absence of a special prior arrangement, the creditor could sell the pledge after giving the pledgor sufficient notice.[64]

In common law America, the public notary was little more than an official witness to oaths and a drawer of affidavits, but in civil law Louisiana he was a major public officer whose duties and functions required substantial legal training and experience. Many legal undertakings—deeds of property, inventories of estates, marriage contracts—required notarial authentication. The notary was expected to establish the legal capacity of the parties and to inform them of their rights and of the consequences of their intended acts. Such acts, once attested by the notary, became official public documents, copies of which were available as evidence whose probative force was beyond challenge by disputants.[65]

In addition to these substantive and formal differences separating the two bodies of law, there were procedural and philosophical distinctions as well. The growing point of the historic common law had been the higher courts of justice, and though legislation had, by the eighteenth century, become an important source of new law, case law maintained its position of primacy. The development of professional law reporting, the emergence of an independent judiciary, and the rapid growth of business and commerce brought forth novel kinds of litigation and forced judges to play an ever-increasing role as creative lawmakers.[66] But Louisiana law was rooted in a tradition that looked to agencies other than law courts for definitive statement of the law, new or old. Civil lawyers would have difficulty adjusting to a system which depended so heavily upon judicial output. Moden civil law codification was still in its infancy, but "civilians" were accustomed to researching the commentaries of legal scholars rather than case reports for expositions of the law.[67]

Moreover, the compartmentalization of law differed substantially in the two traditions. The great fault line in the common law was that which set *law* apart from *equity*. Each of these systems had its own body of decisional law, its own remedies, its own procedures, and, in a few states, even its own separate law courts. But civil lawyers were hard put to understand a legal system in which "equity" was distinct from "law" and in which litigants could not pursue both simultaneously.[68]

The distinguishing feature of the common law was that the jury, not the judge, determined the facts in a legal dispute. In the developing common law the existence of the jury had profoundly affected the law of evidence, the manner and form in which evidence could be presented at trial, and the method and scope of appellate review. Moreover, before the procedural reforms of the nineteenth century, the common law still adhered to an almost ritualistic observance of procedural regularity at every stage of civil litigation or criminal prosecution. In contrast, in civil law the evidence was evaluated by trained jurists, and, consequently, there were fewer restrictions on the kinds of evidence admissible in a legal proceeding. In addition, civil law appellate courts could review the factual record assembled below, whereas common law petitions for review could only be based upon procedural errors or legal rulings made by the trial judges, and original findings of fact could not be set aside. Thus while some formalism was present in civil law trial procedures—and certainly Spanish criminal proceedings were noted for their prolixity—procedure was somewhat devalued. Both systems attempted to achieve a just solution in every legal contest, but where the common law taught that it could only be secured through faithful observance of proper form, the civilian tradition more willingly sacrificed procedural regularity to the interests of substantial justice. In the common law, there was no right if a remedy did not exist, but in civil law, if a right existed, then a remedy would be found.[69]

In Louisiana awareness of these general philosophical and procedural characteristics, as well as the particular substantive oddities of each system, was naturally keenest amongst legal practitioners. Lawyers and judges, after all, were the people who by training, experience, and profession had the greatest stake in the continuation of the legal regime which they understood and of which they were a part. But we should not minimize the immediacy of the lay public's involvement in the whole question of legal change.

V

That the general population of Lower Louisiana was alert to these questions can be documented from the record of the territorial period. Thus Louisianians carefully discriminated between the introduction of the common law jury trial in criminal cases, which they heartily welcomed, and jury trials in civil causes, which they just as ardently opposed. American criminal law and criminal procedure, with its devices for the protection of the individual against arbitrary authority, had obvious advantages over the administration of criminal justice under the Spanish, and Louisianians were quick to see this. But they also preferred the simple forms of written petition in civil suits which they had known from the days of the French, and they resisted what seemed to them to be the unnecessarily complicated and wasteful procedures of American private law including the constant resort to jury process. The Americans were known for their litigiousness, and the sudden appearance of what seemed to be "swarms" of lawyers reinforced local fears that Louisiana was about to be sacrificed to the rapacity of an unscrupulous cadre of common law attorneys ready to take advantage of the people's ignorance.[70]

In the Louisiana Remonstrance of 1804, the first organized protest against American rule, objections to legal innovations figured large among the major items on its agenda of complaint. The Remonstrance received wide support. Public gatherings were called to draft and adopt the memorial, many signed it, and a delegation of three well-known local notables was deputized to present it to Congress. But the Remonstrance was only one of a number of important efforts to quicken sentiment and channel support behind specific grievances having to do with the legal question. Pamphlets, editorial commentaries, manifestos, and instructions to deputies in the first territorial legislature indicate that public interest in these matters was wide and deep.[71]

Local fears were also in evidence in the reluctance of Louisiana landowners to follow American regulations governing the survey and registry of title. The Spanish, in order to encourage settlement, had pursued a very liberal policy based upon verbal declarations of intent to settle followed by three years of actual cultivation. By 1803, however, the situation had become badly confused primarily because of the uncertain validity of Spanish grants made after Spain's retrocession of Louisiana to France, secretly agreed to in 1800. But when the Jefferson administration inaugurated a strict program of title registration to straighten things out, it ran into considerable local opposition. Landowners simply refused to submit their titles for review by American registrars and land commissioners for fear that they were about to be deprived of their properties. The old inhabitants of Louisiana perceived these new regulations not as a mere change in policy but as still another instance of the general threat to property rights which the new legal order portended. The protracted question of unsettled land claims, therefore, reinforced the widespread belief that the American regime was bent upon overturning the legal basis of the Louisiana way of life.[72]

Finally, the legal fight between Edward Livingston and the city of New Orleans for the possession of the Mississippi Batture is especially interesting and important. The Batture controversy was more than just a contest over title to a valuable parcel of real property. Partly as a result of editorial misrepresentation, the fight over the Batture awakened a general anxiety over the kind of treatment the people of Louisiana could expect in American law courts at the hands of American judges ignorant of local customs and usages. The large and sometimes violent demonstrations that occurred on the Batture itself, the profusion of printed treatises—some of exorbitant length—on the legal questions at issue, for which there was an apparently insatiable appetite, and the eagerness with which the latest bit of news or the most recent publication on the controversy was awaited at the exchange coffee house all show that in a curiously distorted way the Batture question served to dramatize the ethnic, cultural, and legal conflict as did no other single dispute in the territorial period.[73]

Thus a fundamental question of legal change facing Louisiana in the Jeffersonian period was not an esoteric issue which only concerned the professional elites. Rather, it touched upon many public questions, some of which were fairly remote from the strict confines of legal cases and conflicts. For the clash of legal traditions encompassed the interests, the value system, and the very identity of a diverse people who now, for the first time in their history, had to unite in defense of the common elements of their heritage.

The Problems of Colonial Rule

[2] *William C. C. Claiborne and the Politics of Territorial Government*

Louisiana was America's first imperial possession. The purchase of the vast and uncharted lands of the trans-Mississippi at the opening of the nineteenth century restructured America's priorities and transformed its interests, potentialities, and resources in land, power, and people. The acquisition of a western empire changed the dimensions of America's development, but it also challenged the nation's fundamental political, cultural, and legal institutions.[1]

The Louisiana Purchase proved to be Thomas Jefferson's most durable achievement in the presidency, but in its time it raised as many problems as it solved. The most obvious of these was the strategic vulnerability of New Orleans. Located on the "island of Orleans" and surrounded on nearly every side by navigable waterways, the city was exposed to naval or amphibious attack. Geographically, New Orleans was part of the Gulf Coast and the western link of a developing chain of river outlets which connected southwestern settlers with Caribbean and Atlantic trade routes. Indeed, Americans in the Mississippi territory would have gladly exchanged Louisiana for Florida in order to guarantee access to the gulf via the Pearl, the Tombigbee, and the Alabama rivers.[2] The principal negotiators of the Louisiana cession treaty, Robert R. Livingston and James Monroe, were specifically instructed by Jefferson and Secretary of State James Madison to acquire New Orleans and Florida precisely because New Orleans without Florida would be difficult, perhaps impossible, to hold. The negotiated purchase of New Orleans and Louisiana, therefore, came not only as a surprise but as a problem.[3]

With West Florida still in Spanish hands, most of the important access routes to the city were under foreign control. Baton Rouge, eighty miles northwest of New Orleans and occupying the last high ground overlooking the Mississippi, was the site of Fort San Carlos. This position gave the Spanish the potential to sever communications between the settled part of Lower Louisiana and the rest of the mainland.[4] Spanish naval units patrolled Lake Pontchartrain and could easily fortify Fort Petites Coquilles which guarded the Rigolets, the most important strait connecting the lake and the gulf.[5] Ship Island, off the Florida coast, was a major staging area for military operations on the Gulf Coast until the Civil War, and in 1803 it too was a Spanish possession.[6] In addition, both overland routes from the northeast—the Natchez-Fort Adams road and the Pearl River route—had to traverse Spanish West Florida. Clearly, the Spanish presence in the vicinity of New Orleans could be troublesome.[7] When, in the summer and early fall of 1806, a Spanish-American conflict seemed imminent, the United States' position in all of Lower Louisiana appeared to be in danger of complete collapse.

Soon after the transfer of Louisiana to the United States, James Wilkinson, the supreme commander of American military forces in the west who was stationed in New Orleans, warned the Secretary of War that "Every Hour evinces more and more the necessity of a strong garrison here . . .—our puny force has become a subject of ridicule, and the old women begin to exclaim 'quel triste Governement'."[8] Wilkinson feared "for the preservation . . . of our immense Acquisitions in this quarter." The general had accurately surmised the dimensions of the difficulty confronting the United States. Coupled to the problem of exterior exposure was the hair-trigger volatility of the local populace, whose reaction to the recent change in sovereignty was still not fully known. Wilkinson was pointing to the urgent need for additional military support to shore up the tenuous American position in that remote corner of the continent.[9]

The isolation of New Orleans was one of the most acute and persistent problems facing Jefferson after 1803. In the remainder of his first term in office and throughout his troubled second term, he returned again and again to its strategic vulnerability and the need to take remedial measures there. A variety of actions was attempted to reinforce the American military posture in Lower Louisiana. The number of troops in the area was increased, so that by the end of 1804 there were more than twice as many regulars in the region than in all of Upper Louisiana, an area many times its size. Key fortifications on the water approaches to New Orleans—in particular, Fort Plaquemines below the English Turn and Fort St. John on the southern side of Lake Pontchartrain—were strengthened. Part of the gunboat fleet was shifted to the Mississippi, and, in order to improve the mobility of naval craft on station there, Jefferson urged the completion of the Carondelet Canal, which would link the river and the lake via Bayou St. John.[10] Finally, the President proposed an elaborate scheme for resettling tens of thousands of American frontiersmen—yeoman farmers in peace and citizen-soldiers in war—in this weak and exposed territory of the United States.[11]

In addition to bothersome boundary questions and Spain's

continuing reluctance to recognize the legitimacy of the Louisiana cession—both of which directly affected the fundamental problem of America's strategic position in the area—a vexing set of internal questions threatened the viability of American rule in Louisiana. What was to be the relationship between the territory to the west of the great river and the new nation to the east? Was the United States to become a colonial power within a generation of its own anticolonialist revolution, or would the ceded territory be incorporated into the Union on some basis of equality, as called for in the treaty with France? If so, then on what terms would the cultural accommodation between Anglo-Americans and Latin-Creoles be made? Eleven hundred miles from Washington, surrounded on every side by Spanish colonial power, inhabited by a largely French-speaking population whose allegiance was unclear, Lower Louisiana became the unlikely setting where America had to work out a host of problems so basic that they went to the heart of what the new nation was all about.

I

Into this storm center of empire Jefferson sent William Charles Cole Claiborne, twenty-eight years old, a man of ordinary talents now in an extraordinary situation. As the governor of Lower Louisiana, Claiborne became one of the most important public officials in all of the United States. He certainly was among the highest paid. His annual salary of five thousand dollars was second only to that of the President in the federal government and equal to that of Cabinet secretaries and the Vice President.[12] His experience in public life was long for one whose years were so few. While still in his teens he had clerked in Congress; by the age of twenty-one he had become a successful criminal lawyer and judge in the new state of Tennessee, and he was elected to Congress in his twenty-second year. His executive career began with his contribution to the presidential election of 1800, for as Tennessee's solitary representative in Congress he held that state's vote for Jefferson in the crucial balloting for President in the House of Representatives. In return he was appointed governor of the Mississippi territory.[13]

Jefferson chose Claiborne, the nearest high civilian official in the region, to go to New Orleans late in 1803 to receive the cession of Louisiana from France. His military counterpart was General James Wilkinson, who, with a sizable troop of men, accompanied him in order to overawe the local populace while convincing the Spanish garrison still in the city of the futility of resisting the transfer of the territory. Claiborne and Wilkinson both aspired to head the civil government to be established in the area, but it was Claiborne who stayed on as the provisional governor pending the appointment of a more acceptable candidate.[14]

Claiborne was capable, energetic, and efficient. Whatever weakness or vacillation he displayed was inherent in his position. The decisions facing American government in what was to be called the Territory of Orleans were too large, delicate, and portentous to trust to a young and untested public man. As a result, Claiborne acted more as the American representative to Lower Louisiana than as a genuine governor with real powers of decision. His correspondence with the national authorities is replete with the routine details of administration and those minute reports of public events so typical of emissaries of one state resident in another.[15] His instructions—though often not defined in explicit terms—left him with little room for independent maneuver with respect to either policy or appointments. On the other hand, his legal powers relative to the territory were so great that the citizens of Louisiana likened him to a despot. In short, Claiborne's position was not unlike that of the British colonial governors before the American Revolution—great in theory but modest in fact.[16]

II

The delivery of all of Louisiana to the United States on December 20, 1803, was anticipated by the local inhabitants with anxiety and hope. They were apprehensive that the Spanish garrison still in the city might resist the change even as they expressed the wish that the Americans would bring them a new political life sweetened by liberty and peace. "The sun's clear," one observer wrote, "the air gentle enough merely to float the banners of [our] triumph; but our political scenery I fear will not be so serene."[17] The ease with which the imperial transfer occurred surprised everyone. That it was so peaceful was the result of the elaborate precautions which had been taken since November. But now, with the establishment of the nominal authority of America safely accomplished, policy had to be determined and implemented. This was the new government's major task.

Isaac Briggs, the surveyor general for the Mississippi territory and one of Jefferson's chief informants in the southwest, thought much of Claiborne's potential. He reported that the new governor's difficulties would be great and his duties "irksome," for much was expected of the Americans after years of Spanish bureaucratic mismanagement and corruption. But the work of reform would have to be slow and the reformer a man of integrity, firmness, resolution, intelligence, and patience. Thus far, wrote Briggs in early January, Claiborne's decisions had been well received. "Disappointed characters are as yet few, nor have they had time to form a party, nor to put, in motion, the engines of calumny and misrepresentation."[18]

Political opposition was the inevitable by-product of change, but the "calumny and misrepresentation" to which Briggs referred was the gratuitous badgering that accompanied the expression of genuine grievances. In the beginning Claiborne had difficulty distinguishing between the two. He tended to confuse legitimate opposition to his policies with personal attacks and the snipings of political rivals. As a result, his early years in the territory were often marred by fumbling leadership. Crankiness, irritation, and nervous self-righteousness were qualities ill suited to his tasks, but they were characteristic of the man. He was open and honest to a fault, however, and his personal shortcomings were mirrored in great detail in his frequent reports to Jefferson. Only when Claiborne learned to differentiate between legitimate complaint and plain backbiting could he manage real problems.

Ethnic conflict stirred the first disharmony. Early in January 1804, at a public ball held in New Orleans, American and French military officers argued over whose dances were to be played first. Claiborne faithfully reported the incident to Secretary of State James Madison, thinking it revealed "a political tendency"; but he also believed it to be of only passing concern.[19]

It was not. Dances and festivities played a large part in the social life of New Orleans in the midwinter season, then as now, and the governor increasingly encountered difficulty in keeping these occasions from becoming violent. "I fear you will suppose that I am wanting in respect in calling your attention to the Balls of New Orleans," he wrote Madison apologetically some weeks later, "but I do assure you Sir, that they occupy much of the Public mind, and from them have proceeded the greatest embarrassments which have heretofore attended my administration."[20] Claiborne tried to sidestep the responsibility for these intramural dances by having the New Orleans municipality regulate them, but clashes recurred. On the twenty-second of January another riot erupted over the playing of an English country dance. The French called for a waltz. A commotion ensued. General Wilkinson apprehended the chief mischief-maker, but this only heightened the tension. A rendering of a throaty "Hail Columbia" was answered by the "Marseillaise." Several arrests were made. The following day Pierre Laussat, the former French prefect for Louisiana, intervened and insisted that one of those arrested, a French officer, was not subject to American jurisdiction. Claiborne replied by calling for the immediate evacuation of all remaining French troops in the province.

A few days later the breach between the French and the Americans widened when the mayor of New Orleans, Etienne Boré, complained to Jefferson that the governor had acted rashly at the public festivity. Boré also used the occasion to challenge Claiborne's overall fitness for his post.[21] He failed to mention, however, that New Orleans had long been the haunt of numerous criminals, vagabonds, and temporary residents, as well as Spanish and French soldiers. The governor had done all in his power to maintain order without precipitating open revolt. The French settlers had overthrown the Spanish when they first took command of the city in 1766, and the Americans had no wish to risk a similar upheaval now. Aware that the residents doubted America's ability to retain Lower Louisiana, given the added presence of high French and Spanish officials in command of troops, and the rumored return of all of Louisiana to France or Spain, Claiborne showed real finesse in riding out the squalls of ethnic conflict during his first weeks in office.[22]

Claiborne tried to follow a middle course in the disturbances occasioned by the public dances. At first he attempted to avoid the question by leaving its resolution with the municipality. When the major outbreak erupted on January 22, Wilkinson and not Claiborne made the arrests. The governor scrupulously asserted his neutrality and rightly attributed the commotion to the presence of foreign soldiers. He tried to hasten their departure. Otherwise he remained aloof, showing partiality to neither the French nor the American side in the dispute.

III

The second public controversy involving Claiborne happened early in the spring of 1804. Once again the major cause was largely beyond his control, but this time Claiborne was partly responsible for it. In January Claiborne reported to Madison on the condition of government in the territory. Among his recommendations he reiterated the need for more permanent political institutions in the province. He urged that its character "be as republican as the people can be safely intrusted with." But, he continued, "the principles of a popular Government are utterly beyond their comprehension."[23] The representative system was "an enigma that at present bewilders them." They were used to authority and ill prepared for self-government.

Claiborne, as governor, had every reason to report his impressions to Madison and to assume that the information he imparted would be kept confidential. But an unidentified Federalist newspaper published the letter, and news of the leak reached New Orleans early in April.[24] The resulting outcry was predictable. Despite Claiborne's efforts to minimize the letter's importance, his official conduct was subjected to its first sustained attack. Joseph Dubreuil, one of Louisiana's wealthiest planters, wrote: "It is not unknown here, after reading over Northern public papers, that the ceded territory has been described to Congress as some sort of Tower of Babel, suffering from the confusion of tongues, and the Louisianians as men stupefied by despotism or ignorance, and therefore unable to elevate themselves for a long time to the heights of a free constitution."[25] Dubreuil attributed these characterizations to Claiborne whom he considered wholly incompetent and entirely dependent upon the English-speaking population for his information. Dubreuil described the governor as "a stranger here, a stranger as far as the soil itself is concerned, its local interests, the customs, habits and even the language of the inhabitants, and who is therefore without even the most absolutely necessary knowledge. . . ."[26] Claiborne's advertised opposition to immediate statehood outraged men like Dubreuil and triggered a resentment that would not soon subside. The Administration had erred in permitting the governor's correspondence with Madison to reach the press. The blunder damaged the governor and intensified resistance to his measures for several years.

Meanwhile, on March 26, 1804, Congress had passed the first organic law providing for the government of the territory. The act delineated the physical boundaries of Orleans and the duties and powers of the governor and other public officials. In addition, Congress established a legislative council of thirteen notables plus a rudimentary judicial system.[27] From the point of view of the general government in Washington and its agents in Orleans, the act was an important first step on the road to political maturity.[28] In setting up the basic elements of American government, Congress was moving in the direction of orderly administration and eventual statehood.

From the point of view of the French inhabitants of Lower Louisiana, however, the act of March 26 was a disappointment. The treaty of cession of April 30, 1803, had specifically provided in its third article that "the inhabitants of the ceded territory shall be incorporated in the Union of the United States, and admitted as soon as possible, according to the principles of the Federal constitution, to the enjoyment of all the rights, advantages, and immunities, of citizens of the United States. . . ."[29] Not only did the act fail to provide for immediate statehood: it was not even mentioned.[30] Furthermore, Congress severely circumscribed the powers of the embryonic legislature by maintaining the right to disallow local statutes.[31] Moreover, while laws inconsistent with the Constitution and statutes of the United States could not be enacted, the governor, with the "advice and consent" of the legislative council, was empowered "to alter, modify, or repeal" local laws still in force.

For many in Lower Louisiana, the most distressing provision of the act of March 26 was the embargo on further slave importations into the territory. According to the enactment, neither slaves from foreign ports nor those from the United States that had been imported from abroad after May 1, 1798, could be brought into Orleans. The only slaves permitted to enter were those accompanying American citizens "removing into said territory for actual settlement."[32] This violated the language and spirit of the third article of the treaty of cession, which had guaranteed to the original inhabitants of Louisiana "the free enjoyment of their . . . property." Louisianians viewed the continued importation of slaves as a necessary condition of their economic prosperity.[33] The United States Constitution barred statutory interference with the foreign slave trade prior to the year 1808, so that here again the inhabitants had evidence of Congress acting discriminatorily and in violation of the Louisiana treaty. As a result, when in early March 1804 rumors began circulating that the forthcoming congressional enactment providing for territorial government would prohibit the importation of slaves, meetings were held, speeches were delivered, and a memorial to Congress was prepared.[34]

These events lowered Claiborne's standing. In letters to Madison he challenged the imputations made against him and dismissed the movement to petition Congress as the scheme of ambitious and vengeful men. His reactions to this first manifestation of political discontent were colored by his belief that persons rather than policies were to blame. Claiborne first reported that the memorial idea was inspired by a recently arrived Mr. Tupper of Boston.[35] He explained Tupper's success in organizing the public meeting called to consider the petition as "a strong proof of the mischief a designing unprincipled Man may do in Louisiana."[36] The governor's emphasis was not upon genuine grievances, such as the rumored prohibition on slave importations, but upon the subversive activities of purposeful individuals. In a subsequent communication analyzing the sources of public support for the memorial, Claiborne again singled out Tupper as the "troublesome Man" who was "the prime mover of this business," dismissed him as "a swindler," and hoped "that his real character will soon be known and that he will sink into contempt."[37] While Claiborne did note that the inhabitants viewed the continued importation of slaves as essential to the welfare of the province, his effort to undermine criticisms of his regime with *ad hominem* references was characteristic of his early approach to political problems.

The results of Congress's labors were well known by June 1,[38] and the worst fears of the people of Louisiana were realized: self-government had been withheld. As a result, the pace of political protest quickened. Spurring it on were the two most formidable political opponents Claiborne would ever face—Edward Livingston and Daniel Clark. Livingston had arrived in February from New York, where political scandal had short-circuited his promising career. The Republican victories of 1800 had led to his appointment as U.S. attorney and mayor of New York. During the summer of 1803 yellow fever struck the city, and Livingston fell ill. Upon returning to his official duties, he discovered that one of his assistants had absconded with federal customhouse bonds later valuated at $43,000. Livingston immediately resigned his offices and set out for Louisiana, determined to clear his debt and redeem his reputation. As part of the effort to restore his solvency, Livingston interested himself in the rich Bastrop lands along the Ouachita River.[39] In the spring of 1804 he was busily negotiating the acquisition of these properties, fully convinced that their value as a speculative enterprise depended upon the availability of black slaves whose importation into the territory Congress had embargoed. Thus Livingston had a direct interest in protesting the act of March 26.[40]

Daniel Clark, an old resident of Irish extraction, had come to New Orleans in the 1780s as a partner-agent in a Philadelphia firm. Clark owned a cordage factory in New Orleans and a plantation near Natchez. In addition he had bought an immense tract of land along the Ouachita. In 1803 Clark was performing consular services for the United States in New Orleans. It was Clark who recommended a show of force at the time of the transfer. He advised the American commissioners in November and December of 1803 and was the man chiefly responsible for the smooth delivery of the territory on December 20. Clark wanted to be governor, but Claiborne's appointment thwarted his ambition.[41]

Livingston and Clark took the lead in the composition and circulation of the draft memorial known thereafter as the Louisiana Remonstrance. Livingston wrote it, and Clark solicited signatures for it throughout the territory. By July 1 the Remonstrance was ready for approval at a large public meeting. At a second public assembly, held soon afterward, three delegates were chosen to convey the memorial and the sentiments it embodied to Washington.[42]

Claiborne attributed these events to "aspiring Gentlemen." He insisted that New Orleans remained tranquil and that the opposition to the act of Congress was confined to "a small portion of the society" and that "at present it is certain that the mass of the citizens have not fallen into their views; but how far the exertions of a few may in time create a general sentiment in favor of a complete representative system I cannot tell."[43] He wrote Jefferson that whatever were the motives of the principal agitators, "they have caused a flame in the District which will not (I fear) shortly subside."[44] Claiborne's analysis of the movement to memorialize the Congress, from first to last, was confusing. He failed to clarify whether or not the wish for greater self-government and the maintenance of the slave trade was a genuine and widespread desire or the fabricated arguments of a few disgruntled agitators.[45]

The memorial itself listed a number of grievances besides the opposition to the slave embargo. It condemned the extensive powers of the governor's office and Claiborne's inadequacy for that post. It criticized the legal innovations undertaken by the new regime.[46] But above all, the Remonstrance emphasized that the necessary precondition for correcting these grievances was early statehood for the territory. Claiborne's known opposition to statehood opened him to criticism from the great mass of Louisianians.

The memorial exposed Claiborne's political isolation. He looked to Washington for political support rather than to the people he had been commissioned to govern. He saw himself as the instrument of an imperial power whose policies he would implement, the true colonial governor answerable only to those above him. His evaluation of local conditions was formulated so as to coincide with broad national policy, but it was also affected by his desire to create the appearance of a prevailing tranquillity. "Political tendencies" would reflect badly upon his competence. As a result, Claiborne was reduced to petulant criticism of opponents. He tried to discredit their activity rather than respond positively to real grievances.

Claiborne's political decline during the spring and summer of 1804, therefore, stemmed from decisions beyond his control, from his own inflexibility, and from his tendency to treat political opposition as personal criticism. Congress had denied immediate statehood to Lower Louisiana, and Claiborne's advocacy of such a postponement had been allowed to reach the press. Placed in an awkward position by these disclosures, he refused to alter his early judgments. His stand put him in direct opposition to the general sentiments and aspirations of Louisianians. In the early dispute over the public dances the governor had adopted a middle position, seeming to favor neither the Americans nor the French. In the ferment over the Louisiana Remonstrance Claiborne again was caught, but this time he was identified as having supported the policy of the general government rather than local interests.

IV

In addition to the criticism which he encountered as a result of his publicized opposition to early statehood, Claiborne also aroused resentment with his appointments policy. Here again the governor was only partly at fault, for he was trying to adhere as strictly as possible to Administration guidelines. According to the act of March 26, the President was required to fill the thirteen seats on the legislative council, and, in the spring of 1804, the Administration turned to the task. Jefferson requested from Claiborne a list of names of the most prominent people in Lower Louisiana "with short sketches of the material outlines of their characters." [47] He advised that the council ought to be composed "of men of integrity, of understanding, of clear property and influence among the people, well acquainted with the laws, customs and habits of the country, and drawn from the different parts of the Orleans district in proportion to their population." His final criterion, however, resulted in the greatest difficulty, for it contradicted his other specifications. "I think a mere majority should be Americans," the President wrote, "and the rest French or Spaniards."

Claiborne's first recommendations singled out two of the old inhabitants and two native Americans. [48] They were Julien Poydras, the leading planter at Pointe Coupée, Colonel Bellechasse Deville Degoutin of the German Coast, the commandant of the militia, Benjamin Morgan, a merchant formerly of Philadelphia, and John Watkins, a Claiborne favorite at this time, a man who had earlier undertaken important responsibilities at the governor's request. [49] All four were well disposed toward the American regime. Poydras and

Bellechasse were to be pillars of pro-American strength in the French community in the years ahead.

Jefferson waited impatiently for more names, but finally concluded that his original letter to Claiborne of April 17 had never been received. He renewed his instructions in early July, this time with an added warning against extending patronage to Federalists. Jefferson wished that it would be possible to abolish all political distinctions, "but while the [Federalist] party throughout the U.S. retain and even increase their bitterness they must not be nourished by office, or enabled to turn the patronage of the government against [its] own existence."[50] It was natural for the President to look to Federalism as a breeding ground of political trouble in the remoteness of Orleans, but his fears did not materialize. The Federalist party never achieved a foothold there. Jeffersonian Republicanism was dominant, and few undertook to challenge its universal attraction. Even the opponents of Claiborne considered themselves Republicans. Political affiliations tended to be transitory, factional, and personal. Party labels were sometimes used as a convenient shorthand, but parties as such did not exist.[51]

On his own initiative, General James Wilkinson submitted a very extensive list of recommendations to the President on July 1. It was compiled by Evan Jones and Peter Delabigarre, both of whom were to become enemies of Claiborne.[52] The governor himself was ill at this time and unable to attend to the task assigned him. His private secretary, Joseph Briggs, sent a brief list on to Washington, and Claiborne amplified it when he was back at work.[53]

Meanwhile, Jefferson had not been idle. Acting upon the list submitted by Wilkinson, the President completed his appointments to territorial office on August 30. Included among these was Claiborne's commission to continue serving as governor after October 1. Jefferson explained that he had hoped to enlist the services of the Marquis de Lafayette—a choice that would be acceptable both to the nation and to the local inhabitants. However, since circumstances did not so permit and as Claiborne's "services have been so much approved as to leave no desire to look elsewhere to fill the office," Jefferson had decided to keep him at his post.[54]

Jefferson designated James Brown of Kentucky, Dominick A. Hall of South Carolina, Mahlon Dickerson of New Jersey, Ephraim Kirby of Connecticut, and John Prevost of New York to the posts of territorial secretary, the U.S. District Court, the U.S. attorney's office, and the Superior Court respectively.[55] The President also enumerated the ways in which Claiborne should proceed with vacancies left to his discretion. He advised the governor that of the thirteen council members seven ought to be American and six French. Moreover, he wanted a mixture of planter and merchant interests and representation to be duly apportioned among the parishes. The President chose three of the six French members—Boré, the former mayor, Poydras, and Bellechasse.[56] He listed five others from whom Claiborne was to choose three. For the American majority he chose Morgan, Clark, Watkins, and Jones, plus John Roman of Atakapas (whom Jefferson thought, mistakenly, to be American), and William Wykoff, a wealthy resident of Opelousas. He left the seventh choice to Claiborne. He said that he had tried to choose men who knew both French and English, although this was not an absolute prerequisite for appointment. He urged the acquisition of the other language upon those conversant in but one.[57]

Claiborne was flattered by his commission as governor, although he did suggest, with typical self-effacement, that James Monroe was better suited.[58] As for Jefferson's other appointments, the governor was generally in agreement and voiced no objection to the policy of establishing an American majority on the legislative council. He was forced to make certain modifications of the President's list, however. He declined to select Pierre Derbigny, Pierre Sauvé, or Jean Noël Destréhan, the three memorialists to Congress, on the grounds that they would be unable to attend the council's early session in New Orleans. William Kenner, a merchant and native of the United States, took the place of John Roman in order to increase the American contingent on the council as Jefferson had directed. Finally, Le Breton D'Orgenois, a young Creole who was to play an important role in the Batture controversy, was Claiborne's choice for U.S. marshal.

Everything seemed to be going smoothly until Evan Jones declined to serve. Jones, a resident of New Orleans since 1765, informed the governor that it would have been inconsistent for him, a signatory of the Louisiana Remonstrance, to join in a government of which he disapproved. Claiborne blamed Edward Livingston for instigating Jones in this course of action and feared that others would follow his lead.[59] Altogether eight of the appointees had signed the memorial to Congress. Should all eight decline their commissions, the wheels of territorial government might cease to turn.

Claiborne was justified in his fears. Jones published his letter of declination in the local press and thereby raised the standard of political revolt.[60] Certainly Jones desired to do more than maintain his own consistency. Otherwise there was no point in publicizing his letter to the governor.[61] "He thought this a favorable opportunity," wrote one observer, "while the public mind was agitated, to put himself at the head of a party, which, at any other moment he could not have hoped for. To create that very party spirit which he feigns to deprecate is the object he has in view."[62]

While sentiment in the English-speaking community was divided on Jones's action,[63] he did rally support among some who had been offered places on the legislative council. By October 22 Etienne Boré and Robert Dow, a Scottish physician long resident in the territory, had declined their appointments.[64] John Watkins, Benjamin Morgan, and Gaspar Dubuys, a judge in the new court of common pleas, had accepted. The rest had still to be heard from.[65] Within a short time Daniel Clark and Michael Cantarelle, commandant of the German Coast, had joined with Jones. Claiborne was heartened, however, that Julien Poydras had consented to be a councilman. "The acceptance of Mr. Poydras is a fortunate occurrence," Claiborne wrote to Madison, "and his Conduct and reasoning form a happy contrast to the part acted by Mr. Jones, Clark and others."[66] Claiborne considered Poydras "the wealthiest and most influential man in the Territory," and while he feared he would not soon be able to fill the remaining vacancies on the council, the knowledge that Poydras would cooperate was consoling. Altogether Claiborne had managed to collect a total of five acceptances. Dubuys had withdrawn, but William Kenner and William Wykoff had agreed to serve. Claiborne was anxious to appoint two other "judicious prudent men" to form at least a quorum so as to set the machinery in motion, for much work needed to be done. On December 2 Claiborne filled two blank commissions with the names of Eugene Dorcier, a man thought to favor the American administration, and George Pollock, a Claiborne supporter. To ensure a quorum he appointed an eighth member, James Mather, an Englishman of long residence destined to become mayor of New Orleans within a few years.[67]

On December 4, 1804, the legislative council held its first session. "The meeting of the Council has had already a happy effect," Claiborne wrote with relief. "The few Intriguers who have laboured to stop the wheels of government are greatly discouraged, and the well disposed Citizens highly satisfied."[68] Poydras was elected council president, a recognition of his public stature. Claiborne addressed the new body in very general terms, mapping out specific areas where legislation was necessary.[69] Then Poydras delivered a message of his own. He commented at length upon the relationship between the territory and the United States, defended congressional wisdom in putting the inhabitants through a period of political apprenticeship prior to statehood, denied that the council would be unduly subservient to the will of the governor, and explained why he believed Evan Jones and his followers to have been misguided.[70] In general, Poydras struck the needed note of harmony that retrieved Claiborne from the first serious challenge to his leadership. In the days and weeks that followed, the council strove to do its work. As one keen observer noted, the counselors were "hammering away at Laws as fast as they can—".[71]

The meeting of the legislative council, and the support which it received from Julien Poydras, aborted the premature bid for power of the Livingston-Clark-Jones faction. This failure, however, was by no means a victory for Claiborne. The governor was still under a cloud. On this particular matter he had some support from the press and from leading notables like Julien Poydras, but, in general, his fitness for his post was still in doubt. Moreover, besides the Louisiana Remonstrance, other pamphlet literature pointedly critical of Claiborne—his appointments policy in particular—was circulating in New Orleans at this time.

The *Esquisse de la Situation Politique*, composed by Pierre Derbigny prior to his departure as one of the Louisiana memorialists, charged the governor with giving an insufficient number of offices to the natives and appointing too many Americans.[72] In reply Claiborne detailed the many lucrative posts he had given to the "ancient inhabitants,"[73] but he failed to appreciate two telling points. First, his argument that appointments had been divided evenly was self-evidently weak, since the population was still overwhelmingly French. Second, while it was true that many local government jobs such as in the municipality, the militia, the lower courts, and the mayor's office were left in the hands of old Louisianians, the offices in the higher echelons of administration were dominated by Americans. To be sure, on this level the matter was beyond Claiborne's control. The Superior Court, the legislative council, the governor's office itself, the U.S. District Court, the offices of U.S. attorney and U.S. marshall and all other offices created by congressional enactment were in the gift of the President, and Jefferson filled them on the basis of his own national political commitments and with only one ear attuned to the local situation. Nonetheless, Claiborne was the President's political lightning rod, attracting whatever resentment Jefferson's decided partiality for Americans generated.[74]

Claiborne still remained very much isolated, and his position was to worsen before it would improve. The Livingston-Clark-Jones faction was jolted by its failure to enlist greater public support. Livingston would continue to strengthen his ties to the settled population, but Clark and Jones moved closer to the American community. As for Claiborne, he was truly alone at this time. Only the national Administration was behind him The President was, to be sure, a formidable variable in the political equation, but given Jefferson's unremitting search for a replacement for Claiborne, even this was not a dependable power base.

V

New Orleans supported a lively brand of journalism during the first years of the American regime. The *Moniteur de la Louisiane*, the well-established French-language journal, though conservative in outlook, occasionally opened its pages to polemical material. In general, however, it was on the periphery of public debate. The other French-language paper, the *Telegraphe*, which began publication one week before the American takeover of Louisiana, accommodated its new American readership with an English translation. The *Telegraphe* did not adhere to the *Moniteur's* fastidious standard of journalism, but displayed much more vigorous interest in politics.[75] In 1807 the French press was joined by the *Courrier de la Louisiane*, a paper of high political content and decided editorial positions.

The English-language press in New Orleans had no venerable forbears like the *Moniteur*, but it was rooted in the full-blooded traditions of eighteenth-century American journalism. The first paper was the *Union*, which appeared on December 13, 1804, a counterpart to the *Telegraphe*. Published by James Lyon, it lasted for one year under its original ownership. During that time it took moderate positions on public questions and was generally supportive of Governor Claiborne. Then the *Union* was purchased by James M. Bradford of Kentucky. Renamed the *Orleans Gazette*, it appeared under its new publisher on the first anniversary of the establishment of American sovereignty in Louisiana, December 20, 1804. The *Orleans Gazette* transformed the style of the *Union* and raised the temperature of New Orleanian journalism by several degrees.

James Bradford was the son of John Bradford, an early Kentucky printer who had established one of the first newspapers west of the Appalachians. James had gained experience in Frankfort on his father's *Guardian of Freedom*. Interested in acquiring a political appointment in the new territory of Orleans, perhaps as territorial secretary, James sought the patronage of John Brown, the U.S. senator from Kentucky, unaware that James Brown, the senator's younger brother and a future draftsman of Louisiana's first legal digest, was being considered for the post. John Brown advised Bradford that the recommendation of John Breckinridge, the other senator from Kentucky, was needed. Breckinridge and the Bradfords were then at odds, however, the elder Bradford having blamed Breckinridge for his loss of the post of public printer in Frankfort. James Bradford failed to get the appointment he sought.[76]

Bradford remained cordial with James Brown despite their rivalry for territorial appointment. From Nashville Bradford wrote Brown of his intention to buy Lyon's *Union* in New Orleans and requested that Brown use his influence in the territory to secure the public printing for him. He also asked that Brown find him a French family with whom to board, as he wished to learn the language as soon as possible. Brown himself was still not arrived in New Orleans and had yet to receive word of his appointment from Jefferson. Bradford told Brown to expect him in New Orleans by mid-October 1804.[77] Bradford would arrive somewhat soured by his failure to secure a political position, but he did obtain the important and lucrative position of public printer.

The third major English-language paper was the *Louisiana Gazette*, a weekly which began on July 24, 1804. More restrained than Bradford's journal, the *Gazette* preferred wide news coverage to local politics. Its relation to the *Orleans Gazette* was that of the *Moniteur* to the *Courrier*. Both the *Orleans Gazette* and the *Louisiana Gazette* backed the interests of the growing American community as they saw it, but neither supported Claiborne. Bradford's paper was Jeffersonian in its national orientation, whereas the *Louisiana Gazette*, at least according to Claiborne, was Federalist.[78]

In addition to the local press, newspapers from outside New Orleans flooded the territory. Natchez was the nearest population center, and its papers had a wide readership in Orleans as did the New Orleans press there. Moreover, the important national papers were regularly received. The local editors and publishers used them as their chief source of world and national news. So extensive was this traffic in newspapers that Gideon Granger, the Postmaster General, once attributed the delay in the mails to "the vast number of news papers that are transmitted from the Atlantic States to [Orleans] . . . and the Mississippi Territory. They have frequently accumulated in such quantities," he wrote, "that the mail carrier could not carry them at one time with the horses that he had usually employed."[79] Thus the territory of Orleans was not only animated by a considerable and lively local press, but, despite its remoteness from the United States, it was kept abreast of events taking place beyond its frontiers.

Despite the availability of the printed medium, however, the governor of Orleans failed to establish a working relationship with any of the local printers. This was not the least of William Claiborne's oversights. Claiborne appreciated the power of the press only when he was the object of its abuse, and he seemed incapable of understanding how it could be employed to advantage. He complained to Julien Poydras in the summer of 1804 that but for "anonymous writings" everything would be quiet in New Orleans.[80] He regretted that "licentiousness" was the unavoidable evil attending a free press and believed that only patience would instruct Louisianians in how to bear it. Despite the fact that Claiborne controlled the appointment of public printer, he continued to endure abuse from James Bradford and the *Orleans Gazette* for three full years before he apparently realized that the office ought to be given to one more favorably disposed toward the government. Not until 1808 did J. B. S. Thierry, the more sympathetic polemicist of the *Louisiana Courier*, replace Bradford in that capacity.

Probably the journal that came closest to adopting a decided pro-Claiborne position during the early period was the *Union*. On August 11, 1804, the editor felt compelled to deny an allegation that it was under Claiborne's control. But even the *Union* did not escape the governor's censure, for in October, probably because James Lyon was temporarily out of town, Claiborne complained to Madison that of late the paper "has been . . . of no service to the Government here; on the contrary, it has been of great Injury."[81] Nevertheless, in the furor occasioned by Evan Jones's refusal to accept appointment to the legislative council, and later, on the question of the Louisiana Remonstrance, the *Union* would stand by the governor just prior to its sale to James Bradford.[82] Claiborne was to regret its passing.

So indifferent was Claiborne to the possibilities of the public prints that he went out of his way to dissociate himself from newspaper controversy. Imputations that press material was in any way a product of his influence seemed to him to diminish his reputation. In reviewing his conduct during his first year in office, for example, he desired to demonstrate to Madison "that the affairs of this Territory have [not] been administered in [a] slovenly and ridiculous manner." He wrote that he had considered publishing documents which would tend to justify his conduct in the eyes of the public and would answer certain specific charges being made against him. "I at first contemplated a publication of the Documents that went to my exculpation," he wrote, "but I was dissuaded from it by a conviction . . . that the people would soon be aware of the characters and real objects of those who have so wantonly attacked me. Under such circumstances I thought a perfect silence on my part, would not only be the most dignified, but also the most prudent conduct to pursue."[83] To prove that he was in no way sullied by newsprint, Claiborne enclosed a sworn statement by one of the editors of the *Union* denying that the governor had ever attempted to influence its editorial policy.[84]

Such fastidiousness was still characteristic of men in authority in an age when political opposition was not yet recognized as part of the normal process of representative government. The existence of party evidenced division and disaffection. The well-ordered polity was free of such aberrations. For a public official to engage in polemical combat was to legitimate "the spirit of party" while diminishing the dignity of office.[85] Claiborne's refusal to engage in close political infighting bears witness to his belief in these conventional attitudes, but he had to pay a price for his orthodoxy. He was the object of constant harassment—in this case, from the press—and yet he declined to reply. Yet as newspaper attacks became more shrill—" an object of terror" he called them—the fear of press abuse impeded the recruitment of able men into government.[86] The governor's detachment, resulting in part from his adherence to the ideological strictures of his time, confined the range of his political activity to rather narrow limits.

Claiborne's relations with the press typified his whole approach to government in the early period of his career in Lower Louisiana. Caught up in a welter of conflicting ethnic claims, his authority challenged by the presence of French and Spanish officials, beset by ambitious men eager to replace him, criticized for policies which were beyond his control, and badgered from all sides by lively and able journalists, the young governor tried to hold himself apart from controversy.

VI

Eighteen five, the second year of William Claiborne's tenure in Lower Louisiana, was not marked by radical changes either in the structure of politics or in the trends of government. It was a quiet year—a year for building. The legislative council, authorized to start functioning in mid-November 1804, had not convened until December because of the difficulties encountered in persuading local notables to serve. The first half of 1805, therefore, was a period for maximum labor upon the great legislative tasks of a new regime. In its first session the council occupied itself with such matters as county government, practice before the new Superior Court, the criminal law, court costs, the militia, the incorporation of the city of New Orleans, public accounts, and the compensation of public officials. In its second session the council provided for the circuit jurisdiction of the Superior Court and for the fees of attorneys practicing in the counties, regulated public houses, inns, and hotels, defined the functions of public notaries, established a court of probate, improved inland navigation, and incorporated a congregation of the Protestant Episcopal Church.[87] No great event or burning political issue impeded the work of legislative creation. Nothing as serious as the Louisiana Remonstrance of the previous year disturbed the relative tranquillity of the territory. Even the elections in the fall to the new representative assembly, called into being by congressional enactment, did not evoke significant controversy. Rather, 1805 saw a continuation of the political patterns of the first year of territorial life.

Claiborne's relations with the press did not change. More frequently the object of journalistic abuse than of praise, he was above its quarrels. The *Orleans Gazette*, in particular, had become the organ of political opposition. The paper was not one month under its vituperative new manager, James Bradford, when the first of a series of unsettling articles over the signature of "AN INHABITANT" appeared in print. The INHABITANT, whom Isaac Briggs thought to be either Daniel Clark, John B. Prevost, or Edward Livingston,[88] adopted the role of a "Public Accuser" whose accusations were among the most strident ever recited in the territory. Claiborne was charged with clumsy and excessive use of power, but also with having displayed weakness before foreign officials still present in New Orleans.[89] Much play was given to the Hulin-Villamil controversy as evidence of this weakness. François Hulin was a local resident who had purchased, at public auction, the slaves of one Don Pedro Villamil. The sale was authorized by the governor himself, but Villamil later challenged Hulin's right to the property before the Spanish commissioner in New Orleans, the Marquis de Casa Calvo. The Marquis issued a decree purporting to prevent Hulin from selling the slaves in question and directing public notaries to withhold official recognition and authentication of such sales. The press accused Claiborne of having sanctioned this exercise of judicial authority by a foreign agent.[90]

Typically, Claiborne took his case in the Hulin-Villamil affair to the general government. On the very day that Bradford published the Public Accuser's account of the matter (January 19), the governor wrote hurriedly to Madison. He told his chief that he had considered publishing documents justifying his action but finally decided that "a perfect silence" was the best course. He had, however, "determined through your Department to convey to the Executive a few comments upon the subject as next to *an approving conscience*, the approbation of the President, is the first object of my ambition, the most anxious wish of my Heart."[91] Claiborne argued that he had acted forthrightly once he understood that Casa Calvo was attempting to exercise judicial authority, and he had insisted that any adjudication of the legal question would have to be undertaken by an American tribunal. More significant than the particulars of the controversy, however, was Claiborne's style of response in regard to the politics of the question. He felt it sufficient to defend himself in private communications with the Administration rather than in public refutation of press insinuations.[92]

In a third installment the Public Accuser criticized Claiborne for the weakness of the territorial militia, for his imprudent sanctioning of a corps of free blacks, and for his unwholesome endorsement of an illicit love affair involving one of his subordinate officers and the daughter of a local inhabitant.[93] In general, the writer described a pattern of administration "uniformly masked with weakness, vanity and error." The governor was defended by Lewis Kerr, the sheriff of New Orleans and the acting U.S. marshal, and by James Workman, a recent arrival from South Carolina, in articles which appeared both in Bradford's paper and in the *Louisiana Gazette.*[94] Their statements in the public press in opposition to the Livingston-Clark-Jones faction revealed the continued division within the English-speaking community and the ties which Claiborne still preserved with some of its more articulate spokesmen. That bond was not to be severed for another several years.

"You will see by the papers how elegantly the newspaper writers abuse Governor Claiborne, Daniel Clark at their head," wrote James Sterrett to Nathaniel Evans. "What a tax it is to be a *great man*—how the shafts of envy are let loose against them."[95] The shafts found their mark. During the early weeks of 1805 Claiborne commented repeatedly to his superiors on the buffeting he received in the press. His mode of response was to send the newspaper articles to the capital along with a written self defense against the charges. "I enclose you the third number of the Public Accuser," he wrote Madison at the end of January. "You will see the Gall of my Enemies and the zeal with which they embrace every occurrence to annoy my feelings."[96] He apologized for bothering the Secretary with such trivial matters, but assured him that when he had perceived "the malignity of [his] opponents" he would understand Claiborne's desire "to keep the Executive advised of [his] answers to the charges." He held Livingston and Clark responsible for the attacks.[97]

"The Parties here run high," wrote Captain Sterrett with his usual bemused detachment. "The Governor is abused *elegantly,* and some of the writers sting their opponents severely—there was a piece in the *Orleans Gazette* on the 2nd Instant [over] the signature of 'Point blank shot' that bears hard on several of the Governor's enemies and is the best that has appeared on that side."[98] Despite the articles of Curtius, Laelius, and "Point Blank Shot," most of the published material was critical of Claiborne. Isaac Briggs referred to "the torrent of abuse lately poured out upon him in the news-papers . . . compounded of gross misrepresentation, base falsehood and bitter, tho' I trust impotent malevolence."[99]

The political warfare carried on in the newspapers occasioned a number of private duels. Claiborne's own brother-in-law, Micajah G. Lewis, was a fatality in once such encounter.[100] Claiborne unburdened his grief to Jefferson on this occasion and tried to identify the "persecution" he was suffering at the hands "of a licentious press" with Jefferson's own unhappy experience with zealous journalists. The President was not without sympathy. Replying to an earlier letter, he noted Claiborne's apologies for troubling Madison with the articles of the Public Accuser. "We perfectly understand the game which is playing against you,"confided Jefferson. "We know every man concerned in it."[101] He commended the governor for detailing the accusations against him and for forwarding documents in his own defense.

Privately, however, both Madison and Jefferson were a little peeved at Claiborne's bothersome trivia. Madison defended his own transmission of the governor's detailed enclosures to Jefferson by simply saying that he was obeying the governor's wish "in taxing you" with his information.[102] Moreover, their own independent sources confirmed at least some of the public charges being made against Claiborne. Madison reported that James Brown, a fairly credible witness and one without personal motive, seemed "to concur fully in denouncing [Claiborne's] want of talents and weight of character." The President wanted it understood, however, that "in the case of Claiborne we must show that however thankfully we receive personal information as to our officers [from such men as James Brown, Isaac Briggs, and others], we will not permit them to be written down by newspaper defamation."[103] Thus, despite his reassurances, Jefferson was countenancing criticism of Claiborne's performance. Had the governor been aware of this his anxiety would, no doubt, have increased, but with the favorable result of forcing him to reevaluate his political posture. Instead, he continued to rely upon an ever-narrowing political base.

VII

At the same time that Claiborne was being attacked in the press a religious dispute erupted within the Catholic community. Father Patrick Walsh, the vicar-general for Lower Louisiana, had removed the parish priest in New Orleans, Father Antonia de Sedella. Father Antonia was a local favorite, and his parishioners kept him on in defiance of Walsh. Since the vicar-general was of Irish extraction and Father Antonia was Spanish, there was an added tug of ethnic tension to what otherwise would have been a purely sectarian squabble. When Walsh composed a pastoral letter to the parish, the city government tried to suppress its publication. But Bradford, in the name of a free press, printed it in the *Orleans Gazette*. Walsh reprimanded the people for their disobedience and reminded them that only the Church could invest a priest. Their defiance, he said, was schismatic.[104]

Colonel Bellechasse of the militia replied to Walsh in the *Telegraphe*. He challenged the vicar's powers, repudiated his attempt to dictate to the parish, and criticized his past performance in the territory. Bellechasse also played ever so delicately upon the ethnic prejudices of the inhabitants. "It would be well to recall," he wrote, "that an Irishman, one of [Walsh's] compatriots, brought mourning and desolation to our families."[105] This was a reference to Alexander O'Reilly, who had arrived in 1769 in the service of Spain to put down a revolt against the first Spanish governor of Louisiana. O'Reilly had crushed the uprising and executed its leaders. These events were engraved in the living memory of many of the inhabitants. The reminder that Walsh, too, was Irish was an effort to rekindle old hatreds. In addition, the fact that Walsh's viewpoint was aired in the *Gazette* while Bellechasse resorted to the *Telegraphe* reinforced the impression that this was a confrontation not merely among Catholics but one between the French- and English-speaking communities. Despite the fact that the overwhelming number of the English population was Protestant and therefore uninvolved in the dispute, the "ancients" were again impressed with Anglo-American assertiveness and interference.

Claiborne noted the existence of the problem in several letters to Madison in mid-March 1805, but he characteristically played down its importance.[106] Nevertheless, its deeper significance was apparent. Besides the ethnic and purely religious question, there was an even larger problem at issue. Casa Calvo, who was still in New Orleans and an ominous reminder of Spanish pretensions to the province, sided with Father Antonia. The situation was particularly dangerous at this time because rumors were circulating in the Natchitoches area, near the Spanish outpost at Nacogdoches, that the return of all of Louisiana to Spain was imminent. The religious issue, therefore, was seen as a lever to pry the inhabitants from their allegiance to the United States.[107] Meanwhile the commandant in the parish of St. Bernard informed Claiborne that a priest, who had also been replaced by the vicar-general, had accosted his successor at the church door and had expressed the wish to appeal the disputed appointment to the people. Disorder ensued, and a serious riot at the church seemed possible.[108]

From one point of view a breach of good order would permit the governing authorities to move into the controversy. Claiborne had written to a number of influential people that, while freedom of conscience was a sacred liberty, the magistracy was charged with the preservation of civil peace.[109] But Claiborne was not anxious to become more deeply involved. If he chose to support Father Walsh he would push the discontented inhabitants into the hands of the sympathetic Spanish. If, on the other hand, he sided with Father Antonia, he would be undermining the stabilizing authority of the church while at the same time appearing to give in to Spanish pressure. Walsh tried to draw the governor into the dispute by pointing out its political overtones,[110] but Claiborne refused to step in.[111] Even when, during the mounting tension with the Spanish on the Sabine in October 1806, Claiborne became convinced that Father Antonia was, and always had been, a "seditious Priest," he refrained from taking action against him.[112]

Claiborne's coolness in this irritating, tense, and continuing religious squabble could be credited to political wisdom. It is more likely, however, that his neutrality was motivated by customary detachment. In this case, if not in others, his penchant for impartiality was appropriate, for it prevented his entry into an ugly and possibly damaging fracas.

The religious dispute between Walsh and Antonia awakened

the English-speaking community to the absence of a Protestant church in New Orleans. The *Orleans Gazette* noted this neglect and commented that the great number of Protestants who flocked to the new territory expected some provision for their religious needs. The paper urged the establishment of a Protestant congregation.[113] Bradford himself took an active part in recruiting a qualified Episcopalian minister at a salary of two thousand dollars, and by November these efforts bore fruit.[114] The Reverend Philander Chase arrived bearing letters of reference and copies of the Book of Common Prayer. He was duly installed as the minister of the new congregation, vestrymen were chosen, and the first Protestant service was conducted on the seventeenth of the month.[115]

Governor Claiborne played no part in the establishment of Protestantism in the territory.[116] The prejudices dividing Catholics and Protestants were as acute as those separating the ethnic communities, but Claiborne remained seemingly indifferent to both. The governor's policy on the Walsh-Antonia dispute, as well as his lack of concern for the establishment of a Protestant church in Orleans, paralleled his posture toward other public issues. He strove to be above the battle, whatever the war.

VIII

By the summer of 1805 W. C. C. Claiborne had delineated the pattern of his government. He saw himself as an administrator of policy rather than a policy-maker. The needs of the territory were ample. Satisfying them taxed all of his time, his energy, and his imagination. With patience, and a fair degree of tolerance from the population, all would go well. Politics was an annoyance, the whip used by the "outs" to fret the "ins"—the less of it the better. Claiborne was well intentioned, efficient, and honest. He viewed his problems as the work of men who had none of these qualities.[117]

During 1805 and 1806 Claiborne followed the lines drawn in the first eighteen months of his regime. As an administrator his major task was to staff the offices of government with able and efficient men. By the summer of 1806 these offices had been created. The legislative council of 1804-05 had outfitted the new territory with a bureaucratic structure capable of meeting most of its requirements. All that remained was to set the machinery in motion. This was the governor's chief preoccupation, and in appointing men to new positions Claiborne adhered to the policy he had pursued from the very beginning despite lively criticism. He tried to strike a balance between the French and the

English population. "I would wish the Coroner, Treasurer and two Justices of the Peace to be Natives of the Territory or ancient inhabitants thereof," he instructed one local judge. "Two of the Justices of the Peace, I would wish to be Natives or Ancient Citizens of the United States."[118] His appointments policy typified his approach to government in general—to steer between the French and the Anglo-Americans, favoring neither if he could help it. This posture of political neutralism worked as long as a major political crisis did not erupt. For a time Claiborne achieved a kind of precarious equilibrium.

But the delicate balance was upset by the actions of the national government as it attempted to respond to the local clamor for more complete political liberty. On March 2, 1805, Congress enacted a second territorial statute providing for a greater measure of representative government in the Orleans territory.[119] It called for the establishment of a House of Representatives. Once elected, the House would choose candidates for appointment to a new five-member legislative council to be selected by the President. The two bodies would constitute the legislative branch of territorial government. Unlike the earlier legislative council—a purely appointive body acting within a unitary framework of government under a powerful executive—the advent of the new bicameral legislature would mark the real beginning of representative government in Lower Louisiana. A House of Representatives was duly elected in October 1805, and the result was an overwhelming victory for the ancient inhabitants.[120] Its first task was to nominate ten candidates for the legislative council from whom the President would submit five for Senate approval. Eight of the original ten nominees were men of standing in the French community. When the council met in the spring of 1806, all of the members were French.[121]

Claiborne looked upon the new legislature as he had the old—an instrument for carrying into effect needed projects requiring legislative sanction. His opening address at the first session was similar to those he had delivered in the past.[122] But soon he perceived a change in mood and a growing resistance to executive direction. By the second week in April the governor was complaining of the legislature's modest progress "in the dispatch of Business."[123] The political situation was extremely awkward for Claiborne. The old council had been controlled by that slim American majority which Jefferson himself had preferred, but now the governor had to deal with a French-dominated legislature that was no longer answerable to the general government. An early effort was made to alter eligibility requirements for seats in the House and thereby purge the

American minority altogether. Claiborne vetoed the proposal.[124] This broke the surface calm. But the real confrontation came when the legislature passed a bill declaring the civil law to be in force in the territory and citing the legal authorities to which the courts were to refer pending the completion of a civil code of private law. Claiborne's veto of this project elicited sharp protests and threatened a virtual collapse of the government.[125]

In the wake of his successive vetoes of measures clearly reflective of the majority will, the governor had managed to ignite a major political revolt. Motions were introduced calling for the dissolution of both houses. Even more significant, the legislature retaliated by electing Daniel Clark as territorial delegate to Congress. This placed one of Claiborne's principal opponents in a position to pry the governor loose from his national political moorings.[126] In the past Claiborne had endeavored to steer between the ethnic groups, but now, when forced to take a stand, he had come down hard on the American side by refusing to sanction the permanent establishment of a continental civil law system in an American territory. Local sentiment was outraged.[127]

The conflict over the laws occasioned a temporary deadlock in government that threatened to untie the institutional fabric which had been the main task of administration in the early years of the territory's history. But Claiborne's veto not only brought federal policy and local policy into sharp conflict; it also illuminated the ambiguous role of the office of governor as the keystone of a highly fragile and double-jointed edifice of government. As territorial governor, Claiborne wore two hats, one in his capacity as a federal official and the other as local executive. The territorial governor was the focal point in each of two increasingly separate structures of authority.[128] Claiborne's major responsibility as a federal official was to outfit the territory of Orleans with an administrative apparatus under guidelines set by the national Administration.[129] But the more he succeeded in accomplishing this goal, the greater was the tension between local and federal interests. He could not side completely with the federal government, because to do so might undermine his regime by alienating elements whose cooperation was requisite for stability. On the other hand, he could not resist federal policy, because the federal government was the source of his power and the base of his political support.[130]

Thus Claiborne's vacillations and hesitations on almost every issue of substance mirrored the built-in ambivalence of his role as an American colonial governor dispatched to implement federal policies—policies which in themselves were irresolute, since neither Congress nor the Administration desired to act hastily on the major questions it faced in Lower Louisiana. Confronted with the impossibility of imposing the general will by superior force, the central government had to pursue its objectives with circumspection, particularly with regard to the sensitive legal problem. In time, it was thought, as the people of Lower Louisiana became Americanized, so would the laws.

The political crisis of 1806 not only illustrated the delicacy of Claiborne's position; it also signaled the end of political neutralism as a workable political style. For by early 1808 it was clear that the governor had altered his course and changed his approach to policy-making as well as to the substance of policy. Claiborne's approval of the civil law digest adopted by the territorial legislature in March 1808, a landmark in the legal history of Louisiana, was to be uncharacteristically bold and creative.[131] His resolution of the legal question set the terms for Louisiana's subsequent entry into the American union. The establishment of a kind of civil law system in Louisiana forced the new American nation to accept an alien culture and a truly foreign legal code, thereby enriching the nation's heritage. But not the least of William Claiborne's achievement was his redefinition of his own place in territorial government. By his action on the legal question he was, in the end, to repudiate the role originally assigned him and assert a capacity for leadership of which few would have thought him capable just a few years before.

[3] *Burr's Conspiracy and the Orleans Territory*

Vice-President Aaron Burr left office in March 1805 beneath a thick canopy of mistrust. He was under indictment in New York and New Jersey for the murder of Alexander Hamilton in the fatal duel at Weehawken on July 11, 1804. With his national political career in ruins, the dapper, impulsive, and audacious New Yorker traveled westward, hoping to build a base of support in the southwest. Like other Americans before him, he headed for New Orleans.

Burr numbered among his friends some of the most influential men of "the western country," including Andrew Jackson of Tennessee, John Adair, the Kentucky Indian fighter, and John Brown, U.S. senator from Kentucky. Apparently Burr's chief confidant was James Wilkinson, pensioner of the former Spanish governors of Louisiana, governor of Upper Louisiana, and Commanding General of the United States Army in the Mississippi Valley. Wilkinson's complicity in the unfolding "conspiracy" was regarded by Burr as crucial; indeed, the general's decision to break with Burr at the eleventh hour proved to be the key to its failure. On these men, and others, Aaron Burr counted for support in the imprecise designs which he formulated soon after leaving the Vice-Presidency.

Historians have never finally established the meaning of Burr's movements in the southwest. His defenders have argued that he intended nothing more than to revolutionize the Spanish colonies in West Florida and Mexico—ends which most Jeffersonian Republicans would have applauded. Burr's critics have asserted that he purposed treason and subversion, that he hoped to detach all of the southwest and Louisiana from the Union and then establish an empire with Mexico and West Florida as tributary states. Burr himself probably never had a fixed design. He had many brands in the flames and hoped that at least one would catch fire.

Despite the atmosphere of pure fantasy that enveloped all of these rumored projects, Burr managed to obtain financial aid from several private sources. He was an exceedingly persuasive man. He was able to buy into the so-called Bastrop lands along the Ouachita River in Lower Louisiana, ostensibly in order to settle young frontiersmen whose presence in that remote quarter would bolster American military power near the Spanish border—a project not unlike Jefferson's soon-to-be-developed militia plan. But the Bastrop purchase may also have been a front for more ambitious schemes.

In the spring of 1805 the former Vice-President reconnoitered the Mississippi Valley in order to prepare the groundwork for his great adventure. His well-publicized trip culminated at New Orleans, where his visit stirred considerable enthusiasm among transplanted Americans and mild interest among the discontented local inhabitants. By the summer of 1806 the southwest was aflame with rumors of an impending clash with Spain along the Sabine River and alive with suspicion that Aaron Burr planned to use the conflict as a lever for prying the western states from the Union, as an occasion for liberating all of the Spanish provinces, or as an excuse for the invasion of Mexico. No one, not even Burr, knew for sure which it would be.

Jefferson was well informed on Burr's movements but remained ostensibly unalarmed. The President had reason for confidence. Burr miscalculated the measure of southwestern discontent. The Louisiana Purchase, with its guarantee of permanent access to the port of New Orleans, had dissipated separatist inclinations in the region. While the frontiersmen still harbored deep animosity toward the Spanish and would have welcomed the chance to push them further westward, any scheme seemingly tainted with secession or treason invited little genuine support in the Ohio and Mississippi valleys.

In the fall of 1806 James Wilkinson managed to defuse the Sabine border by establishing a neutral ground between the American and Spanish military encampments stationed there. With the threat of a Spanish war thus eliminated, Jefferson prepared to move against Burr. The President issued a proclamation on November 27, 1806, alerting the country to warlike designs against the colonies of a friendly power, warning the citizens of the southwest against participating in unlawful enterprises, and calling upon all state, federal, and territorial officials to aid in the apprehension of conspirators.

Meanwhile Wilkinson abjured his shadowy connections with Burr, hastened to New Orleans in order to ready its military defenses, and there conducted a bloodless "reign of terror" climaxed by the arbitrary arrests of Burr's alleged "co-conspirators"—Samuel Swartwout, Peter Ogden, Dr. Justus Erick Bollman, James Alexander, John Adair, and others. Burr himself surrendered to the Mississippi authorities, but fearing a court martial or even assassination by the vindictive Wilkinson, he attempted an escape. He was recaptured and transported to Richmond, Virginia, for trial.

Following a tumultuous and prolonged hearing, the Richmond grand jury indicted Burr for treason. In August 1807 the trial took place before the federal circuit court in Virginia with Chief Justice John Marshall presiding. The proceedings aroused intense interest, for the trial of Aaron Burr was as much a political as it was a legal contest. Important constitutional questions were at stake. The nation's leading barristers represented the opposing sides, and Jefferson himself, while never appearing in court, was as much a principal as Marshall and Burr. In the end the court narrowly construed the definition of treason contained in Article III of the Constitution and left the jury no alternative but acquittal. Cleared of all charges against him in Washington, Burr was subsequently indicted in Ohio, Kentucky, and Mississippi, but he was never tried again. In June of 1808 he sailed for Europe, a political exile and fugitive.[1]

Burr's enterprise—whatever it was—misfired. But while his aborted schemes did not, in the end, have serious national consequences, the same cannot be said for Louisiana.[2] Lower Louisiana was the projected seat of Burr's new empire. New Orleans was to have been the staging area for his attack upon Mexico. The discontents of the inhabitants of the Orleans territory provided the political basis for Burr's high hopes. And despite the failure of the "conspiracy" to trigger a Spanish colonial upheaval or southwestern secession, the effects of Burr's activities were keenly felt in Orleans. Burrism had important political reverberations there.

I

In the territory of Orleans the second coming of Aaron Burr was not unexpected. For years rumors of conspiracy, secession, revolution, and subversion circulated as the currency of common discourse in the southwest. Joseph Hamilton Daveiss, the U.S. district attorney in Kentucky and a Federalist, was not the first to sound the alarm, and it is no wonder that Jefferson read his repeated allegations in 1806 with skepticism.[3] Even William C. C. Claiborne was aware of the vulnerability of New Orleans to adventurers, but he too had more important things to worry about than the rumored projects of an ex-Vice-President. By mid-November 1806 however, the situation was changed. Claiborne now thought Burr's schemes "injurious"—even "political," a word with a meaning akin to "treason."[4] To Cowles Mead, the acting governor of the Mississippi territory, he spoke of "revolution" in the United States.[5] And to Madison he finally disclosed his worst fears. "I am now advised," he wrote the State Secretary on November 18 ". . . that the union of States is seriously menaced, and that the Storm will probably break out in New Orleans."[6] He named Daniel Clark, his territory's delegate in Congress, as a leading figure among the "thousands" concerned in the plot.

Claiborne had worried about Clark ever since his old enemy departed for Washington. He even considered a trip there himself in order to answer in person the accusations he felt certain Clark was making, but the rising political temperature in Orleans made such a journey unwise at that moment.[7] Now the governor began to see how Clark's long-term association with Aaron Burr might be used to advantage. Thus a new political opportunity was already within the governor's view when the first winds of the Burr storm began to blow. The menace of Burr was not to be minimized, however. No one knew how strong a force he would have when he descended upon New Orleans nor what would be the reaction of the people throughout the southwest. Everything pointed towards precaution, and by the end of November the machinery of a government besieged was already in motion.

Unfortunately, in the first few weeks the position of James Wilkinson was not clear. The general was well known for his duplicity. He too had been a candidate for the governorship of Orleans, and Claiborne knew that Wilkinson harbored little love for the man who had supplanted him. In addition, the news that the govenor had received was hardly reassuring. Cowles Mead reported that the general was believed to be "the soul of the conspiracy." His orders to all military units, both regular and militia, to concentrate at New Orleans, rather than go north to meet the enemy, was interpreted as proof of his treachery. "What is all this for?" asked Mead. "Is it to act for you or against you? . . . Is New Orleans invaded? is it threatened? or is it believed that any Enemy is nearer than the General himself?"[8] Even more alarming was the letter received from Andrew Jackson, then the commander of the Tennessee militia and an early intimate of Burr, who must have been well informed when he wrote, "Put your Town in a State of Defence[.] [O]rganize your Militia, and defend your City as well against internal enemies as external. . . . I fear you will meet with an attack from quarters you do not at present expect. Be upon the alert—Keep a watchful eye on our General . . . I fear there [is] something rotten in the State of Denmark. . . . Beware of the month of December."[9] Claiborne must have received Jackson's warning at the same time he heard from Mead.

On November 25 Wilkinson arrived.[10] He had power and the authority to use it. Claiborne had no choice but to trust him, and in the end the general would prove himself not only loyal but useful. Meanwhile the governor and the general prepared New Orleans for its greatest trial. During the first week in December the dilapidated fortifications at the corners of the city were repaired, pickets were constructed, and the troops were mustered and made ready. The navy was strengthened, and the merchants of the city were requested to cooperate in measures to increase the numbers of men and vessels.[11]

Military preparedness alone was not enough, however. The real menace of Burr was not that he would win by a military invasion but that his arrival in strength would ignite the kindling of political and social discontent. Wilkinson's readiness to undertake political action established his loyalty and made him serviceable to Claiborne's long-range purposes.

II

The political overtones in Burrism were audible from the beginning, and as the military threat subsided these increased in volume. Claiborne perceived the advantage he could gain over Daniel Clark by identifying the territorial delegate with Burr, but Clark's absence reduced the likelihood that he was fully engaged in a project to set up a Burrite empire in the southwest.[12] Yet, as Clark moved from the center of Claiborne's vision, at least for the moment, Clark's friends in New Orleans came into better focus.

The incriminating cipher letters between Jonathan Dayton and Aaron Burr which were delivered to Wilkinson first at Natchitoches and then in New Orleans by Samuel Swartwout, Peter Ogden, and Dr. Bollman spoke of "associates" and "agents" engaged in the great enterprise to which Wilkinson was privy.[13] Wilkinson showed these letters to Claiborne soon after his arrival in New Orleans. The words "associate" and "association" must have caught the govenor's attention. Ever since the early days of the territory, a semisecret organization of some three hundred men called "the Mexican Association" was known to exist in New Orleans. Its members and its purposes were public knowledge. The group prepared for the expected war between the United States and Spain when the "associates" would liberate the Spanish provinces, Mexico above all.[14] When Aaron Burr visited New Orleans in June 1805 he contacted the association and managed to enlist the aid of the organization in his projects.[15] As the conspiracy unraveled and the intimate connection between Burr and the Mexican Association was revealed, the membership—some of whom were leading figures in New Orleans—was exposed to the damaging libel of treason. Letters written in early December from Claiborne and Captain John Shaw, the naval commander in New Orleans, indicate that the men knew of the connection between the association and Burr. Thus, at the very outset, Burrism was linked to well-known local figures.[16]

Wilkinson suspected everyone, even James and Samuel Brown, the brothers of the senator from Kentucky, an intimate of Burr.[17] In the first few days following his arrival in New Orleans, the general interviewed a number of the local notables including the then mayor, John Watkins, Edward Livingston, and James Alexander, Erick Bollman's attorney. Wilkinson made a mental note of everything said, particularly of Livingston's and Alexander's offer to introduce him to Bollman. According to the general, his own public silence during the first two weeks of his stay in the city was a feint designed to trap the conspirators. New Orleans, he thought, was honeycombed with Burrites, and their belief in his own complicity was the one weapon he had to use against them.[18]

The flurry of activity in the city, the mysterious conferences, the fantastic rumors, and the military preparations made further delay impossible if the general was to act effectively, however. On December 3 Wilkinson revealed everything he knew to Claiborne and Captain Shaw, and on December 9 he informed the business community of what he would require of them. The general had shown his hand. Now he had to play it.

On December 14 Wilkinson ordered the arrest of Dr. Bollman. This was the beginning of a "reign of terror" in New Orleans. It consisted of a number of military arrests commencing with Bollman's and ending with that of John Adair, Burr's lieutenant, one month later. "The bubble has at length burst with an explosion that has agitated the public mind to a violent degree," observed Captain James Sterrett. "There is nothing talked of or thought of but secret expeditions, plots, plans, and conspiracies."[19]

On December 15 James Alexander filed for a writ of habeas corpus in the Superior Court to obtain Bollman's release. Judge Sprigg postponed the hearing until the following day. Livingston assisted Alexander in a second attempt to free Bollman, but it was now too late. Wilkinson snatched Bollman from the reach of the court and shipped him off to Baltimore for trial. Meanwhile, Lewis Kerr applied to James Workman, the county court judge, to free Samuel Swartwout and Peter Ogden, whose arrests at Fort Adams had been ordered some days before. Workman complied on the seventeenth. Ogden was released, but Swartwout, like Bollman, had been sent to Baltimore. On the eighteenth Wilkinson made a grand appearance in Superior Court to answer the writ ordering the release of Bollman. He used the occasion to accuse Edward Livingston and James Alexander of abetting the alleged conspirators. On the nineteenth he arrested Alexander and rearrested Ogden.

Subsequently Livingston filed for a writ of attachment against Wilkinson.[20] Judge Workman twice called upon Claiborne, as commander of the militia, to back the courts with military force, but Claiborne would not comply. On January 12 Workman adjourned the county court and applealed to the territorial House of Representatives for help. On the fourteenth both Workman and Lewis Kerr were arrested following their indictment on a charge of high misdemeanor by a grand jury summoned at Wilkinson's request.[21] On the same day James Bradford, editor of the *Orleans Gazette*, was apprehended for publishing incendiary accusations against the general, but he was later released without trial. Finally, John Adair, Burr's chief military aid, arrived in New Orleans not suspecting that the conspiracy was exposed. He was seized and shipped to Baltimore following Bollman, Swartwout, and Alexander.[22]

In addition to the military arrests, the illegal abductions, and the defiance of court writs, other extreme acts were committed. The city council imposed strict regulations governing the movements of the civilian population. Strangers were interrogated. Members of the volunteer militia were impressed into regular service. Ships were embargoed. Editors were silenced by drafting them into the mounted battalions. Citizens were encouraged to inform upon their neighbors, and public officials were threatened with the loss of their positions if they displayed opposition to the general's high-handedness. The excitement was great.

But by the middle of January the storm had subsided.[23] The failure of a plot to materialize in New Orleans, the news that the Mississippi authorities were alerted and preparing to apprehend Aaron Burr himself, the publication of Jefferson's proclamation of November 27 calling for the suppression of the conspiracy,[24] all deflated public interest and anxiety and stayed the acts of repression and intimidation. Nevertheless, the repercussions of the "reign of terror" were felt for many months. The political life of the territory had been transformed.

III

During the height of the Burr crisis Claiborne was immobilized. He refused to take decisive action in any way. When Wilkinson requested a proclamation of martial law, the governor turned him down.[25] His proclamation of December 16 merely announced that treachery was afoot and warned the citizens of the territory that the United States government would punish traitors.[26] On the other hand, Claiborne refused to support those directly affected by Wilkinson's conduct.[27]

The governor continued to have doubts about Wilkinson's absolute loyalty, but to defy the general would have been hazardous, for the regular army was under his command. Claiborne did not know how the local militia would respond if he decided to act resolutely. But most important, Claiborne must have appreciated, as time went on, that Wilkinson's "reign of terror" was generously bedaubing all of his enemies with the stigma of Burrism. Livingston and Bradford, two of his chief opponents, collided with Wilkinson head-on.[28] The thrust of the terror was against the English-speaking community. Not a single member of the French community stood accused of complicity, and throughout the crisis both Wilkinson and Claiborne marveled at their fidelity.[29] Even if Wilkinson felled some of Claiborne's political allies, like Kerr[30] and Workman,[31] this was a small price to pay if by the same stroke the governor's chief enemies were thoroughly paralyzed.

Once the arrests had ceased, the scene shifted to the territorial legislature which convened on January 12. In addressing the delegates Claiborne deplored the fact that citizens of the territory had been engaged in lawless associations.[32] The legislative council's reply noted with pleasure that none of the ancient inhabitants of the territory were among the "proselytes" of Burr, but the territorial House of Representatives was somewhat less gratified by recent events and "the extraordinary measures which have had place for some time past in this Territory."[33] The American delegates wanted a resolution condemning Wilkinson's actions. Simultaneously, Claiborne was pressing for a suspension of the writ of habeas corpus.[34] In the end the Orleans legislature passed resolutions supporting "all such measures as may be necessary to assure the peace of this Territory, and to defeat as well the secret machinations of internal foes . . .," but it refused to suspend habeas corpus.[35]

Meanwhile the treason trials of James Workman and Lewis Kerr proceeded in the U.S. District Court in New Orleans. Both men stood accused not for their direct connection with Burr and his alleged co-conspirators—Bollman, Swartwout, and Ogden—but for their links with the Mexican Association. The prosecution—consisting of Abner Duncan, Wilkinson's attorney, John Gurley, the territorial attorney general, and James Brown, the U. S. district attorney—attempted to show that the association had treasonable designs, that it was linked with Burr, and that it was engaged in warlike preparations against a nation with which the United States was at peace. The defense, led by Edward Livingston, endeavored to sever any ties connecting the Mexican Association and Burr. Livingston argued that the real cause for prosecution was Kerr's and Workman's efforts to guarantee the legal rights of Burr's alleged collaborators. Livingston tried to demonstrate that the Mexican Association was nothing more than a private political organization without sinister or subversive motives. "Vulgar minds are too easily led to believe that all political projects in a mere citizen are nearly allied to treason," said Kerr in his own defense. "Political societies," declared Workman, were not unlawful.[36] Both Workman and Kerr were eventually acquitted.[37]

Claiborne's enemies were encouraged by the defeat of the bill to suspend the writ of habeas corpus and by the government's failure to convict Workman and Kerr. They placed a draft memorial condemning Wilkinson's conduct before the territorial legislature.[38] Livingston drafted the memorial, but it was Dr. John Watkins, mayor of New Orleans and speaker of the House, who led the fight for its passage.[39] Watkins tried to show that the Mexican Association was composed of the best members of society, was patriotic in purpose, and had no connection whatever with Burr's schemes.[40] James Workman, introduced into the record the letters he had written to Claiborne in January and February requesting the use of force to back up his court writs.[41] Workman hoped that his material if adopted in conjunction with the memorial censuring Wilkinson, would display to Congress the consequences of the measures which the general had undertaken. He also calculated that a growing revulsion in Washington against Wilkinson would affect Claiborne too, since they had acted in unison during the crisis. Wilkinson would be Claiborne's albatross.

But Jefferson stood by his general.[42] The attack mounted upon him by John Randolph during the Richmond proceedings against Burr some months later climaxed a growing suspicion that Wilkinson was deeply implicated in the conspiracy.[43] Burr was sidetracked when Wilkinson became the primary target.[44] Burr's personal attractiveness contrasted sharply with the general's flamboyant grandiosity. Marshall's acquittal of the chief of the conspiracy was greeted with surprising equanimity, given the alleged offense and the publicity surrounding it. The resentment stemming from the plot centered upon Wilkinson, and in the course of the next few years he had to undergo the ordeal of two major inquiries into his affairs. But through all this Jefferson supported him.[45]

The attack upon Wilkinson did not succeed in the Orleans territory either. Livingston's memorial was defeated, because it did not truly reflect popular sentiment in the region. Many appreciated Wilkinson and Claiborne for their frequent expressions of faith in the old inhabitants. "A rapid change is taking place in the public mind daily, in favor of Wilkinson," wrote one observer.[46] A public address thanking the two officials for their energetic suppression of Burrism was circulated in the territory. It elicited the support of leading citizens and demonstrated widespread public approval of their actions. Edward Livingston questioned the validity of the address as a benchmark of support, and he charged that many signed out of pure expediency, but this in itself was significant, for it indicated that the political winds both in Washington and in Orleans had shifted in Wilkinson's and Claiborne's favor.[47]

The squalls of December and January were followed by a purge of public officials in the spring.[48] Livingston wrote that "place-men" signed the address to Wilkinson in fear that they would lose their positions, "as more than one had been lately removed from office for the opposition which they gave to General Wilkinson."[49] Another writer expected "that the President will remove from office all those persons who have been engaged in the secret combination with Workman and Co. This is notoriously the case with several who hold the most lucrative offices in this Territory, and their names must have been made known to the President."[50]

The most notable example of the purge was Claiborne's removal of Mayor Watkins. The governor informed Watkins in early March that he had selected James Mather for that position, a man more popular with the French than with the Americans.[51] The sheriff of Orleans county, George Ross, was also dismissed. Claiborne reported to Madison that ties with the Mexican Association were the chief cause for their forfeiture of "all claim to any further patronage."[52] Others in inferior offices resigned to avoid dismissal. James Bradford eventually lost his position as public printer.[53] Judge Workman had already stepped down from the bench in frustration and anger.

IV

"Our war is all over," James Sterrett wrote with some amusement to Nathaniel Evans at Fort Adams. "The troops are all to be parcelled out to different stations."[54] But if the war was over, minor skirmishes continued.

Edward Livingston had emerged as the leading public figure in opposition to the policies of Governor Claiborne. Ever since the Louisiana Remonstrance of 1804, Livingston had been a formidable presence with whom Claiborne had to contend. In those early days Livingston had been linked with Evan Jones and Daniel Clark. Since then Jones had faded from the picture, while Clark was busily promoting his career in Washington. Claiborne's other enemies, Workman, Kerr, and Watkins, were new in the opposition camp. But it was Livingston who went to court to defend Wilkinson's victims; it was Livingston who was the *eminence grise* behind the memorial condemning the general; and it was Livingston who penned the most persuasive pamphlet against him when that memorial failed of adoption.

As always, Livingston took the high ground. He saw himself as the champion of personal liberty against arbitrary officials. "I stood at first almost alone in my opposition to these unconstitutional measures," he confided to his brother. "The Executive, the Judiciary, the People all bent before the storm."[55] He noted with pleasure that "a spark of courage" was beginning to show itself—a reference to the presentment of the grand jury, subsequently suppressed, which, on January 24, challenged the legality of Wilkinson's actions.[56] "What a contemptible idea must the President have of this country to send such Bobadils and swaggering Pistols to govern it," Livingston exclaimed. He described Wilkinson as "a little petty tyrant," arresting everyone in sight, and Claiborne as that "wretched cowardly civil magistrate with an intellect below contempt . . . aiding in these measures and surrendering his own power that he may without responsibility gratify his Vengeance."[57] Livingston, above all, was the man to appreciate the consequences of what transpired. His political friends were being cut down in Wilkinson's harvest of "traitors." Meanwhile, commerce stagnated and land values plummeted. Migrations to the territory had virtually ceased, and those who recently arrived were preparing to depart—all as a consequence of the crisis. Livingston postponed hopes of selling his lands and returned to New York. His prospects had been set back. He prayed for "a speedy change in our affairs."

John Graham, whom Jefferson had dispatched to track Burr and to report his activities, finally arrived in New Orleans in early March and informed the Administration that while all danger had passed, "it had left the People here split up into various Parties." Differences of opinion were not tolerated, and the former friends of the governor were alienated. Graham feared that the continuation of Wilkinson's persecutions of individuals might "lessen the respect of the People for the Government."[58]

The general himself wrote to Daniel Clark, safely ensconced in Washington and still above the battle, that "the animosities which have been excited in this City, by Burr's friends and well wishers, and his Enemies and opposers, are deep [,] rancorous and deadly."[59] He said that their own countrymen—that is, the Americans—were almost exclusively among Burr's friends while the ancient inhabitants were to be found on the side of the government. He listed Livingston, Kerr, Watkins, Bradford; "and the Bar in general" in the first group and Poydras, Bellechasse, Fortier, Boré, the Urquarts—all old Louisianians—as well as Duncan, Gurley, and Benjamin Morgan in the second. Wilkinson assured Clark that he did not doubt the territorial delegate's fidelity, although he did mention that the partnership of Chew and Relf, with which Clark was associated, was implicated. Clark must have been mortified. Burr's alleged co-conspirators were all his closest political contacts.

Meanwhile Governor Caliborne found himself in a novel relationship with the legislative council. Less than a year had passed since the clash over his veto of the projected civil code. Yet the Burr crisis had forced upon the governor and the council a new spirit of conciliation. Claiborne reported that "during the late interesting crisis . . . [he] determined to solicit the Counsel and advice of men in whom the Government and myself could confide." He mentioned, in this connection, Poydras, Mather, Bellechasse, MaCarty, and Fouchet—the five councilors—all of whom were influential in the French community.[60]

The rapprochement between Claiborne and the ancient Louisianians was genuine. When John Graham resigned as territorial secretary in May in order to take up a new post in the U.S. State Department, Claiborne warned Jefferson against naming any citizen of the territory to the vacancy "until you should have ascertained his present politicks." He said that John Gurley deserved the position, but he preferred to pass over Gurley and request either Julien Poydras or John Baptist MaCarty. The office of territorial secretary was a vital one. The secretary was the second man in the government and was often left in charge of affairs whenever the governor was absent.[61]

Claiborne renewed his request that Poydras or MaCarty be appointed secretary several weeks later. The urgency of the matter was suddenly made evident to him by the departure of Wilkinson.[62] For the past few months the general, however erratic his course and devious his aims, was at Claiborne's side—a source of real strength in turbulent New Orleans.[63] Now he and Graham were summoned to Richmond to testify at the Burr trial, and Claiborne, for the first time, felt his deep isolation. The Burr conspiracy had brought home to him the remoteness of Orleans and the distance between himself and those in Washington upon whom he depended.

Claiborne now considered the ancient Louisianians "the best supporters of the American Government."[64] He anticipated that their patriotism would be displayed with enthusiasm when the news of the British attack upon the *Chesapeake* broke, and he contrasted their unanimity on this issue with the divisions within the American community.[65] When the fall elections to the territorial House of Representatives again turned in a French majority he expressed gratification. He rejoiced that "Doctor Watkins and those of his Party, were but partially supported."[66] While some among the Americans believed that Claiborne was allowing himself to be duped by the Louisianians,[67] the governor himself was convinced of their loyalty and confident of the genuineness of their support.

But Claiborne was not yet free of troubles. The discharge of Bollman and Swartwout by John Marshall, the departure of Wilkinson, the continued presence of many "choice spirits" in the city, the flow of testimony from Richmond, and the arrival in New Orleans of Daniel Clark hardened divisions and renewed the hopes of the disaffected.[68] While the Burr conspiracy was dead, "Burrism" was not. It persisted for the next several years with undiminished acerbity. Its major effect was to fix the lines of political demarcation which the conspiracy itself had drawn.

V

"Burr's Conspiracy is at an end," wrote Claiborne triumphantly early in May. "This daring attempt to divide and ruin our beloved Country has been frustrated."[69] However, by the end of the month he must have been wondering if his victory statement was not premature. Wilkinson was gone, and in his place a personage no less familiar to the people of New Orleans was being wined, dined, and toasted. Daniel Clark had come home.[70]

Distance had insulated Clark from the events of the preceding months. He had carefully camouflaged the traces of his contacts with Burr,[71] maintained a discreet relationship with Wilkinson, and, most of all, stayed in Washington at a time when many of the people involved in the conspiracy had opened themselves to exposure and capture beyond the Appalachians.[72]

The evidence against Clark was potentially compromising.

John Graham, the Administration's spy, learned in Lexington that Clark had once authorized Burr to draw upon his account with the firm of Chew and Relf in New Orleans to the sum of $200,000. When Burr discovered that notes drawn on New Orleans accounts were not negotiable in Kentucky, Clark ordered Chew and Relf to relay his funds to New York. At least, this is what Graham had been told. Relf denied that any sums had been set aside for Aaron Burr and even invited Graham to inspect Clark's account with the firm when Graham was in New Orleans. Graham found nothing suspicious and concluded that Chew and Relf was merely an unwitting receiving point for communications between Burr and Erick Bollman. While this was a perfectly plausible explanation, Graham's investigation was superficial. And the triangular relationship between Clark, Chew and Relf, and Burr, even if there was nothing to it, could have been interpreted in more than one way.[73]

Clark was to clever to lose himself in the fantasies which Burr had fabricated in order to entice men like Wilkinson. But his ambition was no less ardent, only more matured, than the general's. Clark tried to use his position as territorial delegate in Washington to best advantage. He criticized Claiborne's militia policies on the floor of Congress.[74] The governor had learned of this, and when Clark returned to New Orleans, after the adjournment of Congress, Claiborne demanded an explanation or a retraction.[75] Neither was forthcoming, and their embittered exchange of notes resulted in a duel. Claiborne was wounded in the thigh and spent much of the summer recuperating. Meanwhile, Clark enjoyed the esteem with which his friends chose to honor him.[76]

Clark's relations with the city were not altogether amicable, however. The municipality wanted to connect the streets in the old city with those in the new suburb St. Mary, the fastest-growing part of town.[77] The trouble was that a ropewalk, extending almost the entire breadth of New Orleans, blocked the street connections between the two districts. The municipality was willing to negotiate a settlement that would permit it to dismantle the ropewalk, but Clark and one Samuel Davis, co-owners of the ropewalk, refused.[78] Clark's inflexibility cast a pall over his public reputation. His obduracy on this particular municipal problem signaled the beginning of his political downfall.

During the summer Clark learned the full details of Wilkinson's "reign of terror," and he was able to assess the long-term effects of those events. The enthusiasm that the most prominent Americans displayed toward him was warming, but

Clark could also discern the new cordiality between the governor and the Louisianians. His own selection as territorial delegate by the legislature the previous year was an act of defiance against Claiborne—probably nothing more. Meanwhile, the present polarization of sentiment between the two communities, his own special relationship with the Americans, and the irritation his ropewalk continued to cause did not augur well for the future. Moreover, during August, Livingston began to encounter the first serious resistance to his occupation and use of his newly acquired property in the New Orleans Batture.[79] Livingston's growing unpopularity could easily damage Clark.

These reflections undoubtedly convinced Daniel Clark that he had to do something dramatic if he was to alter the direction of events.[80] By the time he returned to Washington late in the fall, he had decided upon his next move. Clark broke with James Wilkinson. With Clark's support John Randolph of Virginia charged the general on the floor of Congress with complicity in Burr's conspiracy and for having remained a pensioner of Spain even while serving as commander of U. S. forces in the west.[81] As a result of these allegations, and at Wilkinson's request, the Secretary of War summoned a court of inquiry on January 11. It continued to sit until June 28, 1808, at which time Wilkinson was cleared of all allegations.[82]

Wilkinson's deep involvement with the Spanish was no revelation to the Washington community. Not only had it been long suspected, but it was frequently insinuated in the Burr proceedings, most notably by John Randolph, the foreman of the Richmond grand jury. What Clark offered was proof. His long residence in New Orleans, and his wide knowledge of men and events in the southwest, lent credibility to his accusations.[83] Moreover, Clark's decision entailed few risks. Wilkinson was ripe for a fall. Despite tremendous publicity and fanfare, Burr's conspiracy had led to no convictions either in Washington or in the western states where Burr was still under indictment. Wilkinson's own noxious personality at the Richmond trial had redirected toward himself whatever hostility had originally been aimed at the personable Burr. John Randolph and the Quids in Congress had been howling for action ever since the conspiracy had first erupted. Burr's acquittal not only made further prosecutions unlikely;[84] it seemed to prove the debility of the executive branch in the whole affair. Wilkinson was the perfect target for these resentments. Clark reasoned that Randolph would be pleased and the President himself would not be unduly discomfited by disclosures of Wilkinson's guilt.[85] The trouble was that in the course of the inquiry Clark's own links with Burr were brought out into the open, and he soon discovered that his own record, as well as Wilkinson's , was under intense scrutiny.

VI

The Clark-Wilkinson fight rekindled the smoldering embers of Burrism in Orleans. The newspapers reported the proceedings of the War Department's investigation at length. Burr himself had always been a bit remote. He was a stranger to the territory, having visited New Orleans but once and then only briefly. His "invasion" had been stopped far above the city. But Wilkinson and Clark were familiar figures, and the conflict between them had an immediacy totally lacking in the earlier court trials.

Almost at the same moment that the attack upon Wilkinson commenced in Washington, Clark's friends began publishing a partisan journal in New Orleans to champion the cause at home. It was called *La Lanterne Magique* and appeared briefly in the spring and then in the fall of 1808. Although it was published in both French and English, the paper failed to elicit sufficient subscriptions. It was considered highly inflammatory even by those who might otherwise have supported its point of view. The demise of *La Lanterne Magique* meant that "Clark and Company" had to rely upon the established newspapers to uphold their position.[86]

The papers lined up predictably on the question. The *Orleans Gazette* was very vocal in its attacks upon Wilkinson. Its position was clear even before Clark himself broke with the general; Bradford had personal reasons for denouncing him. In the summer of 1807, therefore, the *Gazette* accused Wilkinson of having been "acquainted with, and engaged in the schemes of Col. Burr, as early as August, 1805." The paper alleged that the general used his knowledge of Burr's plans to good advantage with the Spanish, parlaying his complicity for $80,000 of Spanish gold. "Thus, while he was boasting of his patriotism to the American Government, he was drawing on his royal master for his faithful services."[87] Even Wilkinson's personal life did not escape Bradford's abuse.[88]

The *Louisiana Gazette* was equally dedicated to opposing the wily Wilkinson. The *Gazette* consistently supported Clark while it continued to criticize Claiborne. The paper attributed the governor's failure to address the legislature at the close of its session in April 1807 to "the poverty of rhetorical talent in the privy council, for . . . when the governor lately forsook some of his old friends, his eloquence forsook him."[89] The absence of the usual anniversary festivities celebrating the treaty of cession on

April 30 was rectified by the *Gazette*'s own "St. Pretaboire," whose "readiness to drink" was matched only by the profusion of his toasts—all of which derided both the governor and the general.[90] The *Gazette* dismissed the conspiracy, calling it a mere "intrigue." It said that the strenuous measures of suppression undertaken by the government were unwarranted, especially in a nation with a constitution that guaranteed personal freedoms.[91] The paper defended Dr. Watkins and attacked the "vile, polluted, hireling paper [the *Courier*]" which opposed his reelection to the legislature.[92] Burr's acquittal vindicated its editorial policies.

The inquiry into the conduct of General Wilkinson provided the *Louisiana Gazette* with a steady flow of editorial material once the Richmond trial ended. And when Daniel Clark himself returned to New Orleans in June 1808, it was the *Gazette* which delighted in reporting the event. The dinner prepared at the exchange coffee house was, according to the paper, "a testimonial of public confidence in the patriotism of our delegate, a complimentary tribute to his acknowledged virtues, and a frank expression of attachment to his person."[93] Clark was portrayed as the target of "every shaft of calumny which the subtle arts of skulking treason could level at him in the dark." He was the victim of the persecutions of "the vile intriguers of a domineering party . . . [eager] to screen its favorite culprit from exposure."[94] Though hated by the guilty "whom he drags to light," concluded the *Gazette*, "[Clark] still continues to be most esteemed where he is best known."

Wilkinson's champion was J. B. S. Thierry. While the *Louisiana Gazette* opened its pages to Clark's "proofs," the *Courier* reprinted the general's self-defense. In his address "to the Citizens of the Territory of Orleans" Wilkinson attacked his accuser for his "political versatility"—for having been "alternately Spaniard, Frenchman, Englishman and American, as his interest or caprice directed." He denied that he, Wilkinson, had ever traduced the loyalty of the ancient inhabitants. "Sons of Louisiana, and ye worthy Children of the United States," he wrote. "Be not deluded by this shallow but wicked device, the result of the conjunct labors of my enemies, Randolf, Clark, and Co. . . . Creoles of Louisiana, I have invariably defended you against every suspicion of an attachment to Burr or his plans, and I have as constantly supported your true interests."[95] Wilkinson accused Clark of being a member of the Mexican Association, "that diabolical band, which has meditated your destruction." The *Courier* endorsed his denunciations.[96]

The French-language press was not unanimous in its defense

of Wilkinson. The *Moniteur* took a different view.[97] A series of letters by an "OLD INHABITANT" defended Clark's integrity, emphasized the purity of his motives in attacking Wilkinson, and argued the importance of his continued service in Washington.[98] But the *Courier*, in reply, insisted that Clark was full of deceit, intrigue, and ambition. "The pride of this little Irishman," quipped J. B. S. Thierry, "aspired to the government of this province," and when that desire had been frustrated he had resorted to "political views." "Will you, now, tell us," Thierry queried the Old Inhabitant, "that it is unjust to believe that [Clark's] generosity has a political object in view? That he has not absolutely done good for the mere pleasure of doing it, and that he had in view to create for himself a party?"[99]

Thierry named some of the supporters of Clark whom he considered to be "infected with the mania of their party." He included Relf of Chew and Relf and Samuel Davis, co-owner of the ropewalk, in this list.[100] By and large, however, Thierry believed the Clark faction was honeycombed with litigious attorneys.[101] Certainly many leaders of the bar—Edward Livingston above all—had been alienated by Wilkinson's disregard of legal process. But this fitted nicely into the larger picture Thierry was drawing at this time. The imaginative editor of the *Courier* liked to portray the legal profession as the enemy of the people on all the major issues of his time.

Thierry luxuriated in "editorial altercations." He cut his teeth on the *Moniteur*, but controversy with such a staid journal did not satisfy him. The Clark dinner in June of 1808 gave him the opportunity to take on both English-language *Gazettes* in an encounter which better suited his appetite. Thierry viewed the dinner for Daniel Clark in June 1808 not as a spontaneous outpouring of affection for a returning hero but as a contrived political demonstration. Many had been pressured into attending, but it was "with peculiar pleasure" that he announced to his readers and "to the friends of our General and Territorial Government, that his excellency Governor Claiborne was not at the political dinner given to our *honorable* delegate."[102] The dinner for Daniel Clark, "the would be governor of Louisiana," as Thierry liked to call him, was the major social event of the season, but its manifest partisanship could not be missed. To give it the semblance of public sponsorship "all the bloodhounds of Clark and Co. were put in motion handing about long lists, and inciting every comer to subscribe to the famous dinner which the gang had proposed to give their partisan."[103] Its purpose was a reconciliation of the ancient inhabitants with "the wreck of Burr's faction," but it had to fail in that endeavor because the people were becoming convinced that "the scheme of these Gentlemen was to expose them to slaughter in the act of conquering the mines of Mexico."

In a letter to the editor of the *Louisiana Gazette* Thierry noted that the governor was no longer "under the obsession of the depraving advices of your patrons, those mischievous intriguers whose only aim was to pour upon him the odium of the inhabitants."[104] Claiborne had always been at odds with the leaders of "the dismayed gang of Burrists," but many of the rank and file had once been numbered among his friends. Thierry's point accurately reflected Claiborne's changed political stance.

Thierry's accusation that the *Louisiana Gazette* had the financial backing of the "Burrites" and was nothing but the mouthpiece of "Clark and Company" led to a brief flurry of exchanges early in July. The *Gazette* accused Thierry of venality and inconsistency, but Thierry was less restrained in his reply. The editor of the *Gazette*, John Mowry, was, he wrote, "a despicable calumniator in the pay of the vilest and most stupid of intriguers, past, present and to come."[105]

"Parties for and against Mr. Clark in this City are becoming violent," Claiborne reported to the Secretary of State early in April.[106] The "newspaper war" was raging, but it did not go too badly for the governor. The majority of the people was with him if the majority of the press was not. Thierry, Claiborne's chief and staunchest ally, summed up the situation best:

> If ever since the cession, the Louisianians were happy under the laws of America, I can assure without being exposed to the least grounded contradiction, that it is since Mr. Clark and his adherents have totally lost their influence from ducks and drakes, on the policy of the administration towards the inhabitants of this country. Since K[err], W[orkman] and the host of Burrites, all friends to Mr. Daniel Clark, have been expulsed from the councils of the governor, we have no more seen the Louisianians constantly insulted in the public papers, and the expression of their wishes has commenced to be plainly understood by our general government.[107]

For the first time since the Burr storm broke, the political atmosphere was clear. By the summer of 1808, William Claiborne was more fully responsive to the most dynamic forces in territorial politics than he had been before.

VII

The political consequences of Burr's conspiracy in the territory of Orleans were evident within months of the abatement of the Clark-Wilkinson fight. "Burrites" remained but were no longer cause for real concern. Yet Claiborne exaggerated their importance in order to justify demands for troop reinforcements.[108] The projected menace of still other conspiracies, composed of the same elements, simplified the governor's task in explaining to the Administration his new favoritism towards the old inhabitants.[109] They had proven their fidelity in the past and were continuing to be trustworthy. They deserved outright support in view of the unremitting vulnerability of the territory to subversion from within and attack from without.[110]

But Claiborne smiled at the opposition of Clark and other Burrites when he was not using their presence in New Orleans to demand more regular army units. "The faction, who have so long been opposed to me, in this quarter, have really made me popular in the Territory," he wrote Madison at the end of the summer.[111] The "body of the people" supported him as never before. He enumerated his opponents with relish, happy that he had made the right enemies. The governor thoroughly enjoyed his new-found public esteem. "The exercise of my official duties has neither been unpleasant or difficult," he wrote to a parish judge. "On the contrary I meet with a support and confidence from a majority of the people, which afford me much pleasure."[112]

Claiborne reported on the waning influence of the Burr "faction".[113] He no longer worried about the machinations of his enemies in Washington, nor was he sensitive about his earlier animadversions regarding the local population. "A late news-paper Writer, has reminded the Louisianians, of the Character given them in a letter to the President in January, 1804, and was attributed to me," he wrote to a subordinate in reference to his much publicized letter advising the withholding of statehood. He was happy to discover that his enemies could find no other charge to throw at him. As for this one, he thought, it had been so often repeated that the people must be tired of it. "Whatever may have been my first impressions, with respect to the Louisianians, is now a matter of no consequence," he ended. "I have long since found them to be a most virtuous, amiable people, nor is there a Man in existence, who had more at heart their political happiness and welfare."[114]

Claiborne was much less sensitive to newspaper criticism than he had been earlier. He now thought that their attacks had become "in a great degree harmless" and believed that "a man's reputation must indeed be very brittle, if it can be destroyed by a paper war."[115] Claiborne had also learned that the patronage at his disposal could be put to good use. The single most important office within his gift was that of public printer. Bradford had gained that post when he purchased the *Union*, but by the end of 1808 Claiborne had found a more deserving journalist upon whom he could bestow his favor than the venomous Kentuckian. He selected J. B. S. Thierry as a reward for his ardent and useful support. The *Courier* became the official organ of government, something Claiborne had lacked in his earlier days in Orleans.[116]

The governor was even bolder with Jefferson. In other years when his commission was due for renewal Claiborne had been exceedingly deferential, but in the aftermath of his recent trials he showed confidence. "In eight days . . . my Commission as Governor will expire," he reminded the President early in December. "If on this occasion, it should meet the views of the Administration, to continue to me the Trust . . . such further proof of confidence will be gratefully received and merited if in my power."[117] In the past he never dared suggest a renewal of his tenure. He had always been self-effacing and had written as if expecting a replacement. This too had changed.

The political revolution triggered by the great conspiracy was stabilized when Daniel Clark, anticipating his dismissal, resigned as territorial delegate to Congress in January 1809. Julien Poydras, the leading old inhabitant, replaced him. Poydras's only rival for the office was John Baptiste MaCarty, who had ably represented the interests of the public in Washington in the affair of the New Orleans Batture.[118] But MaCarty died in November 1808, and Poydras became the logical choice of the legislature.[119] With Poydras in Washington and Thierry at home, Claiborne could witness with equanimity the second recall of Wilkinson in the fall of 1809.[120] Claiborne's greater boldness with Jefferson, his lessened interest in what went on behind his back in Washington, and his tolerance of the press all grew out of his new sense of power at home. A political base had solidified beneath him, affording a sureness of footing and a heightened vision which was reflected in his whole attitude toward his office and his work.

The fifth anniversary of the transfer of Louisiana to the United States was celebrated by the discharge of cannon from Fort St. Charles and from the vessels and gunboats in the river. The governor received the civil and military officers of the government as well as the leading citizens of New Orleans, who honored him with their congratulations. "Indeed it was for Mr. Claiborne the most affecting and precious reward to see in the harmony subsisting between this people and the American Government, a compensation for all the calumnious machinations resorted to by his enemies."[121] So wrote J.B.S. Thierry. William C. C. Claiborne had learned in the space of five years that there was more to good government than he had first imagined.

VIII

From the point of view of the national government, the Burr conspiracy represented a major challenge to its authority in Louisiana. America's most sensitive and exposed frontier was under attack—so it seemed—not from an external enemy, as expected, but from dissident political elements within. The consequences may well have been disastrous. For a few weeks the fate of Louisiana was at the disposal of men over whom Jefferson could exercise little effective control. The whole episode forced the Administration to a new appreciation of just how important the loyalty of the masses of the local population was to continued American rule in that remote region.

In Orleans itself Burr's conspiracy rearranged political alignments. Reputations, friendships, and old associations were shattered by Wilkinson's "reign of terror." Men who, like Dr. John Watkins, had been staunch supporters of Claiborne's administration in an earlier day were now numbered among the governor's bitter opponents. Others, like James Workman and Lewis Kerr, less clearly identified with any particular faction, were forced to take sides as political interests polarized. Burrism even destroyed the formidable Daniel Clark. But in the end, William Claiborne was Aaron Burr's chief political beneficiary in the territory. Before 1806 Claiborne had been beset by the alliance of Livingston, Clark, and Evan Jones. Whenever he turned a political corner the "faction" was there fomenting discord and broadcasting dissent. The Burr conspiracy changed much of that. The "faction" remained, but its potential for mischief had been substantially reduced by its odious identification with conspiracy and treason.

Even more significant, the conspiracy was for Claiborne a kind of revelation. Despite the fact that leading "Americans" seemed to be at the head of the dissidents in the early years, the governor and the Administration looked to the incoming American population as bedrock support for unfolding national goals. The precondition for uniting Louisiana to the American union, so it was thought, was the transformation of its demographic character. By introducing a mass of American immigrants, the loyalty of the region to the United States would be assured. Burrism, however, threw this axiom of policy into doubt. Claiborne was surprised at the degree of loyalty the local community displayed. He reported to Madison that they were "exempt . . . from all participation in Burr's Conspiracy. [B]ut," he continued, "of that portion of our society whose native language is English, I cannot speak so favorably."[122] He seemed to realize that the whole orientation of policy might have been misguided. One thing, at least, was clear: the national interest had much to lose by slighting local sentiment.

Finally, the Burr episode taught Claiborne other important lessons. In his first years in office, the governor had consistently adopted a posture of political neutralism on public issues of moment. He had proceeded as if government operated in a political vacuum. He tried to push through plans and projects which would succeed upon their inherent merit without creating the political lines of force necessary to render their reception attractive. But a change in Claiborne's political style was evident within months of the conspiracy. It was manifested in his greater selectivity in patronage distribution, his appreciation of the importance of the press, his confidence in his dealings with the national administration, and, above all, his new cordiality with the Louisianians.

As a "colonial governor" Claiborne had always been caught between national and territorial needs. Few of the American territorial governors—or the British governors in the late colonial period, for that matter—had been able to identify with one without slighting the other. In this Claiborne had been no exception. But the Burr conspiracy was the decisive event in making him an effective advocate of local interests. Claiborne's acceptance and then his open support of the civil law digest of 1808 was the most fruitful result of this dramatic change.

[4] *Edward Livingston and the New Orleans Batture*

On May 23, 1807, the Superior Court of the territory of Orleans rendered a unanimous decision in the case of *John Gravier* v. *The Mayor, Aldermen, and Inhabitants of the city of New Orleans.* The court hoped that its judgment for the plaintiff would extinguish a smoldering and potentially explosive public question—a hope not soon realized. With the aftereffects of the Burr storm and the Wilkinson "terror" still lingering, a new and inflammatory public debate commenced in the highly volatile political atmosphere of Orleans. The controversy enmeshed men and government on every level, but, even more significantly, it dramatized the importance of legal questions in public life. The problem was that of the New Orleans Batture.

The Batture St. Mary [1] was part of a land parcel granted to the Jesuit Order in 1726 by the French Crown. In 1763 the Society of Jesus was suppressed in France and its lands in Louisiana were sold. The grounds in question were divided into separate lots. The lot nearest the city was sold to one Jean Pradel, who passed it on to an André Renard. The widow of Renard married Bertrand Gravier in 1785, and upon her death the entire estate was left to him. In 1788 Bertrand Gravier established a suburb on the part of the estate that fronted the Mississippi River, sections of which were sold during the 1790's. Bertrand Gravier died intestate in 1797, and the remainder of his property went to a brother, Jean Gravier, whose title to the property was later contested by the other heirs of Bertrand.[2]

The "Batture," or alluvial ground which the Mississippi deposited on the suburban lots fronting the river, remained unimproved prior to 1800. The inhabitants of New Orleans used batture soil and sand to fill in streets, to construct sidewalks, and to maintain the levee. The Batture itself, through long established custom, was used as a place for anchorage and wharfage.

Traditionally, as the Batture widened, riparian owners moved the levee further toward the water's edge at the high-water limit. By this process of gradual enclosure they were able to increase the size of their holdings. When Jean Gravier attempted this in 1803-04, however, he elicited an outcry from the local inhabitants. The ensuing confrontation between Gravier and the city of New Orleans raised the question of title.[3] Gravier sued the city in Superior Court in an effort to establish his claim, once and for all, but the court postponed a judicial resolution of the problem for more than a year.[4] The difficulty regarding Gravier's title arose from the peculiar fact that his plantation no longer fronted the river but was separated from the Batture by the suburban lots which had been sold by Bertrand Gravier in the 1790's. No one ever challenged the proprietary rights of ordinary riparians to alluvial accretions. The question was whether or not private title to an alluvion formed by a navigable waterway and adjoining a municipal suburb could be enjoyed by an individual whose lands were not adjacent to the river.[5] This, in turn, rested upon disputed points of fact: was a batture already in existence at the time of the original sale of the Jesuit lots in 1763, and did the batture, in the absence of a specification in the deeds of sale, comprise a portion of the properties of those who, by succession or sale, had acquired title to those lots? The court, basing its decision upon the Spanish laws then in force in the territory, decided that an alluvion *had* formed by the time Bertrand Gravier sold his suburban lots, and, since the Batture was not included in the instruments conveying title, the heir of Bertrand, that is Jean Gravier, remained the rightful owner of the property.

I

For Edward Livingston the Batture represented an enormous opportunity to reverse the direction of his declining fortunes. He had come to New Orleans soon after the cession of all of Louisiana to the United States, in order to find some way of liquidating the debt of $44,000 which he owed the federal government. Livingston looked upon Louisiana as a place of voluntary exile where he could reestablish his reputation at the bar while amassing sufficient funds to enable him to settle his accounts, return to his New York home, and retire in comfort. He wrote his sister, Margaret B. Livingston, less than two months after his arrival in New Orleans that he was "engaged in business that will ultimately prove extremely profitable and I am so much pleased with the country that I shall make it my place of abode at least until my labors enable me to re-establish my affairs which, if I am suffered to pursue them without interruption, I hope will be in three or four years at the farthest."[6] He wished merely to be left alone. He hoped the government would not distract him "by pursuing their demands" in New Orleans.[7] Livingston was convinced that Gravier's title to the Batture was good, and that the property had tremendous commercial potential.[8] Possibly at Livingston's invitation,

Gravier engaged him as counsel in his suit against the city. After the court decided in Gravier's favor, Livingston acquired one-third of the Gravier interest, then estimated to be worth $200,000.[9] As time went on the value of the Batture steadily appreciated, but even in 1807 a one-third interest was more than enough to relieve Livingston of his financial obligations. The Batture was a good investment if title could be sustained.

Livingston began a series of works and improvements which, he explained, would benefit the public, but popular indignation was aroused by what seemed to be his impudent interference in the customary use of the ground. To Livingston's surprise, his workers were driven from the Batture on repeated occasions during the spring and summer of 1807. By September of that year public sentiment in New Orleans was inflamed. A crisis had been reached, and Governor Claiborne was once again placed in the awkward position of having to decide between two valid but conflicting claims. He could defy neither the court nor the people without precipitating a breakdown of public order. Claiborne succeeded in quieting the crowd which assembled on the Batture on September 15 by assuring them that the President of the United States would settle the matter equitably. The problem, he informed the people, would be transmitted to the general government in Washington. He agreed to authorize John Baptiste MaCarty to collect affidavits attesting to the public's historic right to the Batture and to convey them to the capital.[10]

Meanwhile, the city of New Orleans initiated the legal maneuver of transferring its alleged title to the Batture to the U.S. government. Claiborne notified Jefferson that he believed the "United States are the legal claimants of the land in question,"[11] but it was not until December 1807 that the city officially requested the governor to intercede in its behalf and to notify the Administration of its desire that the public right to the Batture be defended by the federal government.[12] In November, however, Jefferson decided to review the matter. The President consulted separately with Attorney General Caesar Rodney, Treasury Secretary Albert Gallatin, Jefferson's closest advisor on Louisiana affairs, and then with the entire Cabinet. He then instructed the Secretary of State, James Madison—the Department of State was directly responsible for the territories—to order the U.S. marshal in New Orleans to occupy the Batture in conformity with an act of Congress of March 3, 1807, which empowered the government to evict squatters from public lands. On January 25, 1808, the order was executed. The marshal, Le Breton D'Orgenois, evicted Livingston and his employees. Subsequently, the city passed a resolution calling for the destruction of the works already commenced by Livingston and the restitution of the Batture to its traditional usages.[13] Governor Claiborne himself received the offical thanks of the municipality for his intercession with the U.S. government on this important question.[14]

Jefferson acted hastily in his Batture policy. Madison issued the instructions to the U.S. marshal on November 30, two weeks prior to the city council's decision, and a full month before any offical request could have been received from New Orleans.[15] Three considerations explain the swiftness with which the Administration moved. First, on the basis of the fragmentary material available to the Cabinet at the time, the court decision appeared to be a miscarriage of justice. The only argument Jefferson had was a brief by Pierre Derbigny, the attorney for the city in the original suit. In a note to Gallatin on November 4 the President wrote: "As it will be necessary to decide how this question of the Batture is to be settled, we must of course take the trouble of understanding it. I therefore send you a very able opinion of Derbigny's to be returned when read to Mr. Rodney. Happening to have an Encyclopedia which he quotes, I have turned to it and find it able and satisfactory. Mr. Rodney is in possession of the opinion of the court assigning their reasons."[16]

Derbigny's brief, Rodney's opinion, and a copy of the Diderot Encyclopedia—plus the court's brief opinion—this was the sum of the reference material at Jefferson's disposal when he summoned the Cabinet meeting of November 27 at which the decision to evict Livingston was taken. Early in December Livingston sent Gallatin documents and proofs in support of his title in order to answer the city's argument.[17] But by that time policy had already been decided, and orders were en route to the marshal. Jefferson would discover to his regret that the legal issues involved were not as simple as he first thought—indeed, that the Batture could be a legal quagmire as well as a sandy shoal.

The second reason for haste was Jefferson's antipathy to Livingston. William Hatcher, in his biography of Edward Livingston, lists four sources of this hostility: Livingston's lackluster support for Jefferson in his fight for the presidency in 1801, the financial scandal in New York in which Livingston was involved, the reports the President had been receiving from Governor Claiborne detailing Livingston's political activities, and Livingston's alleged association with Burr and his interference with Wilkinson during the latter's "reign of terror" in New Orleans.[18] For these reasons Jefferson did not hesitate to take a position which he knew would damage a man he had cause to dislike. Personal animosity between the two men deepened as the Batture litigation continued. It abated only on the very eve of Jefferson's death many years later.

The third reason for Jefferson's swift movement in the developing dispute was the political opportunity it presented to the Administration. Political considerations dominated Jefferson's policy on the Batture. His first moves were to freeze the situation, evict Livingston, and halt further construction, confident that the final arbiter in the dispute would decide favorably for the government. The New Orleans public was not uniformly against Livingston, but there is little doubt that a presidential decision in Livingston's favor would have alienated most of the local inhabitants, thereby dissipating the new spirit of amity which the Burr crisis had fostered.[19]

Jefferson presumed that Congress would either leave the matter with the federal land commissioners in the territory or, as he suggested in a note to Gallatin, appoint a special board of higher standing "at least for the batture, which is of too much value and too much involved in prejudices there to be safely trusted to the present Commissioners."[20] By "prejudice" Jefferson meant politics. He wrote this note in March 1808, but he was fully aware of the explosiveness of the issue when he acted back in November 1807. The attitude of the land commissioners was not clear, but Jefferson suspected they were vulnerable to Livingston's allegedly profound and beguiling influence.[21] Consequently Jefferson favored a special commission appointed solely for the purpose of deciding the Batture question "to whom the evidence and arguments in writing shall be sent, without any necessity of their going there."[22] But Gallatin did not like the idea of a special commission. He preferred to have the United States' claim transferred to the New Orleans municipality by an act of Congress, thus allowing the city to continue litigation in the courts.[23] This begged the question, however, since U.S. title would still have to be first established.

Jefferson acted on the Batture with the expectation that he would be sustained by the subsequent decision of either an impartial tribunal or Congress. His order to the U.S. marshal to remove Livingston, an act designed to quiet the excitement until a final decision could be made, was the only decisive action ever taken by the federal government in the matter. Hastily conceived with thin evidentiary support, Jefferson's Batture policy would subsequently have to stand or fall on its insubstantial merits.

II

The Batture controversy generated almost as much heat in the Orleans territory as the Burr conspiracy. Several local newspapers devoted much attention to it. The *Orleans Gazette* was sympathetic to Livingston even though Bradford opened its pages to advocates for the city. The paper defended the decision of the Superior Court, condemned MaCarty's mission to Washington, linked the Gravier-Livingston Batture with the battures of other riverfront proprietors in the hope that this would enlist their powerful support behind the cause, and strenuously condemned the city for transferring its claim to the U.S. government.[24]

The *Louisiana Courier* defended the municipality. In fact, the first appearance of the *Courier* in mid-October 1807 was occasioned by the absence of an adequate vehicle for presenting the public's position on the issue. The *Courier's* ardent and continuous advocacy of the public right to the Batture during the ensuing months was the result of editor Thierry's conviction that he was the solitary defender of the community against the "usurpers" of its property.[25] Indeed, the appointment of Thierry to the office of public printer in November 1808 was due in part to the position he took on the Batture question.[26]

In addition to the "warm newspaper discussion,"[27] a pamphlet war was fought over the disputed alluvial grounds of the Mississippi. Great bodies of law were marshaled by each side. Leading legal luminaries took part, some from as far away as Philadelphia, and their briefs were exchanged in volleys of argument and counterargument. Livingston was his own best advocate, but he also solicited the help of Peter S. Duponceau, then one of the great legal minds in America. The scholarship of Pierre Derbigny and Louis Moreau Lislet and the argumentative skill of editor Thierry were arrayed on the other side.

Pierre Derbigny published the first pamphlet in the summer of 1807. Derbigny opened his argument with general remarks concerning the great utility of the Batture in the life and commerce of New Orleans and its importance both to the inhabitants of the city and to the people of the United States. He then proceeded to raise the pivotal point which would serve as the connecting link between the Batture problem and larger legal questions:

> The peculiar situation of this territory, newly acquired to the United States, governed by the civil law, so different from that which rules the rest of the Union, so lately transferred from a government which manifests the sovereign authority more frequently by ostensible acts than by writings, must surely, it

> should seem be powerful motives to induce the General Government to bestow on the examination of this cause, all the attention and consideration it deserves! Will not the general government reflect that Louisiana, by the very nature of the Provisional government which rules it, is deprived of a part of the advantages enjoyed by the other citizens of the Union, in their judiciary contests, and that the fate of their fortunes, and their lives is definitively submitted to one sole tribunal, composed of three judges, who decide at once in the first instance, and in the last resort, in a country whose languages, manners, usages, and even sometimes whose laws are little familiar to them; and that the acknowledged integrity and information of those three judges are not always a solid security for the irrefragability of their judgment?[28]

Duponceau, in a very persuasive brief, would later reply that the civil law itself—that is, those very same elements of the civil law to which Derbigny would refer—supported the contentions of Gravier and Livingston and that the decision in favor of private right was not in violation of the accepted customs, usages, and laws of the country but rather derived from them. Nevertheless, Derbigny's point was critical. Public opinion, unfamiliar with the legal sources, unimpressed by scholarly citations, unpersuaded by the logic of learned counsel, and unprepared to understand lengthy and difficult legal treatises, would remain convinced that the Batture decision, rendered by judges trained at common law, was a corruption of justice resulting from the adulteration of the community's traditional practices by an alien legal system.[29] The questions raised by the Batture furor stimulated a social awareness of the importance of legal issues in general and a hostility to common law in particular.[30] The Batture controversy was crudely perceived as a conflict between two diverse legal traditions. This misconception was reinforced by at least some legal opinion, in this case that of Pierre Derbigny.

Derbigny's second point was also important. He argued that the original sale of the Jesuit lots occurred while Louisiana was still under French dominion and governed by French law. Therefore, he wrote, "the French laws must . . . direct our judgments as to the effect of those sales, and the extent of the right which they could transfer to Pradel and other purchasers of the Jesuits' property."[31] The question of property in a batture formed adjacent to those lots existing at the time of the original sale, he argued, should also be decided by French law. After reviewing the history of the Batture from the time of the Jesuit proprietorship, Derbigny explained that alluvions or accretions along navigable rivers belonged to the sovereign, according to the civil law of France. To support this contention he cited the French legal commentators Pothier and Denizart and the Encyclopedist Larasle. He attempted to demonstrate that the Batture St. Mary was a kind of alluvion whose possession was governed by the edicts of successive French monarchs. Its existence at the time of the sale of the Jesuit property, the existence, also, of a royal road separating the river and the Batture from private lots, the subsequent acts of Spanish governors in controlling public access to the Batture, and the acquiescence of the Graviers to these regulations all supported Derbigny's major contention. Thus the burden of the rebuttal would have to be directed toward the main point that French municipal law clearly provided for battures and that, in the absence of written evidence of a grant to private owners, the Batture St. Mary continued to be the possession of the sovereign power, which had now become the United States government.

Derbigny's brief was the most efficacious. In particular, his contention that French law would have to be the rule of decision in the Batture question—a contention which the Superior Court did not accept—and that French law favored the sovereign was the theoretical foundation underlying Jefferson's action in dispossessing Livingston. Subsequently, other writers abandoned Derbigny on specific points, but until the end of the dispute, and despite cogent refutations, Jefferson himself adhered to this first published brief with a doggedness and tenacity at which Edward Livingston himself marveled.

Livingston was the first to rebut Derbigny. His *Examination of the Title of the United States to the land called the Batture* was published on December 10, 1807.[32] On the questions of fact Livingston argued that the lots of the old Jesuit plantation extended to the river itself and were not bounded by a public high road on the levee, that the Graviers never abandoned their claim to the Batture, and that, since the sale of the Jesuit lands occurred after the cession of Louisiana to Spain on November 3, 1762,[33] the Spanish Crown could not acquire rights to those properties by virtue of French law.

On questions of law, Livingston challenged the accuracy of Derbigny's contentions. He argued that the custom of Paris, in conformity with both Roman and Spanish law, bestowed upon owners of riparian estates all soil accretions made by changes in the courses of rivers.[34] In any case, Livingston wrote, Spanish, not French, law was the rule of decision in the Batture case, and Spanish law held that although the public retained prescribed usages in riverbank alluvions, the alluvions themselves belonged to the riverfront proprietors.[35] He emphatically denied that customary usage of the Batture established public ownership. According to the civil law, he wrote, the public had a perfect right to the use of the banks of navigable streams, but private title remained unimpaired. Livingston admitted that it was unlawful for riparian owners to erect structures that would impede access to the grounds and that it was within the power of the authorities to order the demolition of such structures. Legal title, however, was not affected by such decrees.

The lines of argument between Livingston and Derbigny were clearly drawn. They differed on whether the river or the levee bounded the lots of the front proprietors, which body of law governed title to the Batture, and the meaning of acts undertaken by the local government prior to 1803.

Louis Moreau Lislet, Louisiana's leading civil law authority, supported Derbigny. As one of the attorneys for the city in the original Gravier suit, Moreau Lislet was familiar with both the facts and the law in the case. In one important respect he broke through the forensic mold set by the original court decision, Derbigny's attack upon it, and Livingston's defense. Later on, both Thierry and Julien Poydras would make it the keystone of their position in the aftermath of Duponceau's definitive demolition of Derbigny's position. Moreau Lislet wrote: "The city's claim was maintained in a law of the *Partidas* which expressly declares that sand-banks or sandy tracts, (*arenales*) on the borders of rivers, in the front of towns, make part of the commons of those towns (Partida 3, Title 28, Law 9.)"[36] This citation of the Spanish *Partidas* was important. It represented a wise tactical switch from French law to Spanish law as the basis of argument. Moreau Lislet wrote that "whether the Batture belonged to the king, as we have proved, or were the property of B. Gravier, as was pretended, it must have changed proprietor at the time B. Gravier established a suburb on the front of his plantation." For a suburb was a part of the city, and by the law governing cities, as defined by the *Partidas*, the sandy banks bordering rivers were part of the commons. In the future, defenders of the public's claim would no longer rest their case upon the law of alluvions but on the fact that the Batture constituted part of the port of New Orleans, and hence could not be owned privately.

Moreau Lislet's analysis of the Superior Court's decision was significant in one other way. He noted that the court was composed of judges trained in common law. "Whatever be the integrity of the judges who rendered this judgment," he wrote, "still must we deplore the situation to which they have reduced New-Orleans, possibly through an imperfect acquaintance with our usages and laws, which made it difficult for them to apprehend the arguments of the Counsel for the city."[37] Defenders of the decision tried to disprove this charge by showing that the Gravier case rested on a foundation built of Roman, Spanish, *and* French legal materials. Nevertheless, the allegation survived the disproofs. Moreau Lislet and others fed the suspicion that the Batture decision represented another triumph of foreign over local justice.

The pamphlet war over the Batture continued unabated for the next few years. Peter Duponceau contributed a lengthy and well-argued brief in the summer of 1808.[38] He riveted his attention upon Derbigny's basic argument: that French law favored the sovereign's title. So thoroughgoing was Duponceau's refutation that no writer, with the exception of Jefferson himself, ever again founded his case for the public's right upon this point. As a result, J. B. S. Thierry, in answer to Duponceau, discarded Derbigny completely and developed a new approach.[39] Thierry argued that the Batture was not an alluvion at all, but the bed of a river which could never belong to a private proprietor. He defended Jefferson's expulsion of Livingston as an exercise of sovereign power over rivers and harbors. Later on, when Julien Poydras presented the case for the public to Congress, he too would use this argument.

Subsequently, all of the major contributors to the public debate over the legal questions at issue in the Batture controversy submitted rejoinders to their respective critics. Derbigny sent the still-uncompleted manuscript of his own *Refutation* of Duponceau to Jefferson in order to reassure the President that his Batture policy was well-founded in law,[40] but Derbigny's new pamphlet added very little to what he had already published.[41] Duponceau came out with his second work on the subject early in 1809. He ridiculed his opponents, pointed to the divisions within their ranks, scolded Jefferson for not having reinstated Livingston, and admonished the government for hiring Thierry as its new advocate.[42] Otherwise there was little in Duponceau's second published work that he had not already set forth in his first. Nor did Thierry add to the debate in his reply to Duponceau.[43]

The newspaper debates and the pamphlet war revealed the depth of public interest in the Batture question. The city council ordered 500 copies of one of Thierry's briefs for distribution. Claiborne reported that public interest in the legal debate was lively and that some of the briefs were "exhibited on the Exchange, and read for the instruction of the bye standers."[44]

The fact situation was complex, and the legal arguments became increasingly prolix. The simplicities to which they were reduced by publicists like Thierry, and later by Poydras, distorted accurate perception. For example, Thierry wrote that "the judges of the Superior Court were not sufficiently versed in the study of the Roman law to render, in such an important matter, a judgment founded upon the principles of that sacred code,"[45] despite Duponceau's attempt to demonstrate that both Spanish and French law provided ample support for the court's decision.

Duponceau's first brief was undoubtedly the most persuasive, and yet there was a dimension to the city's position not susceptible to scholarly refutation. The whole notion that a question of such transcending importance as that of the Batture St. Mary could be settled by parties in court was an alien one. The old inhabitants could not understand a legal proceeding which equated public interest and private right. Learned treatises alone would never convince them that their rights had been adequately safeguarded in an ordinary law court, especially one in which the judges were newcomers to their region. Moreover, the frontier between law and politics had been crossed when Jefferson expelled Livingston from his property, and legal scholarship availed little against the consequent array of power, interest, and reputation. It was on this level that the Batture question had to be decided. Edward Livingston was already aware of this by the spring of 1808.

III

Although Livingston was surprised by Jefferson's course of action in the Batture case, he hoped that difficulties could be resolved by mail. He forwarded documents and proofs to Gallatin in the early part of December 1807 and had even offered his share of the Batture in return for a financial settlement with the government.[46] The Administration's reply had come in the form of the *posse comitatus* led by the U.S. marshal, who drove Livingston's workers from the Batture on January 25, 1808. Three days later Livingston wrote to his brother in New York that "a most extraordinary event [has] again suspended my hopes for independence."[47] Livingston recalled how he had gained possession of the property the previous May, and that he had commenced improvements at a personal cost of $12,000. Now he expected his investment would be swept away by the violence of the river. "What makes it more extraordinary," he wrote, "is that my property and Mr. Delabigarre['s][48] are singled out while there are hundreds of alluvians in the territory depending on the same title and a long quantity adjoining mine held under the identical title by which we held that [remain] untouched." He was shocked at the government's reaction to what he considered his own conciliatory approach. He wrote, "I am so astonished at the . . . despotic nature of the attack that I have yet formed no plan. I can scarcely believe myself in a country that boasts of having a constitution."

Livingston realized that a negotiation by mail was now out of the question and that he would have to go to Washington. Professional commitments delayed his journey until mid-April. Meanwhile Claiborne alerted Madison to Livingston's impending trip and warned that his purposes were "several subjects private and political: Among the former the case of the Batture will be introduced; among the latter, the acts of General Wilkinson during the winter of 1806, and of Governor Claiborne generally are to be much complained of."[49] Claiborne was trying to deflate criticism by anticipating it.

Livingston arrived in Washington on May 5, and Gallatin immediately scribbled a note to his chief, "what shall I do with E. Livingston . . .?"[50] Jefferson replied, "if you can possibly have him arrested here for his public debt, the opportunity ought not to be lost."[51] But that was for Gallatin to decide. As for Jefferson, he was leaving. Livingston wasted no time in contacting the elusive President. He wrote to him from his hotel in Georgetown on the very evening of his arrival, hoping for "a short audience."[52] Jefferson's icy response was composed the next day. He referred Livingston—"whatever be the subject of [his] application," pretending not to know it—to the appropriate department head.[53]

Livingston was indefatigable. He composed a long letter to Madison on the same day, May 6, and recounted the circumstances which brought him to Washington. Livingston could not understand the "peculiar Displeasure of the Executive." He reminded the Secretary that he had not appealed to the public "in a case which [he] could easily have shown regarded every individual in the community."[54] He chose not to spare Madison some evidence of his displeasure, however, commenting on his "ill fortune in arriving after a voyage of some thousand miles at a moment when the President's affairs would not permit him to give half an hour's audience." Livingston was convinced that within that time he could have persuaded Jefferson as to the justice of his petition. Nevertheless, in spite of the President's absence, Livingston was willing to have the Attorney General examine his documents and issue a counterorder to the U.S. marshal restoring his property to him. If, on the other hand, the government was still adamant in its position, Livingston would be glad to place the matter before a competent tribunal. He closed his letter to Madison with an offer to supply an attorney trained in the civil law to aid Rodney in his deliberations.

Both Madison and Jefferson, by the brevity of their notes to Livingston and their pretense at unfamiliarity with Livingston's business, feigned disinterest. In fact, they were nervously preoccupied with Livingston's appeal. Letters exchanged later in the month between these two principal officers of the government betrayed their true feelings.

After examining papers and documents which Livingston presented, Madison wrote to the President that he had "not had time to do more than skim over his pivotal argument."[55] His examination must indeed have been perfunctory, for the analysis which followed was opaque and confusing. Madison wrote:

> I observe he labors more to establish the identity of the French with the Roman and Spanish law, than to show that the proceeding on which his title depends, was under the Spanish, not the French law. At the time this took place France retained the possession, after having executed a Treaty of alienation. If France had a right to do what was done, it would seem, that the French not the Spanish law, would be the rule in that as in all other transactions during the interval of non-delivery of the ceded country: If the proceeding was not of right, the title derived from it must be a nullity also; unless made good by some subsequent sanction under the Spanish authority. To consider France as the Trustee of Spain, would make the Spanish code her guide, and vitiate all proceedings under the French code. To consider France as the sovereign de facto, not de jure, would make the French law, equally the law de facto, tho' not de jure, and exclude the Spanish law as the criterion in the case. Unless therefore the French law of alluvian, be in reality the same with that of Spain, the title of Mr. E. will depend on the course of things relating to it, after the possessory transfer to Spain. These are very hasty ideas, and would not be hazarded without a knowledge that if incorrect they will be superceded by your better view of the subject.[56]

Jefferson's reply was somewhat clearer:

> Your observations on [Livingston's] allegations that Gravier's grant must be under the Spanish law, because after the cession of the province by France to Spain, tho' before delivery of possession, are conclusive, to which must be added that Louis XIV having established the Coustumes de Paris as the Law of Louisiana, this was not changed by the mere act of transfer; on the contrary the Laws of France continued and continues to be the law of the land except where specially altered by some

> subsequent edict of Spain or act of Congress. He has not in the least shaken the doctrine that the bed of the river, and all the atterrissements or banks which arise on it by the depositions of the river are the property of the king by a peculiarity in the law of France, so that nothing quoted from those of Spain or the Roman law is of authority on that point.[57]

Madison's uncertainty on so fundamental a matter as the law in force in Louisiana is an indication of the untidiness of the government's legal position at what was, by May 1808, a very late moment in the unfolding drama. His confusion on a vital part of the government's case reveals how ill-conceived that position was when policy was determined. Jefferson's grasp of some of the fundamentals was better, or at least clearer, but his avid search for weaknesses in Livingston's opinion revealed deep vexation.

The decision to remove Livingston from the Batture had been made in the Cabinet on November 27, 1807. The grounds for his removal was the act of Congress of March 3, 1807, authorizing the eviction of squatters from public lands; this, together with the opinion of Pierre Derbigny, constituted the legal basis for Jefferson's action.[58] He little suspected that his policy would later be vigorously contested. It was not until after Duponceau's opinion was published in July 1808 that it proved necessary for the government to find additional grounds to sustain the action undertaken the previous November. Thierry's *Examen* partly answered this need. Meanwhile, from November 1807 until July 1808, the government felt assured that Derbigny's case, built upon his particular interpretation of the French laws of alluvion, would stand up in possible future litigation. From the exchange of letters between Jefferson and Madison in May 1808 it is clear that the President, at least, felt that his policy in regard to the Batture was legally sound.

Livingston waited for Jefferson and Madison to respond to his personal petition. They tried to divert him by saying that the Batture question had been referred to Congress and was out of their hands, but he was not satisfied.[59] On the eve of his departure for Philadelphia to embark for New Orleans, Livingston wrote again to Madison, this time allowing his mounting irritation to show through his transparent self-restraint. "It having been deemed inconsistent with official duty to examine my proof or listen to my argument, I must at present content myself with having done everything that a sense of justice and the extreme of moderation could require," he wrote, intimating that they had not seen the last of him.[60] Livingston's patience was at an end. He wanted to know if the President seriously intended to submit the entire business to Congress who, in turn, would determine whether or not the President had been invested "with the power of reviewing the decision of a court, of opposing the execution of its decrees, and depriving a citizen of his property without even the form of trial or affording him the means of defence." Livingston warned Madison that unless some satisfactory arrangement was worked out between them, he would charge Jefferson before the bar of public opinion with having committed serious violations of law. He had refrained from such action until then, he wrote, to avoid a confrontation between the executive and judicial branches of the government—a conflict that would unsettle the public mind. He had hoped for a chance to demonstrate amicably and in good faith the error which had misled the Administration, but his appeal had failed.

Madison was obdurate.[61] From Philadelphia Livingston remained in communication with Administration officials. Jefferson had informed him, through Madison, that the Attorney General concurred in the government's position. Livingston desired to examine Rodney's opinion in order to demonstrate its weaknesses. He still hoped for a settlement short of a full congressional and public debate. Despite his warnings to Madison and his confidence in the soundness of his position, Livingston realized his disadvantage in any open battle with the President. He sent Caesar Rodney a note requesting a written opinion on the Batture. In his reply the Attorney General explained that the original was not in Madison's office but had been sent over to Congress with all of the other relevant documents. Not having a copy for Livingston to see, he merely noted that it coincided with Derbigny's opinion in the case.[62] Livingston was astounded at Rodney's blissful admission to having based his opinion upon Derbigny's brief when it directly contradicted the decree of the Superior Court of the Orleans territory. He queried the Attorney General as to which was more deserving of credence, "the solemn deliberate decision of three judges, . . . sworn to do justice between the parties, or the ex parte statement of a lawyer feed to maintain a contrary opinion?"[63] But Rodney was unshaken. In a short note a few days later the Attorney General promised Livingston that he would write to him in New Orleans. He mentioned Moreau Lislet and John Gurley as having concurred in Derbigny's opinion—another anemic defense of his position.

Livingston's appeal to Rodney failed; the Administration was immovable; the visit to Washington accomplished nothing. In spite of this, Livingston remained hopeful. He planned to return in the fall of the year to renew his petition,[64] but by October he had changed his mind. Professional obligations and living expenses forced him to remain in New Orleans. There was little he could do.[65] Frustrated in his efforts to secure his property and redeem his name through a direct appeal to the government, Livingston decided to lay his case before the nation.

IV

In his *Address to the People of the United States*, Edward Livingston arraigned Thomas Jefferson for what he called his oppressive, unconstitutional, arbitrary, and illegal policy in regard to the New Orleans Batture. "Private injuries," he wrote, "when offered in violation of Constitutional principles, become proper objects of public attention. . . . The selection of a remote scene for the exercise of arbitrary power, and of an unfriended or unpopular individual for its object, render the case more dangerous. . . ."[66] Livingston was attempting to utilize his unpopularity to his own advantage. For a year he had experienced the consequences of political isolation and the insufficiency of logic, truth, and justice—as he understood them—to restore him to his fortune. Now he was throwing himself upon the people in a last effort to win public support.

In the course of his long review of the events following the decree of the Superior Court of May 23, 1807, Livingston reflected upon the reasons for the injustice he had suffered. He knew that the malice of his enemies was active against him. He considered Claiborne "the most malevolent among them."[67] The governor had staked his reputation on the cause of the Batture and had convinced the people of New Orleans that his influence with the President would counteract the decision of the Superior Court. He, Livingston, was alert to this, but he still

> found it difficult to believe that the First Magistrate of a great people would quit the care of a nation to participate in the petty disputes of a corporate town; or, to secure the popularity of a favorite, that he would have set at defiance the very forms of law, braved the authority of the courts, and broken through the most important barriers of that constitution he had sworn to defend. If he had only effected my ruin, I should not have been surprised; for I am no longer in a situation to serve him; but that the suffrage of a party in an inconsiderable town should be purchased at this prodigal expense of principle, I own astonished me.[68]

Here Livingston was hitting one of the touchstones of affairs in the territory. The Burr storm had subsided, but the ominous clouds of defection in Lower Louisiana, the proximity of the hostile Spanish, and the remoteness of New Orleans had indeed transformed a local dispute into an urgent national issue. Instances of personal injustice carried little weight in such great affairs of state. This was no "petty dispute of a corporate town"; the "suffrage of a party in an inconsiderable [place]" was not insignificant. Livingston was beginning to realize that the politics of the Batture controversy warranted even more attention than the legal merits of the Batture case.

Livingston planned to send copies of his *Address* to Congress. He asked his brother Robert to help win over the members of both houses.[69] Peter Duponceau and Livingston's other brother, John Livingston, advised that he suppress the work, but Livingston disagreed. For one thing, the *Address* had already appeared in all of the local newspapers. Secondly, he did not see the value of further self-effacement. "I tried moderation and silence longer than I ought," he wrote to his brother Robert in January, "and I found that they produced nothing but insolence and an accumulation of injuries."[70] Livingston contemplated the effect upon Jefferson of a renewed personal petition but concluded that "his tyranny will have increased with my submission." Yet, while Jefferson was but six weeks away from retirement, Livingston did not lose sight of the possibilities which the incoming Administration offered. He suggested that his brother might intercede with President-elect Madison. He himself would not ask for favors. "If he [Madison] should persist in the measures of his predecessor," he speculated, "I will not be the only sufferer—, but I hope better things from his character."

Livingston demonstrated in his *Address* a growing awareness that the causes of his troubles over the Batture lay deeper than mere questions of law or fact. But it was J. B. S. Thierry, editor of the *Louisiana Courier,* who first perceived the full political dimensions of the Batture controversy. The Burr conspiracy was still a live issue in the Orleans territory. If its energy as a catalyst of political change showed any signs of depletion by the end of 1807, the Clark-Wilkinson confrontation, early in 1808, rejuvenated it. Meanwhile the Batture controversy had burst out into the open. On both questions Livingston was vulnerable, and Thierry was quick to punish him for it. Entries in the *Courier* in April and May of 1808 sought to damage Livingston by linking him with Clark and Watkins, the well-known Burrites, thereby connecting Burrism with Batturism. Thierry viewed Livingston's

Batture misfortune as another defeat for the "swarm of locusts from the United States."[71] Thierry attributed Louisiana's political troubles to a fundamental fact: the existence in the territory of "the ambitious members of [Burr's] broken faction." Clark as well as Livingston was subjected to his withering rhetoric. Thierry contrasted Claiborne's devoted service in behalf of the public interest in the matter of the Batture with Clark's fecklessness.[72] Thierry used Burrism to damage Livingston and Batturism to damage Clark, as if further injury could cause additional wreckage to already well-battered reputations.

In his response to Livingston's December *Address*, Thierry commented upon a number of its allegations and again endeavored to connect the Batture affair to the other public issues agitating the territory.[73] In the December 12 issue of the *Courier* he alluded to the Burr imbroglio and tried to entangle Livingston with all the others who had unluckily been caught up in those events. Thierry likened Livingston's declamations against invasions of individual liberty to the cries of those against whom Wilkinson had acted in suppressing the cohorts of the infamous Burr.[74] A week later Thierry addressed himself to the political observations in Livingston's *Address*. He defended Claiborne as a champion of the Louisianians and attributed Livingston's "implacable hatred" of the governor to his failure to gain appointment as a director of the Louisiana Bank when it was first established in 1805. At that time, Thierry wrote, Livingston plunged himself into "the artful intrigues of Clark and Co."[75]

Thierry attributed Claiborne's popularity not to his Batture policy, as Livingston alleged, but to "his firm and wise conduct whilst he was almost involved in the elements of the Burrite faction." This established Claiborne's right to the affection of the inhabitants and the confidence of the Administration. "Such a popularity could not receive any increase from the affair of the batture," argued Thierry. The governor was merely doing his duty. But whether it was duty or popularity that directed Claiborne's policy, he had acted properly both during the Burr conspiracy and in the Batture controversy. Thierry was applauding the governor's peformance.[76]

V

At the urging of his brother Robert, Livingston made another trip to the northeast in the spring of 1809.[77] Duponceau was very active in his behalf at this time. Robert suggested that a final settlement with the government could be reached if Livingston indicated a readiness to accept a cancellation of his claim to the Batture.[78] His brother believed that Congress would be glad to "find some way out of the scrape" and was hopeful that the Madison Administration would not be difficult about it.

The optimism which Robert conveyed to Livingston was contagious. Apparently the mood in Washington in 1809 was not unfavorable, and Livingston reported in May that he believed a satisfactory arrangement was possible. "I am well received by the President and my old Congressional friends," he wrote to his brother some time after arriving in the capital. "[My] misfortunes have arisen from some prejudices excited against me in Mr. Jefferson's mind of which I can neither discover the substance nor the certain author—as they do not seem to have affected me with my former friends!"[79] He felt sufficiently confident to pursue his claim more immoderately than he had the previous year. Livingston composed a letter which he distributed among a number of the members of Congress in which he restated his position, recounted his trials and sacrifices, and requested legislative aid. He asked for Congressional interference "as a matter of the highest public duty, which in my present position, I am content to *solicit* as a private favor."[80]

In the spring of 1809 Livingston did have some cause for optimism. In June resolutions were introduced in the House of Representatives by Daniel Sheffey of Virginia calling for a temporary restoration of Livingston's rights to the Batture and the appointment of a presidential commission consisting of three referees to decide the question. In an alternative proposal, the President would be empowered to reach a compromise settlement pending a hearing in the federal courts. Livingston was prepared to accept either of these suggestions. Sheffey's resolutions were put before the House repeatedly in 1809, but no action was taken.[81]

By January 1810 the buoyancy of the previous spring had evaporated. Livingston lamented the absence of leadership and men of talent in the Congress.[82] Debate was desultory. His own cause had been relegated to the discussion of private claims which took place every Friday. He had little hope that Congress would act in his favor. "Should I be disappointed at this session," he wrote sadly, "I must abandon it forever—a life of solicitation is of all others the most insupportable." One month later the situation was unchanged. Congressional debate continued, but interest flagged. Arguments long since refuted were refurbished and advanced anew. Livingston wrote to his brother that "the wretches have caught some tag ends of ten times refuted arguments in the case and after repeating them gravely say that the title of the United States is so clear that they cannot reconcile it to their consciences to subordinate it to a trial." [83] He contemplated a return to New Orleans and a sale of his lands at one-quarter their value in order to free himself of debt.

The Batture debate in Congress in the spring of 1810 centered on the proposal introduced by George Poindexter, the delegate from the Mississippi territory, on March 1. [84] It provided that a suit be brought by the petitioner in the U.S. District Court in New Orleans against the United States; that the nearest federal circuit court consider the case on appeal according to the law and the forms of law then in force in Orleans; and that the Supreme Court of the United States review the decision of the circuit on a writ of error. [85] In opposition to this proposal Julien Poydras, the territorial delegate from Orleans, lectured the Congress on the subject of the Batture.

Poydras had written and spoken on the question before. His past arguments in defense of the public's right to the Batture were based upon Thierry's *Examen*. Poydras himself was a planter, not a lawyer, and he added little to the prodigious heap of law that had already been unearthed. His published work on the Batture, however, was notable for its rhetorical flourishes. His writings were studded with those hyperbolic epithets so characteristic of the style of Livingston's opponents. The "usurpers" of the Batture, Poydras had written, were "artful adversaries" and "griping attornies" supporting "illegal claims." They "packed juries" and made "poor clients" suffer through "the cunning of chicane."[86] He called the Batture decision an "atrocity" unparalled in human history, [87] and an impossibility had the judges been familiar with the local language, customs, and laws of Orleans. [88]

Poydras's views sharpened public suspicion in the Orleans territory that the Superior Court's Batture decision in favor of Gravier and Livingston was an abortion of the bench delivered by the midwives of the bar, a suspicion that was the one constant factor amidst the variables of legal argumentation in the protracted controversy, [89] a suspicion which had quickened the opposition of the settled population to the introduction of the common law. This hostility to judicial proceedings in general—"judicial piracy" as Poydras once called it—animated Poydras's last speech on the Batture. Opening with an eloquent restatement of "the sacred right of the public to the property of the port of the suburb St. Mary," Poydras quickly went to the heart of the question:

> The honorable delegate from the Mississippi Territory [Poindexter], has told us in a very soft and persuasive tone,

> that he had a resolution to offer to the consideration of this honorable house very conciliatory indeed, and which he hoped would prove satisfactory to all parties, being calculated to insure an impartial and fair investigation of the titles of the invaders of the port of the suburb St. Mary. How has he fulfilled this promise, so engagingly announced in his soft sounding preamble? By a resolution, sir, objectionable in every point of view; the artful production of the combined exertions of practitioners profoundly skilled in all the tricks and windings of deceitful chicane. It is a master piece of duplicity. Its style is natural and flowing, like the limpid water of a gentle stream. Its language fascinating as a magic charm. "*Impartial trial . . . investigation of title, etc.*" Who can oppose himself to propositions seemingly so just? I, sir, do, and will be joined by everyone who knows that the language of a pleader is always calculated to conceal his real intent. It is the artificial blaze which dazzles the eye of the understanding. It is the melodious but bewitching voice of syrens. It is the smooth but perfidious current which dashes the unwary voyager against the rocks of Scylla or plunges him into the whirlpool of Charybdis. It is the golden sheath which conceals the dagger ready to stab you.[90]

For Poydras what must have been particularly exasperating was the absurdity of equating private and public right to the property. Such an equation was built into the adversary procedure of a common law court. The civilian in Poydras rebelled against what he conceived to be the inherent inequity of having a question such as the Batture decided in ordinary courts of law.[91] In view of the decision of the territorial court in *Gravier v. The Mayor, et al.* Poydras was profoundly distrustful of American law courts in general, but the Poindexter proposal was all the more outrageous because it would have moved the forum for a final disposition of the Batture problem to the courts of the United States, thereby subverting his territory's right to have "every suit originating within its jurisdiction decided according to the local laws and in the ordinary way of judicial proceedings."

Poydras's stated fears were specific. He dismissed the "impartial trial" gambit as "mere pleading." Only in New Orleans, were there "people sufficiently acquainted with the civil law, and with the facts and circumstances of the case able to give a just and legal verdict." Elsewhere ignorance would prevail. Jurors would be vulnerable to "artful adversaries" interested only in misleading them.[92] Poydras did not concede that a good argument had been made for private ownership of the Batture. He spoke in behalf of the special nature of the case and of the peculiarities of the law governing it. The ambiguity of the whole question, the fact that the laws were subject to interpretation and the facts to dispute, was unacknowledged. Any other opinion represented ignorance of local "law, customs and manners." Thus Julien Poydras interpreted the Batture decision in favor of Livingston as a thinly disguised effort to overturn the civil law itself. Despite the fact that the rule of decision had been Spanish law, Poydras insisted upon depicting the issue as a conflict between common law and civil law: "A spurious monster, the mongrel offspring of injustice and chicane, has been introduced into my country by our usurpers, who endeavor to pawn it on us as the lovely child of truth and justice; but we have with horror rejected this hideous imp, this illegitimate monster. Its foster parents are now attempting to have him regenerated, and legitimated, and for this purpose they pursue means which are new, circuitous and dark; but I ardently hope their schemes may once more prove abortive."[93] What was this "monster," this "imp," this "mongrel offspring of chicane" if not the common law? Poydras could not say so outright, for he was speaking before an American congress, many of whose members were common lawyers. And yet it is certain that this was his meaning. The Batture had become, for him, a symbolic issue—a test to see whether Congress was willing to recognize some kind of cultural distinction in the territory of Orleans.[94]

VI

Meanwhile, having failed to stir Congress into action, Livingston turned to the courts for relief. In the spring of 1810 he brought an action of trespass against Le Breton D'Orgenois, the U.S. marshal, in the U.S. district court in New Orleans and against former President Thomas Jefferson in the federal circuit court at Richmond. Livingston was determined to have a trial of his cause one way or another.[95]

To defend himself in court Jefferson requested the legal aid of some of the leading men of the Virginia bar.[96] He was advised to seek a full hearing of the case so that the U.S. title to the Batture would be established beyond question.[97] But Jefferson preferred a dismissal of the case on any technical point of pleading that would spare him a judgment of the merits.[98] He was no longer confident that the removal of Livingston and his workmen from the Batture back in 1807 had been legal. He now believed that the federal statute authorizing the eviction of squatters from public lands did not cover him.[99] And with respect to local law, he had already confessed to Claiborne that "we are all ignorant, except so far as instructed by the counsel of that place [Derbigny] who have written on the case," but in view of the published arguments of Livingston and Duponceau he realized that Derbigny's brief was not the last word.[100]

During the summer of 1810 Jefferson explored the whole question of the Batture and prepared what he hoped would be the definitive treatise on the subject as an aid to counsel.[101] He understood that the case against him rested on Spanish municipal law, and so he requested Claiborne to mail him Moreau Lislet's "compilation of the laws of Orleans" plus "the book of Spanish laws called the Recopilacion de Indias and the Partita [sic] of the laws of Castille . . . . I suppose they would be very important!"[102] Jefferson recognized that French civil law gave some color of legality to the position he had taken on the Batture, and the brief he composed, and later published, was a most elaborate argument purporting to prove that the law of France was the law in force in Orleans.[103]

Probably because of his uncertainty over the legal questions at issue, Jefferson did everything possible to guarantee a favorable disposition of his case. This went beyond erudite legal treatise-writing and included the deployment of his considerable influence in the Madison Administration to tilt the courts in his favor. Two crucial vacancies on the federal bench would directly affect the outcome of the litigation.[104] The declining health of Judge Cyrus Griffin of the Virginia district would soon open a seat on the circuit court of appeals where the case would be tried. Jefferson considered Griffin a "wretched . . . fool" and "a cypher," probably because he was a Federalist, and, even worse, likely to be in sympathy with Marshall, whom Jefferson despised and feared. Virginia was part of the Chief Justice's circuit, and the ex-President was convinced that Marshall's "twistifications of the law in the case of Marbury, in that of Burr, & the late Yazoo case show how dexterously he can reconcile the law to his personal biasses: and nobody seems to doubt that he is ready prepared to decide that Livingston's right to the batture is unquestionable, and that I am bound to pay for it with my private fortune."[105] Jefferson urged Madison to appoint Governor John Tyler of Virginia to the District Court. He thought Tyler would have the "character of firmness enough to preserve his independence on the same bench with Marshall."[106] In pushing Tyler's candidacy Jefferson was not above reminding Madison that in 1807, as a member of the Cabinet, Madison had been one of Jefferson's "associates in the proceedings" against Livingston and therefore liable to summons as a material witness in the case—a source of possible embarrassment to the new President.[107]

The other key vacancy occurred in September 1810, when Justice William Cushing died, leaving the Supreme Court evenly divided between three Republicans and three Federalists and opening up to Madison the first opportunity to create a Democratic-Republican majority. But Jefferson's concern was more personal than political because of the possibility of an appeal from the Virginia circuit, should the Batture decision go against him.[108] He recommended Levi Lincoln, his former Attorney General, who declined because of failing eyesight, and Gideon Granger, the Postmaster General since 1801.[109] Jefferson was determined to get a friend on the Court. Madison's fourth choice to fill Cushing's seat (Granger was unacceptable, Alexander Wolcott of Connecticut was rejected by the Senate, and John Quincy Adams, the ambassador to Russia, declined) was Joseph Story, a Massachusetts Republican whom everyone, except Jefferson, trusted.[110]

Meanwhile Jefferson turned to Congress for additional support. With the Cushing replacement pending and Griffin's demise distressingly protracted, Jefferson requested William Branch Giles, a leading Senate Republican, and John Wayles Eppes, his nephew and son-in-law (Eppes married Jefferson's daughter Mary, his first cousin), a staunch Administration supporter in the House, to stifle congressional action on the Batture question despite Livingston's repeated petitions.[111] At one time Jefferson had been amenable to a congressional settlement of the issue, but he now feared that any legislative undertaking even partially favorable to Livingston would preiudice his defense in court.

Jefferson sent the two congressional leaders copies of the brief he had laboriously prepared over the summer, cautioning them to show it only to trusted intimates such as Julien Poydras of the Orleans territory. "I have thought that I might rely on your justice as well as your friendship to attend to this case," he wrote, "so far as to prevent his [Livingston's] obtaining there [in Congress] any vote injurious to a fair trial."[112] But Jefferson was not interested in a "fair trial" as that phrase is commonly understood. He had already agreed with his counsel to try for a dismissal on technicalities, and he was, at the moment, busily engaged in a concerted effort to manipulate the personnel on the courts about to try the case and likely to hear it on appeal. No doubt Jefferson had persuaded himself that the bench was inveterately opposed to him. He assured Eppes and Giles that "were this case before an impartial court it would never give me a moment's concern . . . . [But] the deep-seated enmity of one judge [Marshall] and utter nullity of the other [Griffin] . . . lessens the confidence which the justice of my cause would otherwise give me." But it was one thing for Jefferson to believe that all he wanted was a fair trial—quite another to try to win the sympathy of others by passing himself off as an innocent victim of an oppressive bench. One month later, Griffin died and Tyler was appointed to the Virginia District Court, thus consummating Jefferson's disingenuous bench tampering.

Tyler understood Jefferson's role in getting him onto the federal bench and, more importantly, what was expected of him. Jefferson had spelled it out in May 1810, when the possibility of replacing Griffin first arose. Referring to the Virginia district, to Marshall's "base prostitution of law to party passions," to Griffin's "imbecility," and to the need for a judge to extend the protection of law to all citizens, he admonished Tyler: "I believe you will do it, and where you cannot induce your colleague to do what is right, you will be firm enough to hinder him from doing what is wrong, and by opposing sense to sophistry, leave juries free to follow their own judgment."[113]

Jefferson was not to be disappointed. On December 5, 1811, the federal Circuit Court for the Virginia district rendered decision in *Livingston* v. *Jefferson*. The court found that an action for a trespass committed on lands within the United States but outside the jurisdiction of the Virginia district was beyond its cognizance. Refusing to overturn an ancient rule of English common law, the court said that a trespass was local in nature and had to be tried where the land in question lay. The proper venue for an action of trespass involving the Batture, therefore, was a court of competent jurisdiction in the Orleans territory, not one in Henrico County, Virginia.

Both Tyler and Marshall concurred on the venue question, but Tyler congratulated Jefferson's attorneys for their "Herculean strength of forensic ability which . . . sheds luster over the bar of Virginia," while accusing John Wickham, Livingston's advocate, of trying to make "the worse appear the better cause" and using "high-sounding words . . . [to] fill up a vacuum in . . . argument."[114] Marshall, on the other hand, implied that a decision on the merits would have been in favor of Livingston. This was blocked, he said in effect, by the defendant's assertion of the technical distinction between transitory actions and local actions which the weight of previous judicial opinion forced Marshall to uphold. Whatever the reasons for the technicality, however, said Marshall, "[t]hey are countervailed, and more than countervailed by the opposing consideration, that if the action be disallowed, the injured party may have a clear right without a remedy in a case where a person who had done the wrong [i.e., Jefferson] and who ought to make the compensation, is within the power of the court."[115]

Tyler later informed Jefferson that the Chief Justice was eager to adjourn and remove the case for hearing before the United States Supreme Court. He would have done so, he said, had Tyler—at the time, gallantly resisting the "severe . . . paroxysms" of a bladder condition—not insisted on a decision at the circuit level "letting the parties act as they pleased, by appealing, if they disliked the decision, to which he [Marshall] consented." [116] Tyler's moral debt to Jefferson for his judgeship was thereby paid in full.

Having been unwilling to risk a legal trial on the merits but eager to establish his innocence in the courtroom of public opinion, Jefferson published the lengthy brief he had prepared as an aid to counsel once the legal proceeding was behind him. [117] The work was a clever but unoriginal synthesis of old arguments plus some new ones concocted by Albert Gallatin. [118] The following year, in a characteristically exhaustive reply, Edward Livingston would marvel at how Jefferson could "persevere in the same pretence of understanding the laws of France better than gentlemen bred to it from their childhood, and who, engaged on the same side of the controversy with himself, have abandoned the ground he has taken." [119] To Livingston's gratification, the eminent James Kent, Chancellor of New York, wrote him that, on the merits, Livingston's case was stronger and that he had been the victim of an "atrocious injustice." Joseph Story would later declare that Jefferson's conduct in the matter of the Batture was regrettable. [120]

Meanwhile Livingston had reoccupied the Batture in November 1810, a year before his suit against Jefferson came to trial. This time he deferred to local custom by permitting the unloading of boats and the filling of watercarts, but he warned that anyone caught digging in or carting off batture soil would be sued. [121] Nevertheless, Livingston's gesture, however conciliatory, was resisted—by Thierry in the *Louisiana Courier* and by the United States attorney, who ordered J. M. Fortier, the new U.S. marshal in New Orleans, to retain possession for the government. Livingston promptly sued Fortier. [122]

Batture litigation continued for another decade. Livingston remained hopeful and energetic throughout, despite personal grief and continued legal harassment. He was partially vindicated by a Supreme Court decision ordering the U.S. District Court in New Orleans to restore him to his property, but the local authorities blocked effective implementation of the court order, and litigation went on. [123] Not until 1823, after a compromise settlement with the city of New Orleans had been reached, did Livingston begin to enjoy the fruits of his numerous trials and arduous labors.

In time, Livingston even regained the sympathy of men who had opposed him during the bitter fight. Bernard Marigny, one of his strongest opponents in the Batture affair, expressed warm admiration for Livingston's "imperturbable constancy" and "personal courage." "Such a man," he thought, "inspires interest and deserves consideration even from those who oppose him."[124] Even the aged Jefferson was eventually reconciled. In 1824, in a letter to James Monroe, he wrote that Livingston "may be assured I have not a spark of unfriendly feeling toward him . . . . Mr. Livingston would now be received at Monticello with as hearty a welcome as he would have been in 1800 . . . . I bear ill will to no human being."[125]

VII

The Batture controversy had wide-ranging ramifications. On the political level it led to the isolation of Edward Livingston.[126] Next to Daniel Clark, Livingston was Claiborne's chief rival in the territory. He was a man of two worlds: an American with important lines to the central government whose own brother had been a central figure in the negotiations leading to the purchase of Louisiana, and a resident of Louisiana who had married a French refugee from Santo Domingo, learned the local languages, specialized in civil law, and championed most of the interests of the inhabitants. Livingston was a serious rival for leadership in the territory. Daniel Clark, Claiborne's other opponent, had been ruined politically by his involvement with Burr and his ugly squabble with James Wilkinson, a local favorite, but Livingston had managed to come out of the Burr episode relatively unscathed. The Batture controversy dissipated his popularity, however, and thereafter he stood virtually alone. It is significant, for example, that Livingston had to reach out to Peter Duponceau and other members of the Philadelphia bar for support. No important local lawyer would help him.

On the level of legal controversy there is no one-to-one relationship between the Batture fight and the larger conflict of legal traditions in Lower Louisiana. The rivals for control of the Batture did not parallel the civil law—common law antagonists. From the very first, Livingston fought for the civil law. The practice act of 1805, which he authored, his translation of some of the books in the Corpus Juris Civilis, and then, in the 1820's, his projects in behalf of legal codification, all attest to long and devoted service to local legal traditions. On the other hand, Thomas Jefferson, the leading proponent of the common law in Lower Louisiana, defended the public right to the Batture. On one issue the President's position coincided with that of the

American minority; on the other he allied himself with the Latin majority.

Still, the struggle for the Mississippi alluvion criss-crossed larger legal questions at many points. Edward Livingston was the best-known American attorney in New Orleans. Because of his exploitation of the Batture, the ancient inhabitants viewed him as the most notorious example of those "vexatious lawyers" which the cession seemed to have produced. The American judges of a common law court had consigned to Livingston public properties of enormous importance and value. The Batture controversy seemed to be the classic instance of how the law could be twisted and the inhabitants thereby deprived of their ancient rights and privileges.

The original decision in *Gravier* v. *New Orleans* may have been based upon sound civil law principles. Yet Thierry's *Courier* articles and Poydras's speeches in Congress showed that the public would perceive the Superior Court's ruling as a legal calamity brought on by the bench's profound ignorance of the customs of the country. The Batture litigation stimulated an awareness, in the popular mind at least, that important public interests could be lost by legal means. Questions of law, therefore, assumed a new gravity and awakened wide concern.

Thus, in its own distorted way, the controversy over the Batture of the Faubourg St. Marie dramatized the confrontation between diverse legal cultures. The political, social, and legal issues raised in the course of the Batture fight impinged with unparalleled immediacy upon larger questions of law and the overall problem of the conflict of legal traditions. Indeed, it seems to be an inescapable conclusion that the Batture controversy solidified local realignments which the Burr conspiracy had precipitated. At the same time it prepared the ground at the territorial and national levels of government for the adoption of the *Digest of the Laws in Force* on March 31, 1808, a moment when the clamor over the New Orleans Batture was still at its height.

The Clash of Legal Traditions

[5] *Common Law vs. Civil Law: First Phase*

I

On December 20, 1803, France transferred Louisiana to the United States. William C. C. Claiborne, the provisional governor of the new territory, was authorized to exercise extensive executive, legislative, and judicial power until Congress could provide for more definitive governmental arrangements. Following the retrocession of Louisiana from Spain to France on November 30, 1803, the French prefect, Pierre Clement de Laussat, had abolished all of the existing Spanish courts and had deliberately neglected to put French substitutes in their place. Confronted with a territory virtually denuded of legal institutions, Claiborne had to create a judicial administration with the materials at hand. He declared that the laws in force—whatever they were—were to remain in force. He established a court of pleas of seven judges exercising civil jurisdiction in cases not exceeding three thousand dollars with each of the judges enjoying summary powers in minor civil suits. The court of pleas also had limited criminal jurisdiction. By executive fiat Claiborne also instituted a "Governor's Court" consisting of a single jurist—the governor himself—which retained original jurisdiction in all civil and criminal cases pending the creation of a regular high tribunal. Claiborne also ordered the military commandants to continue to serve as judges in the outlying districts. The municipality of New Orleans, created by Laussat, would administer the affairs of New Orleans, but it no longer possessed the judicial capacity of the old Spanish Cabildo.[1]

Three months after the commencement of the American occupation Congress acted to fill the institutional void left in the wake of the French. By the act of March 26, 1804, Louisiana was divided into the district of Louisiana and the territory of Orleans north and south of a demarcation line at the thirty-third parallel. The governor, appointed by the President, would be aided by a council of thirteen notables, also under presidential appointment. The judiciary was to consist of a Superior Court of three judges, again selected by the President, and such inferior courts and justices of the peace as might be established by the governor and council. The Superior Court had both criminal and civil jurisdiction. Trials were to be by jury in capital cases and in other cases at the request of the parties. Subsequently the legislative council required the Superior Court to go on circuit. Congress also provided for such familiar common law guarantees as the writ of habeas corpus, bail, and the prohibition against cruel and unusual punishments, but the laws in force were continued in force until altered or modified by the legislature.[2]

The government of Orleans, created by Congress, began to function on October 1, 1804. The legislative council divided the territory into twelve counties, each a judicial district with one judge appointed by the governor. The jurisdiction of these county courts commenced in cases of contract in excess of fifty dollars, and in cases of tort less than one hundred dollars. The county courts also exercised criminal jurisdiction concurrent with the Superior Court with regular jury trials. In addition, justices of the peace were chosen by the governor to replace the commandants. They maintained final jurisdiction in minor civil disputes. Acts passed by the legislative council in 1805 regulated procedure in all territorial courts from the justices of the peace at the base of the system to the Superior Court at its summit.[3] Thus the legal reconstruction of Lower Louisiana began with the institutional innovations so characteristic of the common law system. By introducing the familiar officials, courts of law, and adversary procedures of the common law, the way would be readied for the ultimate reception of the common law itself—such was the hope.

But the oscillations in Louisiana's political history had left a legacy of legal confusion. The clash of legal cultures became one of the most perplexing problems facing the new American government in the immediate aftermath of the cession of Louisiana to the United States. A variety of laws, ordinances, regulations, decrees, codes, and legal procedures prevailed. These had to be identified, sorted out, and accepted or discarded. Congress recognized the problem when it declared that the laws in force at the time of the cession were "to continue in force, until altered, modified, or repealed by the legislature." But would the laws in force be modified or, perhaps, set aside altogether? If set aside, what would be substituted for them? Would the Americans institute Anglo-American common law along with the common-law courts they established in the first months of American rule? How would the ancient Louisianians react to this? Would they stand by and allow settled "laws, usages, and customs" to be abrogated or would they try to preserve them? These important questions the organic acts of 1804 and 1805 would leave undecided, and yet the manner of their resolution would obviously affect the future history and character of the area. Congress did face up to the urgent necessity of providing for a governmental structure, but the major legal questions with which it was preoccupied concerned the constitutional implications of the Louisiana purchase.[4]

The issue of the municipal law in force in the region was a narrower problem, and in the end it proved to be much less resolvable in ways thought favorable to American national interests. Jefferson's position on the legal question was well known. He believed in the necessity of legal uniformity as a strand in the web of national unity. Like many Americans of the period, Jefferson looked forward to the time "when our rapid multiplication will expand itself . . . and cover the whole northern, if not the southern continent, with a people speaking the same language, governed in similar forms, and by similar laws."[5] He believed that the cement of union would not harden if it contained mixed legal systems.[6]

Jefferson did not conceal his ardent desire to reshape the laws of Louisiana. During the summer of 1803 the President wrote Horatio Gates, the Revolutionary War general, that the settled portions of Louisiana, particularly the area in and around New Orleans, ought to be annexed to the Mississippi territory, leaving the rest of Louisiana "locked up from American settlement."[7] His purpose in joining the inhabitants of the new territory to the old was to ensure American political predominance and to guarantee Lousiana's peaceable absorption into the American system under American law. "We shall endeavor to introduce the American laws there," he wrote, "and that cannot be done but by amalgamating the people with such a body of Americans as may take the lead in legislation and government."

Despite warnings from knowledgeable men of the southwest, Jefferson remained committed to a refashioning of the laws of Louisiana. In November 1803 he admitted to Gallatin that innovations "would turn all their laws topsy-turvy."[8] Still, he wanted the new territorial government to introduce trial by jury and habeas corpus as soon as possible and, in general, "to draw their laws and organization to the mold of ours by degrees as they find practicable without exciting too much discontent." Several weeks later, outlining to Kentucky Senator John Breckinridge a constitutional plan for the new acquisition, Jefferson pointed to the necessity of limiting the tenure of prospective judges to four years rather than permitting them to serve during good behavior. "Should judges take a kink in their heads in favor of leaving the present laws of Louisiana unaltered," he reasoned, "that evil will be continued for their lives, unamended by us, and become so inveterate that we may never be able to introduce the uniformity of law so desirable."[9]

Jefferson opened his campaign to attach New Orleans and the

nearby settlements along the river to an adjacent American territory when he appointed William C. C. Claiborne, the governor of Mississippi, as one of two commissioners empowered to receive Louisiana from France. Soon after the establishment of American control, however, he abandoned the idea. At his direction Congress permanently detached Lower Louisiana from Mississippi and created the separate territory of Orleans.[10] Nevertheless, the President remained committed to reconstructing the Louisiana legal system.

II

Jefferson endeavored to gather as much information as possible about the vast new empire he had acquired. In the summer preceding the transfer of Louisiana from France to the United States, Jefferson and Madison made a series of formal inquiries about the region. Knowledgeable men of the southwest including Daniel Clark, William C. C. Claiborne, Evan Jones, John Pintard, and William Dunbar were invited to respond to a long list of queries, some of which had specific application to the legal problem—namely, what were the sources of law operative in the ceded country, the nature of the courts of justice there, the status of the criminal law, the attitudes of the local inhabitants toward the administration of justice, and their probable reaction to the introduction of jury trials?

Claiborne himself, then the governor of the Mississippi territory, was one of the first to respond. He reported that the introduction of juries in civil suits would encounter a hostile reception:

> Some of the oldest and most respectable Inhabitants of this territory are of opinion, that in Civil Cases the Trial by Jury, will at first be unpopular, and I have heard this Reason assigned, 'That Men who have long appealed for Justice to great Personages, whom they looked up to as wise and learned, cannot at first, without reluctance, submit to the decrees of Men, no better than themselves.' And the same Reason is likewise supposed, to operate with some of the old Settlers in this Territory, even at the present day to the disrepute of Jury Trials.[11]

Claiborne predicted less difficulty in the application of the jury method to criminal proceedings, however. He wrote that: "In Criminal cases on the contrary, the Trial by Jury (it is thought) will be entirely acceptable. Indeed it is very observable, that as the people in this District, begin to understand this Mode of trial, their Attachment to it increases." This proved to be an accurate forecast. Virtually no opposition greeted the Americanization of the criminal law of Louisiana.[12] The Spanish criminal justice system was noted for its corruption and brutality,[13] and Louisianians were quick to perceive the advantages of the American system in this area. The opposition to the use of the jury system in civil causes was to be considerable, however.

Evan Jones reported to Madison that innovation in another area of judicial administration would cause trouble. Under the Spanish, the military commanders of garrisons in the outlying districts exercised civil powers. They were responsible for general police and the preservation of order, the certification of land claims, and the determination of minor causes. In suits exceeding one hundred dollars in value, the commandants collected the necessary proofs and submitted them to the Governor General who, in turn, placed them before a regular tribunal at New Orleans. In short, the commandants combined the functions of notary, sheriff, land agent, coroner, auctioneer and justice of the peace with their other responsibilities. Their military and civic duties were mutually reinforcing.

Jones said that any effort to do away with the commandants and to replace them with civil judges or justices of the peace would invite trouble. Conditions in the districts were turbulent even under quasi-military governance. How much more difficult then to preserve stability with, as he put it, "two or three Justices of the peace, or Judges of inferior courts, supported only by a few constables, and of the vicinage too, who in all probability would have as little disposition as powers to execute the orders of their superiors? . . . Its much to be feared that those [powers] usually delegated to Justices of the peace, and to the Judges of the Inferior Courts, will be found too small, and too dilatory, to satisfy a people, accustomed from their first experience to a prompt and generally verbal distribution of Justice."[14] Jones suggested some form of summary justice to avoid protracted litigation until such time "as the Inhabitants acquire a competent idea of the laws, and of the advantages that will result from a due submission to them." In sum, Jones was pessimistic as to how the inhabitants of Louisiana were likely to receive the institutional transition from civil law to common law.

III

The problems facing acting Governor Claiborne were multiple, and those related to law and the administration of justice were among the most nagging. "The state in which I found the Jurisprudence of this country embarrasses me extremely," he wrote Madison shortly after the transfer of Louisiana.[15] Cases commenced twenty years before were still pending. Corruption had tainted the judiciary in the past,

Claiborne reported, and now much was expected of the Americans. Written testimony had accumulated in prodigious quantities—all in languages foreign to him. New procedures of appeal were required, but Claiborne hesitated to innovate. In general the governor feared to change things too swiftly. A rapid Americanization of the legal system could provoke resistance. He warned that " . . . the establishment of a Judiciary on American Principles will have to encounter the most serious difficulties. Not one in fifty of the old inhabitants appears to understand the English language. Trials by Jury at first will only embarrass the administration of Justice."[16]

An example of how this legal confusion affected the old inhabitants came to Jefferson's attention in February 1804. One A. Baudin, a Louisiana planter, petitioned the President to grant sugar producers the same privileges accorded to them by the Spanish "laws of the Indies." He charged that the courts established by Claiborne in New Orleans took no cognizance of these special immunities, because they were staffed by men who knew nothing of local jurisprudence or the special difficulties which planters faced. He warned that unless they were protected by the present government, as they had been by the Spanish under the laws then in force, the sugar plantations would be abandoned.[17] Specifically, Baudin requested Jefferson to order the governor to block further seizures of persons and property for failure to meet obligations of debt. He wrote that earlier petitions for redress directed to the territorial government had been disregarded.[18]

Claiborne outlined the details of the Baudin case in a communication to Jefferson. The suit was for the recovery of one thousand dollars plus interest and had been brought against Baudin by one Labie. Baudin had not appeared in court when summoned, and judgment for distraint had been granted to the petitioner *ex parte*. Baudin appealed to Claiborne to arrest the judgment on grounds that the proceeding against him had been "informal," and because sugar planters were exempt from seizure for debt default, but Claiborne had been informed that local usages permitted such decrees, and he made no effort to stay the judgment.[19]

The custom of the country governing the immunity of plantations from seizure for debt was obviously in dispute. But even more interesting was Baudin's challenge to the whole manner of the proceedings. Acquainted only with the written petitions of the Spanish tribunals, he was unfamiliar with the system of pleadings by which issues were prepared for trial in common law courts. Jefferson, in his reply to Baudin, noted that the latter had contested not the justice of the decision against him but the manner of procedure. He wrote that "every Court has an inherent right to regulate their own forms of proceedings, provided they be not at variance with the substance and general privileges of the Law of the Land."[20] The President chose to overlook the fact that in this case the proceedings and the substance of the law *were* "at variance." Baudin's case indicated the difficulties attending an effort to administer a judicial system when the authorities lacked certain knowledge of local customs while the inhabitants were confused by new legal formalities.

The case is illustrative of another source of misunderstanding. The old inhabitants were used to making appeals to the Spanish colonial authorities in Havana when they failed to obtain satisfaction in the local courts. Quite naturally, then, litigants sought appellate review by the President, since they understood that the territorial governor was a mere subordinate. Thus, when Jefferson informed him that Governor Claiborne was the final arbiter of petty disputes, Baudin was stunned by what he considered the arbitrary character of the new regime. In another case a medical doctor, one Paul Alliot, claimed to have been unlawfully imprisoned by the Spanish in March 1803 and then deported by the French. After gaining his release from prison in Lorient, Alliot returned to the United States. Writing to Jefferson from New York, he appealed for justice and specifically requested the President to see to it that debts owed him for medical services rendered in New Orleans be collected. Jefferson referred Alliot to the territorial courts.[21]

IV

No man was in a better position to know the legal conditions in the territory than Edward Livingston. He had arrived in New Orleans in February 1804 and by May was busily engaged in professional activity. Livingston was acutely conscious of the welter of legal forms, regulations, and usages with which he had to cope as a practicing attorney. He reported the situation in detail to his brother Robert, noting that

> we are in a kind of equivocal state as to jurisprudence that produces the most comic effect. The Spaniards when they took possession of the Province abrogated the French and introduced the Spanish laws. Laussat during his ephemeral reign restored a very important part of the French municipal law, and when he gave over the country to us we promised to preserve its laws until they should be altered by the constituted authorities. The Governor having the powers conferred on him by the president of both Governor General

> and Intendant conceives himself authorized to legislate and his ordinances in English mixed with those of his predecessors in Spanish and French, the laws of Castille, the Customs of Paris, the Leyes de Partidas, les Edits du Roi, the Statutes of the United States and the omnipresent Common Law of England make a confusion worse than that of babel and only to be equalled by the Dissonances of our Court of Pleas where American Shop keepers, French planters and Spanish clerks sit on the same bench to hear them cited by American Attorneys, French procureurs and Castillian Abogados each in his own language. In October this will be reduced to some order by the legislative council to be appointed by the president.[22]

Livingston was to be one of the prime movers in the drive to harmonize this dissonant legal system. He was the main architect of procedural reforms, and the practice act of 1805, which he authored, supplied Louisiana with uniquely simple modes of procedure.[23] Livingston also strove to bring order to the disarray of the substantive law with his translation of parts of the *Corpus Juris Civilis*, work which he undertook soon after his arrival in his adopted home.

Others besides Livingston commented upon the legal confusion in the courts of law. Joseph Dubreuil held Claiborne responsible for much of it. He described the situation vividly:

> [The governor] composed tribunals, half of which consisted of American judges, and half of French Judges! As far as pleadings were concerned, he, at the same time, permitted attorneys speaking either of the two languages to handle them. Now, from the point we have reached you can't help but realize the awful cacophony which was bound to result from such an arrangement. One Attorney, whose case, for instance, was up for trial in court, would argue it . . . in English; the opposing Attorney, who had not heard it, would then answer him right away, in French. A heated discussion or argument would then start between these two fellows and the Judges, none of whom could understand more than one of the two languages. They go ahead boldly and pass sentence just as if they understood perfectly well all about the point which was being argued. Of course the lawyer who would know the greatest number of Judges speaking his language would always be the one who would win. You would have about as much chance by rolling dice as you would with such courts! If such a legal case was shown on the stage, the chances are you might die laughing at such a novel burlesque invention, but a man's heart grows sad and revolts, when he thinks that it is to the judgments of such Courts that the fortune and honor of old Louisiana families are entrusted![24]

The mixed legal heritage of Louisiana continued to perplex the administration of justice right through the territorial period. In 1807, for example, Allan B. Magruder of Opelousas diagnosed the legal condition in Lower Louisiana in much the same manner as had Livingston and Dubreuil three years before:

> There is no country in the world, perhaps, where the science of jurisprudence abounds with such various, complex and contradictory principles, as in Louisiana. As a system it is composed of the most heterogeneous materials. In civil concerns, rules of right, are sought from a thousand sources, often enveloped in the mysteries of unknown languages, and the unwritten customs and usages of the descendants of European nations who have successively occupied the country. To these may be added the whole system of the English precedents,—and the general and local regulations, that grow out of the powers of the new sovereignty.[25]

Claiborne himself was bewildered by the legal problem. He reported to Madison that among all his duties "the most embarrassing are those which I have to discharge in my Judicial character."[26] His imperfect knowledge of French and Spanish and his total ignorance of local law were more than a slight handicap, but he persevered with "industry and patience." He was baffled by "forms of practise as intricate as they are new."[27] He had hoped from the first to simplify matters entirely by introducing the Anglo-American legal system with which he was familiar, but such a substitution had proved to be impossible. He explained to Madison that in the course of his efforts "to introduce the American System of Jurisprudence into the ceded territory," he had experienced many difficulties and excited much dissatisfaction. He said that his Governor's Court had been criticized for attempting to innovate upon the Spanish law. He believed that jury trials, oral testimony, and the admission of attorneys at the bar would "illy comport with the former habits of the people."[28]

V

As close to the situation as Governor Claiborne and lawyer Livingston was John B. Prevost, stepson of Aaron Burr and the new appointee to the Superior Court of the territory. Prevost arrived in New Orleans from New York on October 28, 1804,[29] and convened the court on November 5.[30] In the absence of the two other judges — Congress had allotted a *banc* of three—Prevost would preside alone for many months.[31]

Prevost was keenly aware of the necessity to organize the laws of the territory into some coherence. He desired the establishment of the common law, and yet he quickly realized how awkward a sudden transformation would be. Prevost informed Madison of the difficulty he had encountered in attempting to establish a new system. He said the task of reconciling "the ancient laws of the country with the provisions of the Act organizing the government and with the principles of our Constitution" was a formidable one. He suspected that numerous mistakes had already been made.[32] Prevost explained that he had urged the legislative council to compose a legal digest of some sort. The council agreed to appoint a committee of three—Benjamin Morgan, George Pollock, and Dr. John Watkins—to draw up a civil code and a code of Superior Court practice.[33] Edward Livingston and James Brown were commissioned to work on these projects. But Claiborne opposed the scheme. Prevost suspected that the governor wanted to undertake the task on his own and that he hoped to introduce the common law as practiced in his native Tennessee. In addition, for political reasons he thought Claiborne was reluctant to see Livingston employed in such an important and visible public task.

Prevost tried to get Madison's backing for this early effort to straighten out the legal situation. He considered the adoption of a code the safest and surest way of guaranteeing U.S. control of the territory. He wrote that "a governor possessing firmness could then with propriety reject all bills interfering with this code and thus preserve a system entire[ly] congenial with our government until the people become sufficiently conversant with its principles to legislate or until we can obtain an American representation . . . . [The people] have their habit[s], language and religion and they naturally feel some jealousies on this head which may always become a subject for intrigue and party."[34] Prevost feared that continued uncertainty would hasten a definitive reception of the civil law at a time when the common law forces were politically weak.

James Brown, another key individual in the developing legal controversy, also commented upon the confused state of the law. Brown arrived in the territory late in November 1804.[35] He declined an appointment to the Superior Court,[36] but subsequently accepted the posts of territorial secretary, U.S. district attorney, and land agent. He later served as a jurisconsult in the drafting of the Louisiana digest adopted in 1808. The legal digest of Brown and Louis Moreau Lislet solidified the civil law in the Orleans territory.

Brown agreed with John Prevost's diagnosis and prescription for the legal ailments afflicting the region. He thought the legislative council should assist in the framing of a code of laws, but he envisaged one drawn from diverse sources. As he wrote to John Breckinridge, "The Civil Law—the Spanish Ordinances—the British Statute and Common Law, and the codes of all the states are spread before us, and the people are prepared for the reception of a code ably compiled from these several systems."[37] He thought such a code could be composed "which would meet the approbation of our Jùdges and American Lawyers." Once adopted, it would be guarded by executive veto should a popular legislature desire to modify it by statute. "If such a code is not in operation on the commencement of the second grade of government," he warned, "it is but too probable we shall remain sometime without laws or with a system too motley and complicated to be understood by our ablest jurisprudents."

Brown anticipated a polarization of opinion with the probability that the soon-to-be elected territorial House of Representatives would be dominated by French inhabitants "attached to French Law . . . [passing] only acts resembling the Civil Law and the Spanish Ordinances formerly in force here." With Claiborne favoring the common law, governor and legislature would each checkmate the other's efforts.[38] Brown concluded that action was required, before the legislature was elected. The council, still composed of presidential appointees, was largely under the governor's influence and a code adopted under its auspices was likely to be acceptable to the general government—that is, a code of common law plus the gloss of civil law which Brown had mentioned.

Brown sensed that the time had arrived for the kind of stopgap measure suggested by Prevost. But he also agreed that Claiborne would oppose any code in whose composition Livingston played a part. "Such is the unfortunate dislike of the Governor towards the only man in whom the Council seems disposed to confide as my assistant [i.e., Edward Livingston]," he reported, "that it is believed the measure will fail."[39] As a consequence, Brown prophesied a long period of continued legal disorder.

Brown and Prevost were right about Claiborne. The governor opposed legal codification at this time because he viewed with suspicion any scheme involving Edward Livingston. Moreover, he misconstrued the intent of the codifiers. He believed that they were planning to introduce the common law at a time when the territory was ill-prepared to receive it. He wrote Madison that "the Legislative Council do not proceed to Business, with all the dispatch which *several influential Americans* who are here desire; they are solicitous that a code of Laws and principles of

Practise *to which they* have been accustomed, should be introduced, and are so impatient of delay, that I fear former Municipal regulations will be too suddenly innovated upon, and that the American System of Jurisprudence will be more generally adopted than the present situation of the Territory will justify."[40] In short, the governor preferred to wait. His role in the early stages of the legal conflict was typically equivocal. He desired to postpone a decision for the common law until the conditions had ripened for its smooth reception. He expected that the Americanization of the laws would follow in the wake of the Americanization of the population—a logic that appealed with growing force to the administration.[41] He hoped to forestall the permanent establishment of a civil law system until the overwhelming majority of the people of Lower Louisiana demanded that "uniformity of laws" which Jefferson himself thought so desirable. In the meantime Claiborne would prevent civil law reception by exercising his veto. He did precisely that in May 1806, when a bill declaring the civil law in force and projecting a Spanish code was passed by the legislature.

VI

Discontent among the inhabitants developed early in Lower Louisiana, and dissatisfaction over legal innovations was a salient grievance. The Louisiana Remonstrance, the first manifestation of substantial opposition to American policy, condemned the suspension of the forms of law to which Louisianians had been accustomed and the failure of the present government to substitute an acceptable system in its place.[42] Objection was voiced to the use of English in the courts and to the necessity of employing interpreters for the simplest legal communications, a requirement which increased court costs substantially. These practices were contrasted with those of the Spanish, who had been careful to appoint French-speaking officials whose communications with the district commandants were transmitted in French. Spanish had been the language of the courts, but since most judicial business was transacted in writing, translations had always been readily available. As the Louisiana remonstrators put it: "The great mass of the inhabitants speak nothing but . . . French; the late Government was always careful in their selection of officers to find men who possessed our own language, and with whom we could personally communicate; their correspondence with the interior parts of the province was also carried on chiefly in our own

being carried on altogether by writing, translations were easily made."[43]

Here the Remonstrance touched upon one of the more sensitive areas which differentiated the common law and civil law traditions. Accustomed as they were to written petitions, the ancient Louisianians found the adjustment to oral argument in open court exceedingly difficult.[44] Compounding the problem was the baffling fact that these oral proceedings were being conducted in a foreign tongue. As the Remonstrance described the situation:

> [At] present, for the slightest communication, an interpreter must be procured; in more important concerns, our interest suffers from not being fully explained; a phrase, a circumstance seemingly of little moment, and which a person uninterested in the affair will not take the trouble to translate, is frequently decisive, and produces the most important effects . . . [The] introduction of *viva voce* pleadings into the courts of justice subjects the party who can neither understand his counsel, his judge, nor the advocate of his opponent, to embarrassments the most perplexing, and often to injuries the most serious.

The errors committed by judges "uncertain of what codes they are to decide, wavering between the civil and the common law, between the forms of French, Spanish, and American jurisprudence, and with the best intentions unable to expound laws of which they are ignorant . . ." evidenced the need for "reducing this chaos to order, and calling a system of harmony from the depths of this confused, dischordant mass."[45]

Thus an important segment of the Louisiana Remonstrance was devoted to the complaints growing out of the legal question at issue in the territory. Legal reform was among the major objectives of the three memorialists whom the people dispatched to Washington in the fall of 1804. But while the Remonstrance reflected the most substantial body of opinion in Orleans, its circulation and publication elicited numerous challenges. In a counterpetition, the English-speaking community registered its approval of congressional measures, requested that English be maintained as the official language, and called for guarantees of the rights of American settlers in the territory.[46] Even more significant was the ensuing debate in the local and the national press. For example, the *Union*, the English-language weekly published in New Orleans and the predecessor of James Bradford's fiery *Orleans Gazette*, printed a mocking pastiche of the Remonstrance called "One Declaration of de Independence of de

Louisiane!!!"[47] A more sober critique, originally published in the Richmond *Enquirer*, was also printed locally. The article stressed the unreadiness of the Louisianians for self-government and criticized the parallel drawn between Louisiana's quest for independence and the revolt of the thirteen colonies. The changes occasioned by the War of Independence required no radical alteration in existing institutions, it argued. "The judiciary system was not materially altered . . . . The transition was therefore easy." The case of Louisiana was quite different, the writer concluded. Independence in the case of Louisiana would be the gift of another nation and not a prize dearly bought. Moreover, time was needed "to introduce the same language and the same laws" before Louisiana was ready for self-government.[48] This, of course, was precisely what the memorialists and those whom they represented feared most—a change in language and law. The old inhabitants of Lower Louisiana desired independence through statehood in order to preserve these emblems of their cultural distinctiveness and their identity as a people. In November 1804 the *Union* published an article urging calmness and forebearance upon the Louisianians and reminded them of their good fortune in falling under American dominion.[49]

Even Thomas Paine joined in the lively debate over the memorial to Congress. His reply to the Remonstrance was a critical review in the *Aurora* of Philadelphia.[50] Using his well-known appellation, "Common Sense," Paine scolded the French inhabitants for allowing themselves to be misled into thinking that Louisiana had been purchased for their benefit alone. This, he declared, was not the case. Indeed, it would not be very long before immigrants from America would outnumber them. Paine's reasoning heightened the urgency of the mission to Washington. The people of Orleans were heartened, however, when the *National Intelligencer*, the principal organ of the Jefferson Administration, editorialized sympathetically with their position.[51]

VII

The three memorialists, Pierre Derbigny, a young French Creole who was to have a distinguished legal career in Louisiana, Jean Noël Destréhan, a native of France who would be active in the Orleans territorial legislature in the years ahead, and Pierre Sauvé, a wealthy planter, set out for Washington on October 4, 1804.[52] They arrived in November and immediately were the subject of mess-table talk. Jefferson thought that they conducted themselves "with approbation" and would receive a friendly hearing. Yet, referring to Louisiana's relationship to the Union, he wrote philosophically, "the good of the whole and all its parts" would be the primary object of policy. The interests of the United States would precede those of Louisiana, and the agents would have to be sensible that "in a whole composed of parts, no one part must carve for itself."[53] John Quincy Adams believed at first that the memorialists would be successful in their mission. He reported to his father in the latter part of November that the government was reconsidering the wisdom of some of its policies with regard to Louisiana. He anticipated that the next step would be the early admission of the territory of Orleans into the Union. He himself opposed this, but concluded cynically that "there is a probability favorable to any plans other than that which appears the right one."[54] Within a few weeks, however, after attending a dinner with the three memorialists, Adams changed his mind and concluded that they would not succeed.[55] At the same time, Senator William Plumer of New Hampshire met the deputies and was very favorably impressed. He outlined a number of their grievances in his *Memorandum* and noted, in particular, "that [the Louisianians] have in many instances been convicted of breeches of laws the existence of which they were ignorant."[56] He agreed with Adams as to the probable outcome of their remonstrance, however, for he reported that Jefferson was evasive.

To bolster their position and to answer critics, the three memorialists prepared a pamphlet during their stay in Washington. In it they emphasized the readiness of the Louisianians for self-government. The memorialists recalled the early enthusiasm with which the inhabitants greeted their transfer to the United States, and then their disappointment when a governor "unacquainted with their customs, laws and language" had been placed over them. In particular, they were highly critical of the legal morass into which Louisiana had been placed by the attempted introduction of new laws and forms of law in a language still widely unknown. They warned that unless this "perfect labyrinth" was unraveled and reforms instituted, the people of the territory would accept American governance only with sullen resignation.[57]

Despite these efforts the memorialists did not achieve the end for which they had been dispatched to Washington. The special committee of the House chaired by Randolph of Virginia, to which the Remonstrance had been referred early in December, made its report on January 25, 1805. It denied that immediate statehood was required by the treaty of cession and recommended only partial self-government. It urged the continuation of the ban on slave importations.[58] The memorialists, in a separate report, politely dissented from the committee's recommendations and reiterated their demand for immediate admission into the Union.[59]

The act of Congress of March 2, 1805, was a compromise measure enacted to appease growing discontent in Orleans. A greater degree of home rule was granted to the territory, but complete self-government was withheld. By and large, Congress followed the report of the Randolph committee. Thus the memorialists did not go home empty-handed, but their mission had turned out to be something less than triumphant. They arrived in New Orleans at the end of April 1805 and immediately set about preparing a report to the public.[60] In it the memorialists recited the delays which had plagued them in Washington, singling out Randolph for special criticism. It was his indifference, they argued, which was responsible for the failure of the House of Representatives to do more for the territory. The Senate, they said, was mainly preoccupied with the impeachment trial of Justice Samuel Chase. The final rush to adjournment in early March had left the cause of the Louisianians unsettled.[61]

VIII

By the end of 1804 the legal problems which beset the bar, the bench, and the government in Lower Louisiana were being fully aired in public. In 1804 James Workman wrote a play published in Charleston called *Liberty in Louisiana.*[62] A second edition was printed before the end of the year. There is no evidence indicating whether or not the play was ever produced on the New Orleans stage. It is unlikely, because the English-speaking public was still very small and the only plays performed in those early days were in French.[63] Copies of the work were circulated in the city, however, and a third edition was advertised on February 5, 1807, in the *Orleans Gazette.* Since the play commemorated the transfer of Louisiana to the United States, and as there were celebrations on the first anniversary of that event in New Orleans, it is likely that copies of the work had reached the territory as early as 1804. The author must have brought some with him when he migrated to Louisiana in that year.

The purpose of the melodrama was set forth in Workman's preface. It originated in his desire "to celebrate by some literary performance, the cession of Louisiana to the United States." The author also intended to dramatize "the great principles of general and genuine liberty" and to hold up "despotism to alternate derision and abhorrence." He wanted the play to be "the engine of enforcing his political opinions." Besides containing neoclassical tidbits of mistaken identity, outraged virtue and cliché rescues, the work was significant in its scenes depicting the arbitrary, corrupt, and heavy-handed Spanish criminal justice system which existed prior to the retrocession to France and the American takeover.[64]

Liberty in Louisiana was an American caricature of the Spanish system. The advocates of the common law actually knew little of the administration of justice under the Spanish.[65] Moreover, the legal debate did not concern Spanish criminal justice: nearly everyone agreed that the common-law definition of crimes and common-law criminal procedures were superior to the Spanish system. In any case, Workman's crimes act of 1805 permanently terminated the existence of the Spanish criminal law in Louisiana. But the advocates of common law were able to use this bizarre portrayal of the exotic aspects of Spanish justice to disparage all of the Spanish legal system—particularly among the Americans. To that extent, *Liberty in Louisiana* was a weapon in the arsenal of common-law supporters.

Even more apposite to the civil law—common law controversy than *Liberty in Louisiana* was the *Esquisse de la Situation Politique*, published in 1804.[66] Pierre Derbigny composed the *Esquisse* just prior to his departure to Washington in the fall of 1804.[67] He had prepared it as a further defense of the Louisiana Remonstrance. The *Esquisse* was one of the most widely discussed tracts of the territorial period. Claiborne viewed it as highly unsettling and inflammatory. In it Derbigny contrasted government under the French, the Spanish, and the Americans, but he concentrated his fire upon Governor Claiborne's administration. He scolded the governor for his weak militia policy, his inept appointments to office, and his practice of requiring English in the official business of government. He also blamed the governor for the stagnation of commerce, the paucity of hard money, and the presence of undesirable elements in the territory. Oddly enough, the author was not without some sympathy for Claiborne. The governor had fallen "naked . . . into all this," he explained, "without the least knowledge of the country, of its inhabitants, their ways, their usages, even of their languages, neither of the laws that he was ordered to follow." From this point of view, Derbigny reasoned, many of Claiborne's blunders could be excused, for they were the natural result of ignorance.[68]

But the part of the *Esquisse* that would elicit the governor's most concerned response centered upon judicial administration. Derbigny sharply criticized Claiborne for replacing the old Spanish tribunals with a court of pleas installed "entirely according to the American way." He charged that

> This single innovation would have been·enough to put the Louisianians in great difficulty, even if the care had been taken to give them, in this regard, all the necessary information. One can imagine therefore what was their surprise when it was seen, all of a sudden, transplanted into their midst, the strange system of English jurisprudence, without having taken the trouble to publish any preliminary information, to prepare the people for its introduction. Imagine the astonishment of the peaceful but ignorant citizens, when a sheriff or Constable, came to give him court orders of a new variety, in a language which he didn't understand. Imagine the difficulties of the judges themselves who had the vaguest idea of these strange forms, that they were supposed to follow and that had to be combined with the Spanish laws.[69]

It is somewhat ironic that Claiborne was admonished for "transplanting all of a sudden" elements of the Anglo-American system when he was, in fact, supremely conscious of the need to proceed cautiously. Moreover, just at this time—the winter of 1804-05—the governor faced mounting criticism from Americans like John Prevost and James Brown for a caution that they construed as obstruction.[70] The Louisianians condemned him for intoducing the common law, and the Americans condemned him for delaying its introuction. This was the real measure of Claiborne's political isolation, for in trying to maintain political equilibrium he had satisfied no one.

In the *Esquisse* Derbigny noted the precautions observed by the Spanish in their system of appeals. As an example he cited the use of *assessors*, legal officers present at court proceedings to ensure the rights of the parties and to render legal advice to the judges. In contrast, Claiborne had established his Governor's Court as a court of last resort where he alone presided with no other officials in attendance. "One cannot, help but be seized with fear," argued the pamphleteer, "upon entering this court, to see ONE man, sole arbiter of the fortune and the very lives of individuals! without counsel, without help! What can I say! without a guide to explain unknown laws."[71]

This was not entirely fair. Claiborne had established the Governor's Court as a temporary measure pending congressional action and the establishment of more regular tribunals. He was very much aware of his own shortcomings as a judge and looked forward eagerly to the convening of the Superior Court. One month after the *Esquisse* was published, Judge John Prevost arrived and the Governor's Court ceased to function. Still, Derbigny's argument had merit. The old inhabitants were used to having court officers present to protect litigants against uninformed rulings by judges or, in some cases, to defend public interests deserving of special judicial consideration. The absence of these officials from Claiborne's makeshift Governor's Court, and, later, from the Superior Court was a continuing grievance.

Derbigny also attributed the proliferation of lawyers and of litigation to the Americans.[72] The *Esquisse* pointed to the "prodigious number of lawyers" who controlled all the avenues of justice. "One pleads in English and cites English authorities; the other pleads in French and claims the usages of Spanish laws. Always one group of judges understands but one side of the argument: however, they must decide for or against; it is a throw of the dice." In this manner, said Derbigny, was justice administered in Louisiana. In such confusion were the affairs of individuals entangled while greedy attorneys profited "by digging among the ashes of faded causes or by creating litigation where there was nothing but a shadow."[73] Edward Livingston would fall from favor in the territory for dredging the sands of the Batture. He too would be accused of "digging in the ashes of a faded cause" and litigating where there was but a shadow. Indeed, for a while, Livingston symbolized the evils which legal disorder produced.

James Workman, the author of *Liberty in Louisiana* and an advocate for common-law reception, defended Claiborne against the attacks made upon him in the *Esquisse.*[74] He accused Derbigny, its author, of encouraging discontents and implied that the pamphlet represented one of many "angry effusions of prejudice and passion." And while Workman discussed most of the subjects covered in the *Esquisse*, he concentrated upon the language question and the judicial system.

Workman said that uniformity of language and of laws were the foundation of American national union. "In all the other states," he wrote, "a large majority of the citizens are derived from the same Nation, have adopted the same system of law, and speak the same language. These are the great bonds of their Union." The fact that the Louisiana French were not of the same derivation as their American brethren made the similarity of language and law and even more urgent priority. The language problem was susceptible to changes wrought by time. "Those whose native tongue is English," Workman observed, "though they now compose but a small part, will probably form in a few years, a majority of our population." The only question, therefore, was how swiftly the language of government should be made to reflect that ultimate modification. He concluded that Claiborne's innovations in this area were not unreasonable.

In regard to the "uniformity of law" Workman recalled that

by the treaty of cession, Louisiana was entitled to quick incorporation into the Union. But in all of the other states, he wrote, "the laws are founded on the common law of England, purged of its ancient barbarisms, and the method of trial is nearly the same in all; that is, by jury, on the public examination of witnesses, and the oral as well as written pleadings of the parties or their advocates in open court." The Constitution of the United States prescribed this mode of trial. "This similarity," he remarked, "between the federal and the state laws and tribunals is unquestionably a strong bond of union, and tends to promote harmony and good understanding between the various members of the Republic." The closer the law of Louisiana approximated the law as it was known and practiced elsewhere in America, the tighter would those "bonds of union" be.

Workman was generally uncritical of the substance of the Spanish law then in force in Louisiana. "The laws of Spain," he said, "are generally excellent in themselves; for they are founded on the Roman Code, one of the most perfect and elegant systems of jurisprudence ever promulgated to the world." Its precepts were the maxims of the law of nature applied to civil society. Only the manner of carrying them into effect—in other words, the procedural aspect of the Spanish system—was objectionable, he said.[75] Obviously Workman's position was not an unmitigated attack upon the civil law then in force. He viewed that system as fair-minded, reasonable, and well balanced. Still, national political and cultural necessities required greater uniformity of law: Thus, despite his acknowledgment of its merit, the implications of Workman's essay were that substance as well as procedure would have to change.

By and large, however, in this early phase of the controversy the major sources of conflict were the changes in legal institutions. Claiborne procrastinated on the enactment of a code or digest of substantive law. But law courts would not wait. Forced to act, the governor established tribunals which followed modes of practice to which he was accustomed and to which he was fundamentally committed by high policy and personal conviction. Once the court system was established, the issue changed from the type of court to the type of law that would prevail in Louisiana. Once common law courts had been established, the natural next step was to decide the laws they would adjudicate and administer.

IX

Claiborne defended himself against the attacks made upon his administration in corresponsdence with superiors in Washington. He noted that he had been "charged with making unfortunate Innovations on the Spanish System of Jurisprudence, and with much of the Confusion which ensued. . . . But the formation of a Court System devolv'd upon the American administration.—The necessity for [its] Establishment, was obvious, and the clamours of the people, would not permit me to delay my measures."[76] The exigencies of government demanded immediate action in the judicial field. The "unfortunate innovations" which had been made were, he said, "absolutely necessary" in order to prepare the Louisianians for admission to the Union as required by the treaty of cession. The court of pleas in the city of New Orleans was therefore organized upon principles "somewhat similar to the Tribunals of the United States." In short, Claiborne admitted that he had introduced changes, but he justified them on the grounds that they were in line with the policy of creating what James Workman and Thomas Jefferson both meant by that "uniformity of law" so desirable in a federal union.

Early in December 1804, in addressing the legislative council, Claiborne reiterated most of the points he had made to Madison. He hoped that the council would consider the judicial problem and "provide a system of jurisprudence suited to the interest, and . . . adapted to the habits of the citizens."[77] He called upon the council to fix the jurisdiction, mode of trial, and form of practice of the Superior Court and divide the territory into workable judicial districts. He urged the formation of a comprehensive criminal code. By acting on these matters, he said, the council would complete the work of institutional change. His only reference to a possible code of private law was vague and noncommittal. He outlined "the objects of high considerations devolving on the Legislature, . . . above all, the laws which are to be administered." In the context of his remarks this was an oblique reference to the need for determining which laws were to remain in force. But the governor did not specify which he preferred among the multiplicity of sources available.

The official reply of the legislative council proved to be almost a mirror image of Claiborne's address. Claiborne had encountered considerable difficulty in finding leading men to occupy positions on that body. Acceptance of appointment was regarded as approval of the governor's administration. Refusal was an emblem of loyalty to the opposition which had just mounted the memorial to Congress, the earliest statement of political dissatisfaction. Thus the council was composed of men not notable for their independence, and their answer to Claiborne reflected a generally favorable disposition toward his regime. "Your advice, and our own inclination," the council declaimed, "will make us endeavor to avoid the evils resulting from impetuous or careless innovation, on the one hand, or from indolence or timidity on the other. A system of jurisprudence, suited to the interests, and as much as possible, to the habits of the citizen, will occupy our first attention."[78]

Julien Poydras was the president of the council and unquestionably its leading figure. A man of considerable reputation among the Louisianians, he had also maintained cordial political relations with Claiborne. Poydras was no cipher. He vigorously resented the imputations circulating in the territory that members of the council were the governor's lackeys. In his speech commenting upon the governor's remarks, Poydras struck back at critics. He denied that participation in government signified feckless acceptance of everything the administration said and did. He challenged the dissenters to prove their independence by participating in public affairs and not by abdicating their responsibilities. He denied that the council was failing to represent the true interests of the community.[79]

Even more significant were Poydras's pointed comments on the legal question. He paraphrased what he understood to be national policy toward the Louisianians. The general government had referred to the Louisianians as brothers, said Poydras, and had guaranteed them the privileges of all American citizens, including trial by jury, the writ of habeas corpus, and free religious worship. But, he continued, the national government also said that

> our courts of justice and our laws shall be yours . . . . Your laws, . . . must not be in contradiction with ours, for which reason we reserve to ourselves the right to confirm, or reject them as they may be congenial or inconsistent with our constitution. For as you are to become an integral part of our great union, it is necessary that your laws should as far as possible assimilate with ours; so that the different states of the commonwealth may march in concert, and by their united forces and efforts compose a mighty republic, compact, indissoluble and invincible.

This, said Poydras, had to be resisted.

Poydras's remarks were a part of his general rebuke of those individuals who, for political reasons, had chosen to decline appointment to the council. He attempted to show that the dangers to which the Louisianians were exposed could best be prevented by legislative action and not by fruitless carping from outside the government. Significantly, Poydras chose to use the legal question to dramatize his point. Of all the possible evils to which Lower Louisiana was exposed, Julien Poydras could imagine nothing more calamitous than the threat to its ancient laws and legal institutions.

The Lousiana Remonstrance, the *Reflections on the Cause*, Derbigny's *Esquisse*, and the other documents in the arena of public debate shared a single theme: the transition from civil law to common law caused irritation primarily becaue of the novelty of new procedures. What struck the local inhabitants of long residence most forcefully were the obvious differences in the way in which the common law worked. Substantive divergences were dimly perceived by the general public. These were matters for the professional litigator. Only when a case such as that of the New Orleans Batture intruded with the elemental force of a gulf coast storm did the public at large rouse itself to confront substantive issues.

In the beginning, then, the legal question emerged as a social issue on the level of institutions and procedures rather than substance. This was true on both sides of the growing controversy. James Workman, for example, stressed the procedural superiority of the common law system as did Pierre Derbigny for the civil law. In 1804 the legal controversy was embryonic. Its elements were visible in the memorial to Congress and in the widely circulated *Esquisse* of Pierre Derbigny. Workman's reply to the *Esquisse* indicated that the issue had been joined in the public press. By and large, however, the first year of territorial government had been a year of structural growth and reorganization, and, as a consequence, the clash of legal systems made its appearance as a conflict between those who favored the establishment of American law courts and those who hoped for a restoration of the Spanish system minus the criminal law. On this level a real confrontation never developed. The necessities of government settled the problem almost before it was defined. Despite local complaint, the machinery of judicial administration was soon established and functioning. But with the institutional phase of legal change virtually settled, the way was cleared for the debate over the law itself.

[6] *Common Law vs. Civil Law: Second Phase*

I

The conflict between Louisiana's American future and its Latin past was brought into focus by the conflict of legal systems. Once the question of legal structure had been determined, the debate over the body of law to be administered commenced. Governor Claiborne still feared precipitate action. He knew the sensitivity of the issue and the divisiveness which a decision one way or the other would cause. He wrote to Jefferson early in 1805 that he was "fearful of sudden innovation" and urged "the gradual introduction of the American system of Jurisprudence."[1]

Even Congress was aware of the seriousness of the dilemma confronting Lower Louisiana. The second organic act providing for the government of Orleans, that of March 2, 1805, applied major provisions of the Northwest Ordinance to the territory. The act established "a government in all respects similar, to that now exercised in the Mississippi Territory."[2] But the government of Mississippi was based upon the paradigmatic Ordinance of 1787,[3] which, with reference to the territorial judiciary, had provided that ". . . there shall also be appointed a court to consist of three judges, any two of whom to form a court, who shall have a common law jurisdiction." The Ordinance of 1787 also required "judicial proceedings according to the course of the common law."[4]

By the act of March 2, 1805, therefore, Congress extended major common law provisions of the Northwest Ordinance to Orleans.[5] Yet what it gave with one hand Congress withdrew with the other. The act of March 2 specifically excluded the Ordinance's regulations governing the succession of property.[6] In addition, in the only other provision of the act touching juridical questions, Congress authorized the continuance of the local laws in force until altered by the Orleans territorial legislature. Thus the act of March 2, 1805, did not clearly define a congressional policy vis-a-vis the legal problem in Orleans. The application of the Northwest Ordinance seemed to mandate the introduction of Anglo-American common law, but the important reservation regarding the succession of estates manifested congressional sensitivity to local peculiarities and the desire of the ancient inhabitants of Lower Louisiana to perpetuate their special legal customs.

II

Given this ambiguity of national policy, it is difficult to understand why Claiborne decided to bring the legal issue to a head in June 1805. As late as January of that year he was maintaining his characteristic middle course. Then, rather suddenly, at the opening of the second session of the legislature in June, Claiborne moved from neutrality to advocacy. In his address to the council he urged the consideration of

> such subjects as seem to me to require the immediate attention of the Legislature. The most important of these arises out of the Act of Congress further providing for the Government of this Territory. By the Ordinance to which that act refers, it is declared that the Court to be established in virtue of it, Shall have a "common Law Jurisdiction", and that its Citizens shall be entitled to the benefit of "judicial proceedings according to the course of the common law."
>
> I recommend it to you to consider how far this constitutional provision will necessarily innovate upon your present System, and what measures may be expedient to prevent the inconveniences that might attend an unprepared transition from one mode of practice to another.[7]

In his letter to Madison a few days later the governor gave no indication as to why he had chosen this particular moment to raise the civil law—common law issue.[8] He may have interpreted the act of March 2 as a clear signal from Congress to move forward on the legal question despite the statute's ambiguity. However, Claiborne usually took his cues from the executive branch, and there is no evidence that the Administration was demanding action at this time. Claiborne had desired "the gradual introduction of the American system of jurisprudence" as late as January 1805, but now in June he invited "the immediate attention of the legislature" to common law adoption. What happened between January and June that made him alter course so abruptly?

There is no doubt that the need for some kind of digest, code, or restatement of the law was more urgent than ever. The grand jury, in its published reply to Judge Prevost's charge at the opening of the Superior Court's term, noted that "the want of a certain code of laws has been severely felt in this country, and causes down to the present moment the greatest embarrassments in the administration of civil justice."[9] What the grand jury called "the conflicting precepts of different codes" was undoubtedly troublesome. The governor was mindful of the problem. Moreover, a legislative committee established to draft a civil code had been working since its inception the previous winter.[10] In the spring of 1806 that committee would report a project of a code based upon Spanish sources. The direction the committee was taking may already have become apparent, and Claiborne probably wanted to block a statutory reception of Spanish law by assuming the initiative. Finally, the relatively manageable legislative council would soon dissolve. In its place would be a new bicameral legislature popularly elected and less amenable to executive influence. Possibly Claiborne thought that this would be the last opportunity for carrying through the legal revolution he had been mandated to undertake.

On July 3, Claiborne prorogued the council. His speech on that occasion contained no reference to the legal question or to his own earlier proposal.[11] However, the council president, Julien Poydras, was not nearly as reticent. Despite his obvious effort to maintain cordiality with the governor, Poydras's references to the common law and the legal question betrayed the deep division which had hardened relations between the legislative and executive branches of territorial government. He spoke of "the union and harmony that have reigned among us [despite] occasional differences of opinion" and noted "the good intelligence which has existed between the two branches of government, and the singular aid we have received from his excellency." But Poydras must have been recalling his admonitions of December 1804, which he had addressed to those who then declined conciliar appointment, when he remarked that "vain praises are not what you expect from me, . . . [but] truths of another kind. Permit me then, my dear colleagues, to tell these truths naturally and without disguise."[12] The legal conflict had ripened, and any effort by Poydras to gloss it over would have cost him support in the community he represented. He had said in December that the council was not a rubber stamp, and now he had to verify the fact.

Poydras intoned the virtues of "laws that are simple, natural, clear, and intelligible . . . and adapted to the local circumstances, the necessities, the manner and the customs of the people which they are to rule." He said that law "ought above all to be divested of those complicated, expensive, and unnecessary forms which render the dispensation of justice both difficult and various." He reminded the councilors that the style of the laws should be "pure, correct, and purged of those barbarous foreign expressions that are become obsolete and unintelligible." He spoke at length on the need for law to be up-to-date and appropriate to social circumstances. And then he launched into a bitter attack upon those who tampered with these principles:

We are on the eve of seeing confusion established on the banks

> of the Mississippi, by the forced introduction of a voluminous body of common law to which we are total strangers; laws which are quite foreign to our constitution, our liberty, our circumstances and our manners, and are wholly unknown and inapplicable to us. And why is this to take place? because our ancestors of glorious memory were children of the Thames; had they been natives of Japan or China, the *Bambou* would be justice of the peace amongst us, as it had been for numberless ages amongst the inhabitants of those empires.

Poydras was the highest public offical in the French community. He needed to maintain good relations between it and the territorial administration at a time when that administration was still looked upon as alien and provisional. For this reason the sharpness of his remarks and the warmth of his attack are significant. His speech, delivered within two weeks of Claiborne's proposal, answered the governor and signaled a serious cleavage between the two leaders. Claiborne's faulty timing had precipitated an open conflict on the legal question.

While Governor Claiborne must have felt that his stand for the common law would please the general government, it did not impress his local allies. In mid-September James Brown criticized him in a long letter to John Breckinridge detailing the political conditions in the Orleans territory. Brown emphasized Claiborne's youth, his ignorance of the local languages, his susceptibility to flattery, and his lack of firmness. Brown was an eager advocate for the adoption of the common law, but he gave the governor little credit for having championed the cause in early summer. Rather he felt that with Claiborne at the head of the government the chances of a civil law reception were all too likely. He informed Breckinridge that "a man of talents who will undertake the disagreeable task of governing the territory" should be sent without delay accompanied by a contingent of troops. "A firm Governor will protect us against the introduction of the civil law, the French administration of Justice, [and] the French language," he added.[13]

Elsewhere in his letter Brown noted the increased agitation against American law and government. This had resulted from the presence of malcontents who had stirred the population into thinking "that the established laws of the Country were about to be altered." He reported that the *notables* on the legislative council were incensed at the prospect of such a change. In an earlier letter Brown had warned of the deadlock which would occur when the legislative branch of the territory was delivered into the hands of the people upon the commencement of the second grade of government. He now reported that events had borne out his earlier anticipations. The elections to the territorial

House were underway and, he predicted, the result would be complete domination of both legislative branches by French elements. "The effect . . . upon the friends of America here," he said, "will be serious indeed." The tone of Brown's analysis was pessimistic. It appeared that the civilians had the upper hand and that the common law forces were divided, on the defensive, and, above all, poorly led.

As Brown predicted, opposition to the common law was visible in the Orleans legislature elected in the fall of 1805. On November 11, soon after the opening of the first session, one Hazour Delorme moved "to instruct the committee appointed to draft a memorial to Congress, to pray for a repeal of that part of the act granting to this territory the second grade of government, as provides for the introduction of the common law, owing to the great confusion it will introduce in the courts of justice."[14] Delorme's motion was tabled pending the judgment of the Superior Court in a matter to be argued the next day.[15]

The hearing referred to in the legislative debate was one of the most pivotal ever decided in the territorial period. The issue before the court was whether or not it would be bound by the Spanish laws in force at the time of the cession of Louisiana to the United States. John Prevost, still the court's only judge, called upon the local bar to consider the question for the benefit of the court. After listening to an energetic debate, in which leading legal luminaries of New Orleans participated, Prevost decreed that Roman, Spanish, and French civil law would be enforced as the customary law of the territory in all cases.[16] In the absence of the kind of code or digest whose adoption he had urged a year earlier, and despite his known preference for the eventual reception of common law, Prevost was persuaded that judicial recognition of the civil law was the best temporary remedy for correcting the legal confusion which was particularly bothersome to newcomers like himself.

This judicial recognition of civil law was to be a major step on the road toward final civil law reception, but it by no means resolved the issue once and for all, nor was it so intended. Two years later Judge George Mathews gave a similar ruling which Govenor Claiborne subsequently used to justify his endorsement of the civil law digest enacted soon afterwards. But neither judicial decisions nor legislative statutes satisfied Louisianians fearful for the security of their basic legal institutions. Consequently, the Louisiana constitution of 1811—and every subsequent contitution of the state—barred legislative reception of an alien system of law by general reference.[17]

III

Evidence that the people of the Orleans territory were deeply concerned about the growing legal controversy is furnished by a pamphlet published at the time of the Prevost decison—November 1805. It was a work devoted almost exclusively to legal matters.[18] The pamphlet consisted of published *Instructions* from some of the rural planters to their delegates in the territorial House of Respresentatives which had just convened for the first time. In substance the work attacked the now defunct legislative council for having established, early in 1805, the system of county courts. The planters preferred judicial administration by the old French and Spanish commandants, one for each parish, and they objected to the expense, the new and, for them, complex procedures, and the more extensive jurisdiciton and powers which these new local courts exercised. In particular they complained about the distance litigants now had to travel in order to settle diputes.

> Formerly, all the parishes were of moderate extent; the commandant, or judge, resided in the center, or at least, within reach of the inhabitants. If a new settlement was formed, a commandant was nominated, when necessary; so that every individual who had occasion for the judge, in his official capacity, could fix on his own convenient time; in a few hours he could be with the judge, and settle his business, or terminate his dispute.
>
> Now he has to go several days' journey, on horse back, in spring, when the paths are impracticable: for as to roads, there are none: but at times when the journey cannot be made by land, a boat with oars must be hired at a great expense, to go fifteen or twenty leagues by water, and sometimes more, against a rapid current: to go, where? to a place where there is no manner of accommodation for any traveller; much less, for a parcel of litigants, who assemble together, to suffer with hunger and wretchedness, and ruin one another with costs, that very often answer no kind of purpose; since the absence of a single member of the court prevents its being holden, or the want of one necessary witness; and moreover, the evasive suggestion of wanting time to procure new proof, throws obstacles in the way of your having your case decided. . . . Well might one say, in such a case, that an injust, but prompt decision, is preferable to an equitable one, so dearly bought. . . .[19]

The *Instructions* declared that if not for "the small share of . . . ancient jurisprudence that our fabricators of laws have designed not to meddle with," good order would not have been preserved. Congress had wisely left intact customary rules regarding the succession of estates, but the new county courts were bent upon introducting novel rules of law that would, in the end, destroy their way of life.[20] For nearly a century, the pamphlet argued, Louisiana had enjoyed a judicial system which succeeding governments had adopted as the only one suitable to the "local situation and the necessity of circumstances. Everyone is satisfied; there is no complaint: then, what is this whim of yours? What right have you then, to fall upon a system established already and organized, and which moves of itself; which is made respectable by the usage and attachment of those who are governed by it?" This step was the more reprehensible as Congress had granted to the Louisianians the right to preserve their ancient laws, "of altering them, of modifying them, according to the pressure of circumstances, retaining whatever we might find absolutely essential."[21] In undertaking the destruction of Louisiana's ancient legal system by the introduction of English common law, the council was guilty of an action "more fatal to us . . . than the invasion of the Goths and Vandals was to the Roman empire."[22] The threatened "inundation of new laws" portended nothing less than a comprehensive cultural revolution, likened in its effects to the barbarian migrations of ancient times.

The *Instructions* applauded the old system of justice recently overturned by legislative innovation and contrasted the single commandant with the numerous court officers which the county courts had spawned and the delays in proceedings which had become so onerous. "All is changed," the pamphlet lamented; "the act for dividing the territory into counties has overthrown the whole of the ancient system." The legislative representatives were urged to reestablish "the ancient division into parishes, over which one judge may be appointed in place of the ancient commandant." The pamphlet suggested a series of reforms: simplified procedures, limits on the use of juries in civil cases, and the termination of the circuit function of the Superior Court with its "retinue of lawyers." Finally, in outlining a model of legislative practice, the *Instructions* urged the enactment of laws that are "clear and intelligible . . . so that everybody by plain reading, may understand and follow the law inviolably." While the reference here was to the framing of statutory law, the refrain was a constant among those opposed to the common law—a system unwritten and unkown except to lawyers and judges.[23] "Bear in mind," the *Instructions* warned, "that there is no need of genius nor mystery to enact laws agreeable to reason;

that it is sufficient that the mind be well disposed; and that one drachma of good sense is worth a load of erudition."[24]

The *Instructions from the Inhabitants* is one of the most important documents to have emerged from the legal controversy in Orleans. It showed that debate was not confined to New Orleans but ramified through the country districts; its style indicated the bitterness which the legal question engendered; its timing revealed the importance of the issue in the minds of the old inhabitants; its content reflected the widespread fear that legal transformation portended the unraveling of the very fabric of life in Lower Louisiana.

IV

In 1804 and 1805 the legal debate had centered upon the structural changes generated by the exigencies of judicial administration. Concern focused upon institutional innovation and political control of the machinery of justice. The issue of substantive law emerged from time to time, but until a plan for a code of Spanish law emerged from the legislature in 1806, this side of the debate was muted by more immediate concerns. The tactical advantages during the first phase of controversy lay with the American common law forces. An American-style court system was implanted before effective opposition could be deployed. Louisianians accepted institutional change with some rancor, but even the reforms outlined in the *Instructions* would have left the major American legal innovations intact: the Superior Court would function, though not on circuit; jury trials would continue but with less frequency; parish judges would replace the county courts, but the old civil commandants would not be restored. Memorials, appeals, and remonstrances had done little to prevent major structural modifications of the Louisiana legal system, and despite continuing protests, the local population adjusted to the new order with surprising speed.

But the American victory in the early period did ignite local determination to block the introduction of the body of the common law. Claiborne had encountered this in the summer of 1805, when his attempt to get a common law reception through the old legislative council failed. By November, a turning point in the content of debate had been reached. The Delorme motion in the new legislature, Prevost's ruling in Superior Court, and the publication of the *Instructions of the Inhabitants*—all occurring in November 1805—were clear signals that the civil law forces were alert to the possibility that, unless something was done, the whole of their legal tradition, the substance as well as the institutional structure of their law, would be transformed.

On March 24, 1806, Claiborne opened the session of the new bicameral legislature with a lengthy address that touched upon sundry territorial matters but which was portentously silent on the legal question.[25] The governor sensed that the time was not auspicious for common law reception. Futile recommendations would serve only to trigger renewed dissension. Two months later the storm broke. The territorial legislature passed a bill "declaring the laws which continue to be in force in the Territory of Orleans, and authors which may be recurred to as authorities within the same." The proposed legislation was an open challenge to Claiborne and the United States government. It enumerated the legal sources, chiefly Spanish, upon which the courts were to base judgments until such time as a definitive civil code could be framed for the territory. The purposes of the bill were twofold: first, to enunciate what the law was and thus clarify the legal situation, and second, to block any further attempts to have the common law declared the law in force. The writ of habeas corpus and trial by jury were allowed as exceptions, and laws contrary to federal statutes or to the U.S. Constitution were barred from enactment. The congressional statutes of March 22, 1804, and March 2, 1805, continuing the laws in force in the territory of Orleans were cited as justification for the proposal, although the provisions in the act of March 2 specifically applying the common law provisions of the Northwest Ordinance were disregarded.[26]

The Act of Congress of March 2, 1805, had been ambiguous. It sanctioned the civil law in some respects and the common law in others. Claiborne had tried to use the common law elements of the statute as a lever for overturning civil law and receiving common law, but he had failed in that attempt. Now the territorial legislature was attempting to use the "laws in force" provision of both organic acts to establish the civil law in the territory once and for all. Claiborne was determined that this maneuver should fail. On May 26 the governor vetoed the proposed legislation.[27] The principal legislative leaders immediately resigned, resolutions calling for dissolution were introduced, and a maifesto was adopted and published. In the wake of his decision Claiborne confronted a major political revolt by some of the leading elements in the French community.[28]

The govenor had anticipated trouble in his letter to Madison on the twenty-second of May.[29] He attributed the proposed declaratory act to the suggestion of "some of the French Lawyers," and admitted that it was a favorite measure in both houses. Subsequently, Claiborne informed Madison of his major reasons for rejecting the bill while confessing surprise at the degree of opposition his veto had stirred. "This act of mine has given rise to a proceeding no less unexpected than it is unprecedented and unexceptionable,"[30] he wrote, referring to the council's call for immediate dissolution. Claiborne attributed the resolution to Pierre Derbigny who, he believed, exercised great influence. He was not certain how the representatives would react, but he expected concurrence "since a majority of the members of the lower House are evidently under the influence of men inimical to the Government."[31]

Claiborne's explanation of his veto was imcomplete. He wrote that "if by the Ordinance and Laws of Congress the Civil Law is recognized, the bill was useless." In any case, he thought, the judges of the Superior Court ought to determine the authorities on which to rely. "Their selection would likely be more judicious than any which the Legislature would make."[32] For the governor to say that the bill was needless was disingenous. He, after all, had been the first to seek a legislative settlement of the legal question. It was precisely because the Ordinance of 1787 and the acts of Congress were ambiguous that some agency of government had to define which laws constituted "the laws in force." Claiborne chose not to mention—perhaps he had forgotten—that when the issue had been placed before the Superior Court in November 1805 Judge Prevost had ruled in favor of the civil law. But a judicial determination clearly was insufficient. Both sides to the controversy wanted something more emphatic, permanent, and definitive which only a statutory decision could supply.[33]

To Julien Poydras, Claiborne explained that he thought the proposed measure "might prove injurious." Why he thought so, he did not say. He affirmed his interest in the public good, claimed that his best intentions had been perverted and his best acts misrepresented, and took comfort in what he liked to call "conscious rectitude . . . [a] consolation . . . dearer . . . than popular applause."[34] Meanwhile, the council drafted a lengthy manifesto justifying its decision to dissolve. It received the support of ten members of the lower house and was published in the press. The document constituted a major statement of the civilian position on the legal question.[35]

V

The manifesto opened with the declaration that "the most inestimable benefit for a people is the preservation of its laws, usages, and habits."[36] The sudden political transition from one government to another made legal continuity an absolute necessity. Congress had sanctioned this "sacred principle" by providing for the preservation of the laws of the inhabitants in the statutes establishing their government. "Now, what are these laws which Congress intended to preserve us by this provision?" the manifesto inquired. "The question is not a doubtful one. It is evident that they are the old laws which were in use in this country before its cession to the United States of America." Congress had carefully prescribed those elements of the common law which it desired to introduce into the new territory. The elements were those "two great *palladiums* of civil liberty"—trial by jury and the writ of habeas corpus. The remainder of the body of the common law was left to the inhabitants to receive or to reject.

Public law in a federal union ought to be uniform, the manifesto argued, but there was no such necessity for private law. "Thus the Constitution of the United States and the other Federal laws being general for the whole Union, it would be absurd to claim that this Territory ought not to be subject to them: but as to the laws regarding contracts, wills and sucessions, what difference does it make that here such acts should be governed by the civil law while in the other states of the Union they are governed by the common law?"[37] The common law was, after all, not a part of the Constitution. It had been received piecemeal by the English colonies with such modifications as local circumstances dictated. The result had been wide legal diversity from state to state which the general government had not tried to alter either by constitutional provision or by federal statute. On the contrary, Congress had sanctioned legal diversity by permitting the territory of Orleans to maintain its laws in force with such changes as its legislature considered desirable.

As for the character of the civil law itself, it could withstand a contrast with any body of law. It was a system based upon the Roman law which presented "an ensemble of greatness and prudence which is above all criticism." Its purity, clarity, simplicity, and natural equity was the work of the very "greatest jurists encouraged by the wisest emperors." The manifesto refrained from drawing a specific comparison with the common law, but left to the reader the job of reciting the litany of its defects—its complexity where the civil law was simple, its obscurity where the civil law was clear, and its confusion where the civil law was pure.

The manifesto emphasized the deep attachment which Louisianians bore to their ancient legal system. Had the

Americans overtaken an area denuded of law, no hardship would have attended the introduction of a novel system. But Louisiana was no legal *tabula rasa*:

> We certainly do not attempt to draw any parallel between the civil law and the common law; but . . . the wisdom of the civil law is recognized by all Europe; and this law is the one which nineteen-twenthieths of the population of Louisiana know and are accustomed to from childhood, of which law they would not see themselves deprived without falling into despair. If the inhabitants of this Territory had never known any laws, if they had lived down to the present time without making agreements or contracts, it would perhaps be a matter of indifference to them whether to adopt one system or another system, and it is even probable that their attachment to their new mother country would cause them to prefer that system which would bring them nearest to their new fellow citizens. But it is a question here of overthrowing received and generally known usages and the uncertainty with which they would be replaced would be as unjust as disheartening.[38]

The manifesto then catalogued those particular areas of substantive law where change would occasion the most serious dislocations in legal relations.

> Everyone knows today and from a long experience how successions are transferred, what is the power of parents over their children and the amount of property of which they can dispose to their prejudice, what are the rights which result from marriages effected with or without contract, the manner in which one can dispose by will, the manner of selling, of exchanging or alienating one's properties with sureness and the remedies which the law accords in the case of default of payment. Each of the inhabitants dispersed over the vast expanse of this Territory, however little educated he may be, has a tincture of this general familiar jurisprudence, necessary to the conduct of the smallest affairs, which assures the tranquility of families; he has sucked this knowledge at his mother's breast, he has received it by the tradition of his forefathers and he has perfected it by the experience of a long and laborious life. Overthrow this system all at once. Substitute new laws for the old laws; what a tremendous upset you cause![39]

The legislative manifesto of 1806 thus represents an important transitional document. It is the first major statement in behalf of the civil law tradition which goes beyond the argument over institutions and procedures and fixes upon the substantive law itself. Family law, marriage, successions, property, and the law of obligations—the everyday concerns of people—were in danger of overturn by an alien body of law which was either largely unkown or in serious conflict with established customs. What would be the consequences of an entirely new system? Ignorance of novel legal regulations would discourage entry into contracts, lessen the facility of property transfers, and force the illiterate and the unkowing into the hands of law professionals in order to execute the simplest transactions.

The answer to the problem was obvious; to forestall the introduction of foreign law and to establish the foundation upon which future generations could build, the settled legal traditions of Louisiana had to be cemented in the bedrock of an enacted code: "Now, what is the first law, the most important law in the present situation of this country; what is the fundamental basis of the great edifice of its future legislation? It cannot be denied that it is the matter of giving to it a civil code."[40] In the modern civil law tradition the code of private law has served a function which can best be likened to a written constitution.[41] The law of persons, of things, and of mutual obligation has been the heart of the authentic civil law system. The authors of the legislative manifesto meant to preserve the tradition by preserving the body of the private law. These were the reasons which impelled the action taken by the legislature when it attempted to declare the Spanish laws in force pending the formulation of a finished code. Necessity required the first legislature to build the "fundamental basis of the great edifice of its future legislation."[42] To satisfy the need of both citizen and jurist for a civil code of laws was a natural and compelling responsibility.

Denying Clairborne's argument that a declaratory act was unnecessary, the manifesto explained that confusion was widespread. The hearing before the Superior Court some months before had shown this. The persistence of public argument in the aftermath of the court's decision proved the need for legislative action. The sentiments of a vocal minority in favor of a change in the legal system menaced the welfare of the region with "the frightful chaos of the common law." To dissipate doubt and to register the will of the majority, the declaratory act had been passed, only to be vetoed by the executive, thereby enabling the sentiments of the minority "to mock the desires of the majority."[43]

The manifesto included every major civilian argument from the most general to the very specific, from the dramatic to the technical. It detailed the particular inconveniences which a change in the laws would bring about, but it also recited the larger dangers of cultural annihilation such a change would cause. It had raised the specter of the common law while warmly declaiming the great virtues of the civilian system. It was a statement of position, a subtle political attack, and the most persuasive argument yet mounted by the advocates for an authentic civil code.

VI

The territorial legislature was determined to have its way despite the opposition of Governor Claiborne. On June 7 it appointed James Brown and Louis Moreau Lislet as jurisconsults "whose duty it shall be to compile and prepare, jointly, a Civil Code for the use of this Territory."[44] It was further resolved "that the two jurisconsults shall make the civil law by which this Territory is now governed, the ground work of said code."[45] Thus, despite the veto, the legislature moved ahead on the civil code for which the aborted declaratory act had been meant to prepare the way. The guidelines for the work of the codifiers—"the civil law by which this territory is now governed"—lacked the specificity of the declaratory act, which had enumerated the legal sources that were to be the basis of any future code, but it did serve as a clear expression of legislative will. Thus the legal question remained on the public agenda while the work of Brown and Moreau Lislet proceeded. The legislature set up a special code committee to work with the principal jurisconsults, outlined procedural detail, and provided terms of renumeration and payment for expenses. The legislature also devised a method for modifying the code in the aftermath of its adoption by requiring the codifiers to attend the courts in order to observe how their system worked once it had been put into effect.

Somewhat surprisingly, Claiborne approved these actions. The resolutions of June 7 bore his signature. But this did not represent a change in policy, for the establishment of codification machinery in itself did not settle the question. The commotion caused by his earlier actions undoubtedly dissuaded him from again exercising the veto. Moreover, the legislature's move was harmless, and, in any case, beyond his control. It was, after all, within legislative privilege to appoint committees to perform specified tasks. By seeming to approve this action Claiborne may have been hoping to regain some political ground. The government was already being likened to a despotism,[46] and nothing would be lost by his acquiescence in this project. A second round between the executive and the legislative branches could not come for many months, and by that time the political climate might well have changed.

Claiborne had cause to think that it would. Ever since Congress had detached the territory of Orleans from Mississippi, Jefferson had been toying with alternative methods for guaranteeing the domination of the new region by an American population. The belief was widespread that the laws and institutions of the ancient Louisianians were ill suited to a self-governing polity. By altering the demographic character of Lower Louisiana, the proper conditions for the introduction of American law and American institutions would be created and the way prepared for Louisiana's ultimate admission into the Union. To effect this change, as well as to provide for the military security of the area, Jefferson had proposed that Congress adopt a militia scheme as a variation of the President's general plan for national defense. Back in 1805 the Administration had recommended to Congress that 300,000 Americans between the ages of eighteen and twenty-six be organized into a ready reserve force within the existing state militias prepared to move, at short notice, to combat zones. After age twenty-six these men would be placed in an inactive reserve pool available for call-up by the regular army.[47] This was to be part of a system of classification according to which all able-bodied men were subject to different forms of military obligation and service depending upon their age.[48] The plan conformed to prevailing Republican objections to standing armies. In addition, it fulfilled the Jeffersonian commitment to budgetary retrenchment, a modest federal establishment, and the preservation of state power. Nevertheless, though simple, practical, and consistent, the plan was never approved by Congress, and only portions of it were ever enacted into law.[49]

It is against this background of Jefferson's partiality to the militia concept that his particular designs for the defense of Louisiana can be understood. Early in 1806 the Administration prepared a bill providing allotments of 160 acres in fee-simple estate to white males between the ages of eighteen and thirty-five who agreed to reside in the territory for no less than seven years, during which time they would render two years of active service to the regular army. Recruiters would receive grants of 640 acres for every hundred men they brought into the program. The federal government would carry the costs of transportation and settlement.[50]

The idea was fully in keeping with Jefferson's philosophy. It would solve a pressing military problem at minimal cost, for the project would be funded with that wealth which the government had in superaboundance: the newly acquired lands of Louisiana. As Jefferson once put it to Gallatin, "Satisfied that New Orleans must fall prey to any power which shall attack it, in spite of any means we now possess, I see no security for it but in planting on the spot the force which is to defend it."[51] Lower Louisiana, surrounded on every side by Spanish garrisons, was to be peopled with a self-sufficient and reliable military force.

The idea behind the proposal had been marinating for some time, perhaps from the very earliest days of American occupation of New Orleans,[52] but it was presented for the first time by Senator Thomas Worthington of Ohio in March 1806. Jefferson's attitude toward it is best summarized by William Plumer of New Hampshire:

> The President observed to me that he considered this bill as one of the most important now pending in Congress. That no part of the U.S. was so much exposed as Louisiana—That it was absolutely necessary to provide means for its defence—That near half of its present inhabitants were such that they could not be depended on in case of an invasion. That it would be impolitic and expensive to raise a standing army—That it was very doubtful whether the militia from the States would consent to march & tarry there any time—That we had not the means of compelling them—That the climate of that country would prove unfavorable to the health & lives of our Militia—[53]

Jefferson explained the connection between the military-security problem and the political-legal question in his letter to Gallatin outlining his proposal for "planting" in New Orleans "the force needed to defend it." "If by giving 100 miles square of that country we can secure the rest," he continued, "and at the same time create an American majority before Orleans becomes a state, it will be the best bargain ever made."[54]

The idea was ingenious but not entirely original. There is good evidence that Thomas Paine first suggested it. In a letter written in January 1805 Paine warned Jefferson to beware of the French inhabitants, "for they give symptoms of being a troublesome set."[55] Paine proposed the resettlement of large numbers of easterners plus a wholesome infusion of German redemptioners into Louisiana, which would soon make the Louisiana French a minority in their own country—an end which Paine would have welcomed. "When the emigrations from the United States into Louisiana become equal to the number of French inhabitants," he advised, "it may then be proper and right to erect such part where such equality exist into a constitutional state; but to do it now would be sending the American settlers into exile." Paine cautioned the President that any concessions made to the demands of the Louisianians "would be an incumbrance on the

Union." He suggested that the people of Louisiana should be governed directly by Congress "till there be a sufficient number of American settlers to be trusted with constitutional powers."

Paine's ideas appealed to Jefferson, for almost all of his proposals were incorporated into the administrations's design once the militia scheme had fully ripened. Writing of the plan to John Dickinson in January 1807, one month after Jefferson had again urged congressional passage, the President explained:

> I proposed to the members of Congress . . . the enlisting [of] 30,000 volunteers, Americans by birth, to be carried at public expense, and settled immediately on a bounty of 160 [acres] of land each on the West side of the Mississippi; on the condition of giving two years of military service, if that country should be attacked within 7 years. The defence of the country would thus be placed on the spot, and the additional number would entitle the territory to become a state, would make the majority American, and make it an American instead of a French state. This would not sweeten the pill to the French; but in making that acquisition we had some view to our own good as well as their, and I believe the greatest good of both will be promoted by whatever will amalgamate us together.[56]

Dickinson opposed the idea as unwise and unworkable. He had more faith in persuading the French inhabitants of American affection than in introducing large numbers of armed settlers into their midst. He questioned the effectiveness of the military service to be rendered by these volunteers and doubted their fidelity to the Union.[57]

Despite the doubts expressed by Dickinson, however, Jefferson remained enthusiastic and hopeful. Late in February he wrote to a correspondent: "I have tried for two sessions to prevail on the legislature to let me plant 30,000 well chosen volunteers on donation lands on the west side of the Mississippi, as a militia always at hand for the defence of N. Orleans; but have not yet succeeded. The opinion grows, and will perhaps ripen by the next session."[58] At year's end he was still optimistic. He asked Gallatin to look over a draft of the measure while once again reminding him that "the defence of Orleans against a land army can never be provided for . . . till we can get a sufficient militia here."[59]

Besides its obvious military purpose, the proposal was attractive to the President because it provided a means for settling the major dilemma which, from the very beginning, troubled the administration of government in Lower Louisiana. By peopling Orleans in the manner proposed, Jefferson would overawe the local population and create a preponderance of Americans whose political reliability and fundamental loyalties would be beyond question. Moreover, these Americans would create political and legal institutions similar to those of their native states and would thus transform the character of the territory. When the time came for its admission into the Union of States, the territory of Orleans would be culturally, politically, and legally assimilable.

Jefferson kept Governor Claiborne informed of these proposals. In the early spring of 1806 he reported to the governor that the militia scheme had not yet been acted upon by Congress. In reply Claiborne expressed regret, inasmuch as the plan "was received here with great approbation."[60] It is clear from his response that Claiborne appreciated the wider implications of the militia proposal. He wrote that "besides adding to the safety of the Territory, it would have increased the American population; have facilitated the introductin of the American Government, Laws and Language . . . [and] therefore have liberally compensated the United States for the Donations bestowed on settlers."[61] He urged the President to press forward on the militia scheme at the next session of Congress and anxiously anticipated its adoption at that time.

Claiborne's letter was written one month after his veto of the bill declaring the Spanish laws in force. In view of the high hopes which both he and the President entertained at that time for the eventual implementation of the plan, it is highly likely that the prospect of an early settlement of large numbers of Americans in the territory weighed heavily in the governor's calculations as to what legal policy to follow. He approved the formation of a code committee, confident that, by the time a completed code was submitted to him for approval, it would either conform to his common law predilections or he would again exercise his veto, knowing that behind him would be a much more substantial body of American opinion. By early 1808 it would be clear that the militia scheme for the defense of Lower Louisiana would not be passed by Congress.[62] Its rejection would mark the decline of Jefferson's political influence in Congress in the latter half of his second term. But during the period when it was still a live issue, it is clear that more was expected from the projected transplantation of large numbers of Americans than military security alone. Both in Washington and in New Orleans, American policy-makers were bent upon a quick solution to the dual problem of the American administration of Lower Louisiana: the need for security and for cultural, particularly legal, homogeneity. W. C. C. Claiborne's knowledge of the national government's long-term strategy explains his repeated delays, vacillations, and seeming inconsistencies.

Claiborne's endorsement of the code committee on June 7,

1806, therefore, did not represent a change in his overall posture on the legal question. Nor was it so interpreted. Edward Livingston wrote to his brother Robert some months later that "altho the Governor at the last session of the Legislature sanctioned the appointment of persons to prepare a Code to be formed on the basis of the Civil Law, yet it is now generally understood that he will not approve the system when it is presented."[63] Livingston proved to be a false prophet, for in March 1808 Claiborne signed the act declaring a civil law digest in force. By that time, however, Jefferson's militia scheme was moribund, and a major option of policy foreclosed.

VII

The Jefferson Administration defended Claiborne's veto of the proposed legislation of May 1806, which would have declared the Spanish law in force pending the adoption of a civil code. The *National Intelligencer,* the unofficial newspaper organ of the government,[64] outlined administration policy on the legal controversy in the Orleans territory in a lengthy editorial printed on August 11, 1806. While admitting that remoteness from the scene, imperfect knowledge of the facts, and the absence of Governor Claiborne's explanation of his decision made it impossible to give a definitive judgment, the editorial defended the use of the veto power. Congress had granted that prerogative to the territorial executive with the expectation that it would be used when warranted. Moreover, the paper stressed that the governor was a stand-in for the President. "We must consider his measures," it said, "as those of the Chief Executive, in all cases of a serious collision of opinion."[65] This virtual identification of the governor of Orleans with the President of the United States was an effort to demonstrate that the Administration fully supported Claiborne in the policy position he had adopted. Indeed, in the remainder of the editorial, wherever reference was made to "executive power," the wording adopted was "the Executive of the U.S." In the eyes of Samuel H. Smith, the editor of the *Intelligencer* and a close confidant of the President,[66] the debate in Orleans had ceased to be a mere squabble between local functionaries but instead had become a confrontation between the Louisiana legislature and the general government itself.

Having redefined the terms of debate, the *Intelligencer* listed the arguments which bolstered the "Executive's" position. It was the duty of the President to sanction laws which best promoted the general interest of the United States as well as the special interest of Lower Louisiana. He was bound to favor both, and could not promote one at the expense or to the prejudice of the other. Should the interests of Orleans and those of the nation be in conflict, then the President could not sanction measures favorable to the territory alone. "If this exposition of the duty of the Executive of the U.S. be correct," argued the editorial, "the question whether the civil or the common law shall form the basis of legislation in the Territory of Orleans is a point which, in its present form, can only be settled by determining which code it is most for the interest of the whole U.S. to adopt." The controversy stirring Orleans was not to be looked upon as only of local and passing concern, but rather one which touched "*general interests*, unrestrained by time."

From that viewpoint the wisest legal policy was for the territory of Orleans to adopt the common law. The *Intellegencer* was certain that the American people would agree to such a decision, not because of the greater merit of the common law system but out of a desire to preserve the laws with which they were familiar. While there was no general common law for the United States, the laws of the separate states were sufficiently similar to make the system of one state known to the inhabitants of another. Surely the good of the people of the territory was an important factor to be weighed in the balance, but it was also a question whether "the temporary interest of a few inhabitants of Orleans should be exclusively consulted to the prejudice of the interest of the citizens of the U.S. who have already settled there, and of all those who shall hereafter emigrate to that country." How long, inquired the *Intelligencer*, would the large majority of inhabitants of Orleans consist of those "who have heretofore been under the subjection of the civil code?" Indeed, "before the present generation shall have passed away they will be outnumbered by . . . emigrants from the U.S." The governor, in blocking the establishment of the civil law and in attempting to introduce the Anglo-American common law, was merely acting as surrogate for his absent fellow countrymen.[67]

In the summer of 1806 the Administration still had hopes that Congress would act favorably upon the militia scheme at its next session. Claiborne's decision to freeze the legal question for the time being had been made with this in view. And now the Jeffersonian press had sustained his legal policy by outlining what the future portended for Lower Louisiana.

VIII

The most perfervid reaction to the *National Intelligencer* came from J. B. S. Thierry. In an essay composed but unpublished at this time, the fiery editor of the *Louisiana Courier* attacked what he called the "machiavelism of Mr. Jefferson" and "the insolent paragraph of the *Presidential Gazette.*"[68] Thierry had no doubt that the *Intelligencer* spoke for the Administration. He said that during the American Revolution the French Canadians had been invited to join the thirteen colonies after the English had threatened to extirpate their religion and their laws. At that time the Americans had promised to preserve the unique legal institutions of Quebec, but now, presented with a parallel situation, they were insisting that the inhabitants of Lower Louisiana be governed by American laws rather than their own.[69]

Thierry also lashed out at the militia scheme. He appreciated its political implications. "A redundancy of population . . . of crafty and unprincipled proletair;" he said, "such is the description of emigrants that we must expect to receive among us. Then indeed the machiavelian views of Mr. Jefferson, seconded by the *double-retrenched common law,* will be fully realized." He warned of business failure, property losses, endless litigation, the erasure of ethnic identity, and the eventual expulsion of Louisianians from the land of their fathers. Appeals to Congress to rectify violations of political rights had been ignored. The only refuge from the menace of the common law was an appeal to Napoleon to enforce the terms of the treaty of cession. *"France did not sell us like vile heads of slaves,"* proclaimed Thierry.

Other critical reactions to the position taken by the *National Intelligencer* appeared in the *Telegraphe* early in October. In reply the *Orleans Gazette* hurried to the defense of national policy.[70] After reprinting several paragraphs from the *Intelligencer,* the *Gazette* affirmed that the United States had purchased Louisiana primarily for the welfare of Americans, although it did intend, where possible, to ameliorate the condition of the local inhabitants. The paper then observed that objections to the administration of affairs had arisen as a consequence of the effort of the legislature to institute the Spanish system of justice. "It would appear," argued the *Gazette,* "that the gentleman's *recent* displeasure [a reference to a piece in the *Telegraphe*] originated from the refusal of the Governor to approve a certain act of the Legislative Council, the object of which was, to give to the American people, settled in this country, or who may hereafter come to it, a Spanish system of laws." The paper described this as "an attempt to throw the American people back some half dozen of centuries: If an American governor were to give his sanction to such an act, he would well deserve and would receive the contempt and indignation of his country!" From a journal normally opposed to the governor's policies, this oblique praise was substantial indeed.

The *Gazette* recounted the merits of the common law. Compared to the civil law it was "an infinitely milder system." Even more important, the common law was an organic part of the constitutions and laws of the different states and, as such, was "inseparably connected with the rights of the people, and [was] the foundation of American jurisprudence." Unless its laws were harmonious with those of the nation, the territory of Orleans could not expect to be part of the American Union. The *Gazette* considered the common law an inheritance of the people of the United States which had "contributed largely to their unexampled happiness and prosperity." The paper believed that Louisianians really desired to share in this system of jurisprudence. It implied, despite the overwhelming evidence then available, that the advocates of the civil law did not truly reflect the general will.

IX

The major statement in support of the effort to introduce common law into the territory of Orleans was a pamphlet written in New Orleans late in 1806. Its author was one Jeremiah Brown.[71] In comprehensiveness the work can only be compared with the manifesto adopted by the legislative council the preceding June. In all likelihood, it was written in order to answer that important defense of the civil law. But the most conspicuous theme in Brown's essay was the connection he made between the central legal question and the large political and even strategic concerns to which it related.

Brown's appreciation of the civil law system was notably deficient. He referred to Louisiana attorneys as "little better than mere scriveners." Their only business, he explained, "was to draft petitions . . . for suitors." "The fact is," he went on, "that the pleadings in a cause resembled more an epistolatory correspondence, and that oftentimes in the meanest language, than a matter of judicial record. The military commandants, men wholly unacquainted with judicial affairs, were also judges in their several districts; and the same parlor window practise pervaded the whole province of Louisiana."[72] Here Brown betrayed his deep bias against the civil law system. To refer to civil lawyers as "mere scriveners" and their pleadings as "epistolatory correspondence" was to distort the characteristic modes of civil law procedure which many believed to be superior to the common law and were no doubt more suited to Louisiana. But Brown's error was typical of civil law and common law advocates alike. Whether acting deliberately or out of ignorance, each side failed to evaluate the opposing tradition on its merits. The tendency to measure the performance of one by the standards of the other was natural and apparently hard to resist. As a result, images were blurred, and what emerges from the documentation is often a caricature of the other system instead of an accurate sketch.

Brown rejected the civilian contention that the common law was scattered through countless volumes and beyond the reach or understanding of the layman. He argued that for every volume of common law there were twenty of civil law. But he betrayed his true feeling on this side of the debate when, with reference to civilian advocacy of a simplified code, he wrote: "Could indeed a short code be written and comprised in a few light volumes, in all its parts so complete as to provide clearly and unequivocally for every possible complication of relationship between man and man, comment of course would then be even worse than impertinent, and there would be no contestations to report; law would cease to be a science or its practise a profession; and every man might become his own judge by carrying his counsellor in his pocket."[73] Civil law advocates viewed the common law as providing a fertile field for endless litigation requiring the services of a burdensome legal profession. A concise, simple, and logical code of laws reduced the need for lawyers if it did not entirely eliminate them altogether. The whole civilian spirit—indeed, one of the essential points in the post-Revolutionary critique of the common law from within the common law world itself[74]—was that the law ought to be easily found and simple to understand. Legal professionalism was under attack, at this time, from many quarters in Louisiana as well as elsewhere,[75] and Brown's defense of the profession was, at the least, poorly timed.

Substantive law appears as a minor theme in Brown's pamphlet. He conceded that American policy intended nothing more than to introduce "judicial proceedings according to the course of the common law," the wording of the Northwest Ordinance. As Brown himself put it:

> The reasoning of our *civilians* on this subject are worthy of notice. As the corner stone of their cause they state the affection which every people have been observed to bear towards the ancient laws of their country, and the tyranny of subverting them is insisted on; and so strenuously, that a stranger would be led to believe that such are the laws which they were really laboring to introduce. The general principle is perhaps not incorrect, that it is seldom either good policy or justice to make a violent and total change in the laws of a

> country. But let us see how this principle applies to the present circumstances of this territory. If I understand the [Northwest] Ordinance right it interferes with little else in this respect than our judicial proceedings. Nearly all the other private social relations are untouched. The ordinance declares only how justice shall be administered; a subject never before regulated in this country.[76]

For purposes of argument Brown chose to minimize the very real threat of a wholesale transformation of the substantive law which was undoubtedly the ultimate objective of national policy.

On another level of analysis—where law and high politics met—Brown's comments were pertinent and incisive. Not only was the common law observed by "some of the ablest and purest judiciaries on earth," he argued, but its utility in assimilating Louisiana to the American nation was undeniable. Presumably those opposed to the common law also opposed the attachment of Louisiana to the United States. A swarm of refugee lawyers from the bloodletting on the island of Santo Domingo were responsible, he said, for "nearly all the rancor manifested here against the common law."[77] Not content to practice law *in* the territory, these newcomers desired to dictate laws *for* the territory. That the common law was British in origin, and that it awakened the ancient anglophobia of the people, was but a disguise for the real cause of their opposition—private gain and national prejudice. A "few French lawyers," he charged, were attempting to monopolize legal practice by establishing a system foreign to American attorneys.[78]

Brown claimed that the anti-American contagion had even infected Judge Prevost of the Superior Court. He recalled how, in the fall of 1805 during the recess of court, Prevost had called for a hearing on the extent to which the Northwest Ordinance had mandated common law proceedings. The weight of opinion, Brown believed, fell on the side of the common law, but Prevost deferred to the opinion of a minority of two—Edward Livingston and Pierre Derbigny. In place of the letter and spirit of the ordinance of Congress, therefore, a crude system of practice, in imitation of the Spanish, had been devised and instituted in the Superior Court. "Thus did one judge for the present at least, expel from his court the laws of his country; those in the study of which he was himself bred, or supposed to be bred; and boldly undertake to administer justice according to rules which he never learned, which he never even saw, and which if he had seen would have found written in a language which he could not read."[79]

But Prevost's decision was not enough, Brown continued. The legislature endeavored to prescribe the authorities to which all courts would refer and thus to establish the civil laws as the laws in force throughout the territory. This effort having failed, it then proceeded to appoint two jurisconsults to prepare a civil code. Thus the crucial decision that would affect Louisiana for generations to come, one involving questions full of doubt and uncertainty, was delivered into the hands of two men, Louis Moreau Lislet—"the St. Domingo Lycurgus"—and James Brown, the "mask" behind which the law would be codified on the basis of the Napoleonic model.[80]

The establishment of civil law in the territory, Brown explained, would create great confusion. The United States District Court in New Orleans applied common law. The local courts would apply civil law. In effect, two systems of law would coexist in the same region for the same people. In time, this would build a formidable barrier between the United States and Orleans. At this point in his argument Brown was touching that vital linchpin connecting the legal question and larger political and strategic considerations. The territory, he wrote, was the most valuable segment of the entire province of Louisiana. But because of its adherence to the civil law, Louisiana appeared to him to be "on the eve of eternal alienation from the American union. Your government may at present garrison our forts and for some time exercise many acts of sovereignty over us," he warned. "But with those who so fondly cherish a foreign language and a foreign law, who can cordially unite?"[81]

With reference to Lower Louisiana and New Orleans, the leading problem facing the United States government from 1803 until the Battle of New Orleans in 1815 was whether or not such a remote and vulnerable region—surrounded by hostile garrisons of Spanish troops on the land, threatened by a British invasion force from the sea, and harassed by pirates, malcontents, and plotters—could be preserved as an American possession. Jefferson's advocacy of the militia scheme in the early years of American rule showed his acute concern for this problem. Jeremiah Brown concurred. The bonds of union had to be woven from within. Yet, he feared, the territory was "rather in preparation to form a department of France than an American state."[82]

By failing to drawn the threads of union tighter, America would risk losing its valuable western treasure. By permitting Louisiana to remain a French stronghold governed by "foreign codes imported from Paris or Madrid," the United States would create a refuge for Frenchmen rather than a home for Americans. "[Did] but the general government know how high many a wayward pulse beats in this city at the present important moment they would not long hesitate to think with me that this is not the season when popular affection is to be conciliated by indulgence or concession."[83] The introduction of the common law was, therefore, not merely a legal requirement for the sake of uniformity but a political necessity of high moment. It was a link in the chain of union. America's hold on Lower Louisiana would never be assured "until the territory shall be inhabited by men whose hearts are American; distinction between the American and the Louisianian shall be obliterated from our laws, language and manners; until all the existing motives of mutual jealousy subside . . . and we become in sincerity and fact one people."[84]

Brown concluded on this note of accord with the Jeffersonian program, but in time history would prove the calculations of both to be wrong. The bonds of affection would be strengthened, not weakened, by "indulgence" and "concession." The Jefferson Administration would shortly accept defeat in its continuing effort to plant the common law in the soil of Louisiana. The civil law of Louisiana would soon achieve major reinforcement by legislative enactment. The principle of unity in diversity, more subtle but equally tenacious, would prevail when the territory of Orleans, contrary to Jeremiah Brown's dismal expectations, would cement its political linkages while partially severing its legal ties to the American nation.

[7] *The Louisiana Civil Law Digest*

I

Fifteen months prior to the adoption of the civil law digest the governor of the Orleans territory still gave every indication that he remained committed to the Jeffersonian policy of introducing Anglo-American common law jurisprudence into Lower Louisiana. Anticipating the comming meeting of the legislature, Claiborne wrote to Secretary of State Madison in December 1806 that "the formation of a Civil Code will engage much of their attention," but his letter implied that he was prepared to veto any attempts to establish the civil law as the law permanently in force. He hoped for understanding between the legislative and executive branches of government, but he would not sacrifice policy for the sake of agreement. "The negativing power was given to be exercised, when the occasion required," he wrote, "and of that occasion I must be the judge."[1]

But while Claiborne's position on the legal question remained firm, his attitude toward judicial reform showed considerable elasticity. In his message delivered early in January 1807 he recommended major revisions of the judicial system along the lines advocated by the *Instructions of the Inhabitants* of 1805. Nevertheless, on the question of the laws, Claiborne was immovable. As he told the legislature: "Whatever of the principles of the Civil Law, which are in unison with the interest of a free People, or that is essential to the security of prosperity in this Territory, I am desirous to retain; I have no disposition unnecessarily, or injuriously to innovate on the former Laws and usages of my fellow Citizens; But in my official Character, I can never approve measures, which will tend to bar the introduction of those great political and legal principles which are cherished throughout the United States."[2] Claiborne was trying to sound conciliatory without misleading his audience. He would not be the instrument of radical change, but neither would he bar the innovations he considered salutary.

The answer of the upper chamber to the governor's address came soon afterwards. The legislative council agreed that the session would be short and that it would be difficult to proceed with the civil code. Nevertheless, it hoped that the code committee established by the legislature, aided by James Brown and Louis Moreau Lislet, would continue at their work. Claiborne was told that the project they were preparing was already "far advanced." The message continued: "The Legislative Council agree with your Excellency in the opinion that the preservation of the Civil Laws, now existing in this Territory, is all essential to the security of property and to the tranquility of the Citizen; but your Excellency need not apprehend that the general assembly may ever attempt to revive any law which would tend to bar the introduction of those great political and legal principles which are cherished throughout the U[nited] States."[3] Julien Poydras, author of the message, here displayed his verbal sleight of hand. Claiborne *had not* said that he wished to preserve "the Civil Laws now existing in this Territory." The governor had merely stated his desire to retain "whatever of the principles of the Civil Law which are in unison with the interest of a free people." These were two very different ideas. The first was a statement of maximum support for the civilian position, the second a minimal commitment. Claiborne had been purposefully vague; Poydras purposefully interpolated. The words sounded the same. They struck that chord of agreement which both men desired. In meaning, however, they were each in a separate universe of discourse.[4]

A little more than a year later William C. C. Claiborne, the tried and tested proponent of American common law, signed the Digest that formally recognized the civil law as the law in force in the territory of Orleans. There is little concrete evidence in Claiborne's official papers during the critical months preceding his dramatic change in policy to indicate the new direction of his thinking. The fact that the legislative debates were not recorded, or are no longer extant, increases the problem of historical reconstruction.[5] Yet, it is possible to identify what must have been the decisive factors in the governor's change in policy.

Uppermost in his mind, early in 1807, was the Burr storm just then at high fury. The depth of the conspiracy and the measure of its effects were still little known. Undoubtedly, the governor was anxious to avoid another clash with the legislature over the legal question so soon after the very existence of the territory had been menaced. A year later the ripples set in motion by Burrism were very much in evidence even though the crisis itself had subsided. Related to this were the declining prospects of Jefferson's militia scheme. In 1807, the chances for its enactment—with all that it portended politically—were bright.[6] But as time went on, that possibility became increasingly remote, and by 1808 its unfeasibility was evident. Finally, the ripening Batture controversy presented Governor Claiborne with an opportunity that he could not afford to miss. His position on that inflammatory question was highly acceptable to Louisianians. Had he rejected the Digest he would have dissolved the ties just recently forged.

Thus 1807-1808 was a critical time in the history of Lower Louisiana. Events crowded in on decision-makers in rapid succession. Fundamental problems relating to the future of the area had to be solved in an atmosphere highly prejudicial to ultimate national objectives. Options were foreclosed, choices limited. But it is to the credit of William Claiborne that he recognized necessity and gave way to it. He was, after all, the essential Jeffersonian.

II

On March 31, 1808, the Orleans legislature adopted the *Digest of the Civil Laws Now in Force in the Territory of Orleans* by formal enactment.[7] Like the *Code Napoleon* (or its *projet*) after which it was modeled, the Louisiana Digest was divided into three books: "Of Persons," "Of Things or Estates," and "Of the Different Manners of Acquiring the Property of Things." Book One was preceded by a preliminary title which differentiated law from custom, noted the necessity and set forth the requirements for the present code's promulgation, outlined the prospective and other effects of the laws therein enacted, established fundamental rules of construction, and defined the conditions governing repeals. The entire work was preceded by an alphabetical index of subjects. The Digest was printed in French and English, and in the act providing for its adoption and promulgation the legislature provided that in cases where the text was ambiguous or obscure "both the English and French texts shall be consulted, and shall mutually serve to the interpretation of one and the other." However, judicial decisions subsequently established that since French was the working language of the codifiers, the French version was to be authoritative.[8] Bradford and Anderson prepared the Digest for publication in October just prior to the takeover of the public printing by J. B. S. Thierry—a final irony given the *Orleans Gazette's* consistent advocacy of common law reception.

Governor Claiborne signed the measure adopting the Digest and thus added his official imprimatur to one of the most decisive undertakings in Louisiana's legal history. In a message delivered several days later, the governor pledged that he would put the Digest into force by promulgating it throughout the territory.[9] He pointed to weaknesses in the English translation but was satisfied that no inconvenience would be caused by it. He concluded that "a want of information as to the laws in force, heretofore a source of such general embarrassment, will no longer exist; the code will serve as a guide for the magistrate and the citizen; and, while every member of our society will possess the means of acquiring a knowledge of his civil rights, he will be the better enabled to judge in what manner they may be enlarged, or what further measures are necessary for their security."

Claiborne was bowing to necessity with grace. To Madison he even admitted that there was "much to admire in the Civil Law." However, lest the Secretary think him disloyal, Claiborne hastened to add that "there are some principles, which ought to yield to the common law Doctrine." He protested his good faith, insisting that it had been a high priority of policy to "assimilate as much as possible the Laws and usages of this Territory to those of the states generally." The "work of innovation" was slow, however, and not to "be pursued hastily, nor could it be prosecuted to advantage or with safety until the existing laws were fully presented to our views."[10] Claiborne was attempting to soften the impact of defeat.

The governor also distinguished between a code and a digest. "The 'Civil Code' alluded to in my last letter," he wrote, "is nothing more, than a 'Digest of the Civil Laws in Force in this territory.' " It was an important distinction. A digest is a summary or compilation of preexisting law designed to make that law known and available. Prior law remains authoritative. A code, on the other hand, replaces prior law and itself becomes the definitive and final statement of the law for purposes of adjudication. Despite some formal resemblances to a modern civil code, therefore, the Digest of 1808 lacked the essential element of a genuine work of code law. To describe it as "the civil code of 1808"—or "the Old Code" as it was called in Louisiana for a short while after the enactment of the Revised Civil Code of 1825—is misleading.[11]

There is little doubt that the enactment of a digest rather than a code was the intention of the Louisiana legislature. The language of the preamble to the statute providing for the promulgation of the digest made this plain:

> Whereas, in the confused state in which the civil laws of this territory were plunged, by the effect of the changes which happened in its government, it had become indispensable to make known the laws which have been preserved after the abrogation of those which were contrary to the constitution of the United States, or irreconcilable with its principles, and to collect them in a single work, *which might serve as a guide*, for the decision of the courts and juries, without recurring to a multiplicity of books, which, being for the most part written in

foreign languages, offer in their interpretation inexhaustible sources of litigation.[12] [italics added]

Clearly, a guide to sources was not a finished code. Moreover, section 2 of the act abrogated only those rules of law inconsistent with the new digest and the present system of government: "*And be it further enacted,* That whatever in the ancient civil laws of this territory . . . is contrary to the dispositions contained in the said digest, or irreconcilable with them, is hereby abrogated."[13] The obvious reference was inescapable: all other prior law not so abrogated remained in force.

The Louisiana judiciary carried out the intent of the legislature in a series of decisions starting in 1812. In that year the Superior Court held that "what we call the Civil Code, is but a digest of the civil law which regulated this country under the French and Spanish monarchs."[14] Five years later the state's highest court established "That our civil code is a digest of the civil laws, which were in force in this country, when it was adopted; that those laws must be considered as untouched, wherever the alterations and amendments, introduced in the digest, do not reach them, and that such parts of those laws only are repealed, as are either contrary to, or incompatible with the provisions of the code."[15]

The Digest itself, in its preliminary title, recognized custom as a source of law: "Customs result from a long series of actions constantly repeated, which have by such repetition, and by uninterrupted acquiescence acquired the force of a tacit and common consent."[16] Since modern civil codes are based upon legislative positivism this provision contravened a fundamental requirement of code law. Even the Revised Civil Code of 1825 failed to abrogate this recognition of custom despite the fact that the redactors of the revision advised that it be suppressed.[17]

For contemporaries there was little question but that Spanish law was the custom of Louisiana. Major Amos Stoddard, who served for a time as military commandant in Upper Louisiana, observed in 1812 that the Spanish had changed "almost the whole of the French colonial jurisprudence, and only preserved the principles of *allodium* in their grants of land, and in the settlement and distribution of estates *ab intestato.*" He noted the importance of the Code of the Indies (*Recopilacion de Indias*) and the *Partidas*, two of the major sources of Spanish law. Where Louisiana departed from Spanish law, he said, it did so out of deference to Roman civil law rather than French law.[18] In addition, arguments by counsel and judicial opinion during the territorial period, but after the adoption of the Digest, strongly suggest that the Spanish law was considered to be in force in

Louisiana at the time of the cession to the United States.[19] Later on, the Louisiana State Supreme Court (the old territorial Superior Court) said that a supersession of French law by Spanish law had taken place prior to the enactment of the Digest.[20] This led to the renewal of interest in the old Spanish sources, and, as a result, the state legislature commissioned a translation of *Las Siete Partidas,* probably the most comprehensive single source of Spanish law then available. The preface to that work, coauthored by Louis Moreau Lislet, the principal draftsman of the Digest of 1808, makes it clear that the Spanish laws, including many provisions of the *Partidas,* were still in force in Louisiana:

> It remains now to state, how it happened, that the laws of Spain, are still in force in Louisiana, since its transfer to the United States of America.
>
> The customs of Paris and the ordinances of the kingdom, were observed in Louisiana, while it remained under the dominion of France, and by them all civil and criminal suits were determined. . . . This state of things, existed until the month of August 1769, when count [Alexander] O'Reilly took possession of that country, in the name of the king of Spain, in virtue of the treaty of cession, which France had made to that power. . . . O'Reilly issued a proclamation, changing the form of the government of Louisiana, abolishing the authority of the French laws, and substituting those of Spain in their stead. This proclamation which was accompanied by an ordinance, establishing the several branches of the new government of Louisiana, and defining their respective powers, appears to have been published on the 26th November 1769. From the time of its promulgation until now, the French laws ceased to have any authority in this country, and all controversies were tried and decided conformably to the Spanish laws. . . .
>
> The return of Louisiana under the dominion of France, and its transfer to the United States, did not for a moment, weaken the Spanish laws in that province. The French, during the short continuation of their power, from the 30th November to the 20th December 1803, made no alteration in the jurisprudence of the country; and the government of the United States, left the task of legislation to the people of Louisiana themselves, giving to them, the right to make whatever changes they might deem necessary in the existing system of their laws. . . .
>
> However the legislature of the territory of Orleans, as early as the year 1807, considering that the ancient laws secured to the inhabitants of Louisiana by the acts of Congress, were written in a foreign language [Spanish], and contained in books difficult to be procured, ordered a digest of those laws to be made and prepared in the English and French languages, by two jurisconsults. . . . This code commonly known under

> the name of the Civil Code, is therefore become part of our statute laws. But it is easy to perceive, that a work of that nature, however excellent it may be, can only contain general rules and abstract maxims, still leaving many points doubtful in the application of the law; hence the necessity of going back to the original source, in order to obtain new and additional light. It was moreover perceived that the Civil Code did not contain many and important provisions of the Spanish laws still in force. . . .[21]

Thus the authority of Moreau Lislet himself helps to establish that the Spanish law was the custom of the country at the time of the successive transfers of Louisiana first to France and then to the United States.

III

The ancient Spanish law was the fundamental law in Louisiana both before and after the enactment of the Digest of 1808. This has long been recognized in Louisiana. What is curious has been the persistence of the tradition that the Digest itself was largely a work drawn from French sources. Why should a digest of French law appear amidst an ongoing Spanish tradition? In recent years Louisiana scholars have addressed themselves to this question, and some have suggested that the Digest of 1808 was, in fact, a digest of Spanish law. In 1958 a first edition of the work containing interleaved pages with carefully annotated citations to Spanish, Roman, and some French sources—the so-called de la Vergne manuscript—was made available to researchers and has since been published in a limited edition. One leading commentator, Joseph Dainow, was struck by the "complete preponderance of Spanish authorities."[22] Mitchell Franklin, whose earlier publications had consistently emphasized French influence on the Digest, now concluded that it was designed to divert Louisiana law away from French and toward Spanish law.[23] Another find, this time an edition of the Digest actually annotated in the handwriting of Louis Moreau Lislet, led Robert A. Pascal to the conclusion that "both documents . . . help demonstrate that the redactors of the *Digest* of 1808 did indeed consider it a digest of the Spanish laws then in force in Louisiana even though they cast it in the mold of the new French *Code Civil.*"[24]

The great appeal of this "revisionist" interpretation of the sources of the Digest is that in emphasizing its Spanish origins it helps to establish the continuity of early nineteenth-century Louisiana law whose Spanish character the Louisiana judiciary recognized both before and after 1808. The more traditional interpretation still has adherents, however.[25] In September 1971 the *Tulane Law Review* issued a special supplement, a study by Rodolfo Batiza of the sources of the Digest of 1808.[26] Batiza challenges the importance of the de la Vergne manuscript volume as well as the Moreau Lislet copy of the Digest. He maintains that these are not compilations of sources but what he calls "concordances"—that is, texts of Roman and Spanish law having relation to but not necessarily in harmony with the principles of law in the articles of the Digest to which they correspond.[27] Batiza has gone back to all of the legal sources—French, Spanish, Roman, and English—known to have been available to the redactors and has attempted to establish the exact source for each of the provisions of the Digest. He believes he has succeeded in identifying 97 percent of them, and he is satisfied that while "there is still some room for uncertainty and speculation on some articles" . . . the mystery surrounding most provisions in the Code is almost entirely dispelled by the present investigation."[28] According to Batiza's analysis, 85 percent of the Digest's provisions are French, with the *Projet* of 1800 and the *Code Civil* of Napoleon constituting 70 percent of this total. The remainder of the sources are distributed among Latin and Spanish, as well as English, works.[29]

There are a number of methodological problems which Batiza's work raises, however. His scale for measuring the degree of transcription from source to Digest ("verbatim," "almost verbatim," "substantially influenced," and "partially influenced") sets up a linguistic standard which, as he admits, favors French over Spanish sources, as French was, with English, one of the two original languages of the Digest. In addition, numerical totals may be deceptively conclusive, since the purport of specific legal concepts is not to be ascertained by enumerating provisions but by analyzing their total meaning and thrust in every major field of the private law.

In the field of riparian law, for example—the major area of dispute in the Batture fight—the Digest does seem to be more heavily weighted toward Spanish law despite formal similarities with contemporary French sources, principally the *Code Civil* of Napoleon and the *Projet* of that code produced in 1800. Article 13 (Bk. 2, Tit. 2) of the Louisiana Digest was an exact transcription of the essential part of article 15 of the *Projet* of 1800 which provided that an alluvion formed "successively and imperceptibly to any soil situated on the shore of a river or creek . . . belongs to the owner of the soil situated on the edge of the water, whether it be a river or a creek, and whether the same be navigable or not."[30] However, article 19 of the 1800 *Projet*—"islands, islets and sand bars [*attérrissmens*, sand bars, also means alluvion] formed in the beds of rivers belong to the nation"[31]—

has no corresponding provision in the Digest. On the basis of what must have been a deliberate omission, it is fair to conclude that the redactors of the Digest rejected this provision of the French *Projet* (2.2.19) because it conflicted with the Spanish rules then in force in Louisiana. The Louisiana Revised Code of 1825 would provide that sand bars were public property when unattached to the shore,[32] but the 1823 *projet* of that Revision specifically referred to the Spanish *Partidas* as the legal source.[33] Moreover, the nonattachment of such accretions to the shore was a crucial difference between this provision of the 1825 code and article 19 of the French *Projet* of 1800. Mississippi river battures were, by definition, always attached.[34]

Related provisions in Book 2 (Tit. 1) of the Digest of 1808 reinforce the conclusion that French sources were used as formal models only when they did not conflict with local law. Thus article 6 (Digest Bk. 2, Tit. 1) defined properties belonging to the nation "the use of which is allowed to all members of the nation" as navigable rivers, sea ports, roads, harbors, and highways "and the bed of rivers as long as the same is covered with water." However, as a clarification, article 8 (Digest, Bk. 2, Tit.1) provided that "the use of the shores of navigable rivers or creeks, is public; accordingly everyone has a right freely to bring his ships to land there, to make fast the same to the trees which are there planted, to unload his vessels, to deposit his goods, to dry his nets, and the like. *Nevertheless, the property of the river shores belongs to those who possess the adjoining lands*" (emphasis added). There was a provision in the French *Projet* of 1800 close to article 6 (Bk. 2, Tit.1) of the Digest specifying those public properties insusceptible of private ownership, but there is nothing in the *Projet* equivalent to article 8 (Digest, Bk. 2, Tit. 1) that excepts the proprietary interests of riparians from the category of public properties.[35] Batture ground was of unique importance in Louisiana because of its extent and value, but it was a special problem because it constantly shifted and was covered with water at certain seasons of the year. Articles 6 and 8 of the Louisiana Digest clearly established that while the public had a use in the battures of navigable rivers, property rights remained with the riparian landowners.

But this was quite contrary to French law then and now.[36] It did, however, correspond to Spanish law, and in fact, the de la Vergne manuscript refers to the *Partidas* as the source of article 8 (Bk. 2, Tit. 1) of the Digest which held that while the public had a use in the banks of rivers, "the dominion or property of the banks . . . belongs to the owner of the adjoining estate."[37] Indeed, Louisiana law has consistently provided for private ownership of alluvial accretions formed along the banks of rivers with a use reserved to the public.[38] The foregoing analysis of the relevant texts shows that French models were followed closely only when they did not detract from local law which sustained the rights of private ownership to a particular kind of alluvial formation, a controlling concept more Spanish than French.

The kind of enumerative tabulation which Rodolfo Batiza has undertaken, however, does not lead to such a clear-cut conclusion, for while Batiza does identify the Spanish laws which he believes were sources of Louisiana riparian law as redacted in the Digest of 1808, French sources get almost equal play. Thus, of the articles discussed above, we get one (Digest, 2.2.13) which is an "almost verbatim" transcription from the French *Projet* of 1800 and the *Code Civil*, one (Digest, 2.1.6) which was "substantially influenced" by the French commentator Domat and the Spanish *Partidas*, and one (*Digest*, 2.1.8) which was "substantially influenced" by the Roman Institutes and Digest as well as by Spanish law. The conclusions to be drawn from such information must remain ambiguous. Significantly, in Batiza's numerical summary of the sources of the Digest, *all* of the provisions in Book 2, Title 2, are attributed to French sources even though the controlling principles governing the ownership of alluvial accretions were Spanish and not French.[39] Moreover, *no* numerical weight is given to the important suppression of article 19 of the French *Projet* (*Projet* 2.2.19), deliberately omitted because it so clearly subverted the local law in force in Louisiana which, as declared by the Superior Court of the territory, provided that "the right of alluvion is incident to land which is bounded by a navigable river" and therefore susceptible of private ownership.[40] The "revisionist" scholars never suggested that French models were not used. Their major point, however, has been that French models were accepted only when not in conflict with local law which was, for the most part, Spanish.[41]

Despite some of the problems raised by his method and the curious inconsistency of his conclusions with the fact that Spanish law was in force before the Digest—a fact which Batiza's own research had helped to establish—[42] and was reactivated by the Louisiana courts subsequent to its enactment, Rodolfo Batiza's article remains, to date, the most arresting, ambitious, and comprehensive effort to discover the sources of the Digest of 1808. Until the revisionists come forward with research of comparable breadth, conclusions on either side must remain tentative. What is clear, however—even striking, perhaps—is the wide net which the redactors of the Digest cast. In Batiza's words, "While the impact of the French *Projet,* Code and writers on the [Louisiana] Code of 1808 is clearly overwhelming, the variety of sources used in drafting the Code gives it a cosmopolitan and distinctive flavor that differentiates it from either of its two principal models." [43]

Whether or not the Louisiana Digest was predominantly Spanish or French is important to determine because of the many substantive differences dividing those two members of the civil law family, differences which even today can affect the outcome of litigation. Still, the vital issue confronting the ancient Louisianians in the time of Jefferson was not which of the two would prevail, but whether the elements of the civil law would remain the cornerstone of their private relations or a totally foreign Anglo-American legal system would be received and implanted. Of this there is no better proof than the Batture controversy itself, which did question whether Spanish law or French law was in force in the territory and how each of those systems disposed of riparian estates. Yet, oddly enough, this great issue, which so divided opinion and was forced upon the attention of the United States Congress and the Administration in Washington, was largely perceived by the local community as a conflict not between Spanish and French law but between Louisiana's ancient system of civil law jurisprudence and the novel system of common law which the Americans were attempting to impose.

Thus one is forced to wonder if the interesting scholarly debate over sources is not somewhat misconceived. In the absence of independent manuscript sources, legislative debates, and other traditional documentary materials, it is doubtful if speculations about the actual sources of the Louisiana Digest will ever be resolved. In addition, there is little extant evidence to suggest that there was a significant struggle between proponents of French or Spanish law at the time. Were the Digest of 1808 indeed predominantly a digest of French law, we would expect to find some evidence of resistance to what would have been a break in legal continuity with the past as well as a bold defiance of the legislative mandate that the codifiers "shall make the civil law by which this Territory is now governed the ground work of said code." None has been suggested. On the basis of the historical evidence that we do have, therefore, it is fair to conclude that the real conflict was between legal traditions rather than within the civil law family, a conclusion with which most contemporaries would have agreed. [44]

IV

At the time of the adoption of the Digest a newspaper war was again in progress. This was not unusual for territorial Louisiana, but the rising crescendo of public debate, reflected in the press, illuminated the entire legal-political landscape. There was a brief flurry in late March over the public activities of Daniel Clark. Articles attacking and defending the territorial delegate appeared in both the *Moniteur* and the *Courier*.[45] The Clark-Wilkinson dispute was important news in Orleans, and for months the papers were crammed with charges and counter-charges. The imminent passage of a civil law digest, however, drew the legal debate into the political arena. This joining of the issues betrayed an awareness that politics and law were two parts of the same whole.

Almost simultaneously with the adoption of the Digest Colonel Bellechasse of the militia and a member of the legislative council published extensive extracts from the piece written but never published by J. B. S. Thierry of the *Courier* in answer to the editorial of the *National Intelligencer* of August 11, 1806.[46] Bellechasse told how he had, at that time, prevailed upon Claudius Beleurguy, editor of the *Telegraphe*, not to publish Thierry's savage attack upon Jefferson for fear that it would further defame the Louisianians. Beleurguy had taken his advice and withdrawn the piece at the last moment. All of the page proofs were destroyed except for the one copy still in Bellechasse's possession.[47] The purpose of bringing it before the public now, Bellechasse explained, was in order to show that it was not Daniel Clark who was the real enemy of American interests in Lower Louisiana but the hot-tempered editor of the *Louisiana Courier*. It was Thierry, Bellechasse charged, who had attempted to inflame the demonstrators on the Batture in September 1807. For having attempted to incite the people against their lawful government, Thierry deserved the reputation of the true "Burrite" whose accusations could not be credited.

In reply, and with characteristic passion, the editor of the *Courier* defended his position on the Batture question.[48] Thierry contended that despite constant harassment and "persecutions" he had remained faithful and energetic in a cause near and dear to the interests of Louisianians. As for his supposed oscillation from erstwhile opponent to present supporter of national policies, he wrote that, on the contrary, it was the government that had tailored its position to fit his. Thierry reviewed at length the political history of the territory. Daniel Clark, frustrated in his desire to become governor, had used his influence to deprive Claiborne of popular support and "to sow discord among the inhabitants." Clark, he asserted, had sought to accomplish these ends by placing his own men close to the governor, ostensibly as advisors. These individuals had been responsible for Claiborne's misguided first steps during his early months in the territory.

"At this period," Thierry wrote retrospectively, "the introduction of the common law into this country was in dispute. A population which had been held up as the most ignorant, the most stupid, that vegetated on the surface of the habitable globe, ought not, according to it, to be thought capable of judging what laws were fit for them." The enemies of the Louisianians managed to gain access to "a Gazette [the *National Intelligencer*] printed under the eye of government," there to argue that Louisiana was bought not for the sake of its inhabitants but for that of America, and "that the choice of laws by which they were to be governed depended no longer on them." This theme was pursued in local as well as in national newspapers. In the Natchez press, and then in Bradford's *Orleans Gazette,*"the civil laws by which the country was governed were cried down . . . [The] Justinian Code, as well as the Collection de las perdidas [sic], and the ordinance of Bilbao, were treated as Gothic wrecks, and incoherent, which could not be held forth in comparison with the majestic forms of the English legislation." These newspapers had endeavoured to establish the common law, and it was to thwart their efforts that the editor of the *Telegraphe* had invited Thierry to respond to the *National Intelligencer's* prescriptions. At the time, Thierry explained, he had no way of knowing that Jefferson was "the dupe of a plot contrived by Mr. Clark," so that he had mistakenly attacked the Administration instead of the real source of discord and dissent.

Burr changed everything, said Thierry. The loyalty of the Louisianians had nullified his intrigues. But the current apologists for Clark were the very same men who had abandoned the government at the time of crisis. The Burr conspiracy had revealed the real friends and the true enemies of Louisiana. Of what, then, was he guilty? he inquired. Of making known to the inhabitants the dangers of the common law? Of indicating to them the need for conserving their traditon? Of holding up before them the intrigues of their accusers who desired to block "the essential point, that of conserving the laws of the region?"

Finally, Thierry referred to the unpublished article which

Bellechasse had attempted to use against him. Here he displayed how, in his own mind, political and legal issues had coagulated:

> This piece that I handed over in manuscript to Mr. Gurley, will have probably been communicated to the general government, and if it has arrived as I have every reason to think, how can you say that it contributed nothing towards disabusing us of the common law, since the general government has exposed all the menaces that had been practised here? In any case, I can say relative to that article, that it is not I, but the general government that has changed its mind, seeing that it has permitted us, by a compilation of the old laws adapted to the loyalty of the Territory and to the principles of the American government, to be ruled by the empire of the civil law.

As in the Batture controversy, there always was a vein of truth buried beneath the crisscross lacunae of Thierry's reason. Obviously, the government's position on the legal question had not been changed merely by the reading of an unpublished manuscript. But there was a connection between the political upheaval caused by Burr and the government's new position on the legal question. Thierry recognized this. In spite of the non sequiturs, the undocumented charges, the exaggerated claims, his answer to Bellechasse described that awareness. Burrism had been exposed, the government had amended its legal policy, and a civil law digest had been enacted. Here was a flow of events that *did* bear upon each other. Political realities had affected the outcome of the conflict of legal traditions. Questions of politics and questions of law had been fused by events, and to this conjunction of discrete but related themes Thierry's statement was a contemporaneous testimonial.

V

During the ensuing months the civil law digest was prepared for publication, and by October it was ready. Claiborne issued a circular letter to all parish judges informing them that the bearer, one David Becket, would deliver copies of the work for them and for the justices of the peace.[49] For Becket he prepared a list of the judges by parish, the number of copies they were to receive, and detailed instructions on how to travel and where to go. He sent a copy to Madison with another letter explaining his reasons for approving the work. His "first object," he said, "has been to render the Laws certain; my next shall be to render them just, and to assimilate our system of Jurisprudence as much as possible, to that of the several states of the union."[50] Perspective had changed. He referred to the civil law system as "our system" and ranked the assimilation of civil law with common law third in his list of priorities—a third priority but a possibility more remote than before.

Most of Claiborne's utterances on the Digest dwelt upon the legal necessities which had compelled him to approve it. He told Madison of the confusion that had now been clarified, and to the legislature he confessed the embarrassment which citizen and magistrate had suffered as a consequence of the widespread ignorance of the laws in force.[51] But Claiborne was keenly aware of the setback the American community had received with the formal establishment of the civil law. To a district judge he wrote that "the Code will probably be greatly censured by many native citizens of the United States who reside in the Territory. From Principle and habit, they are attached to that system of Jurisprudence, prevailing in the several states under which themselves and their Fathers were reared."[52] Claiborne regretted that it had not been possible to establish that system of Anglo-American law to which he, too, was accustomed. He remained convinced that unity of law was requisite to national unity, but he recalled "the peculiar circumstances in which Louisiana is placed" and reminded his correspondent "of the respect due the sentiments and wishes of the Ancient Louisianians." Having been reared in the civil law tradition, Louisianians were mindful of its excellence. Therefore, he reasoned, just as Americans preferred their own system of jurisprudence out of habit and prejudice, "we should not be surprised, at the attachment which the old Inhabitants manifest for many of their [own] Customs and local Institutions." He warned of the perils which attended the hasty introduction of a new legal order. It would cause "much inconvenience" and "serious discontents."

Claiborne's letter to Judge White was unique thus far only for its equanimity. He balanced his expression of loyalty to the common law with a sensitivity to the demands of his Louisiana constituents. This was the familiar style of the early Claiborne standing between contending forces and interests. However, the remainder of the letter reflected an altered posture. The governor warned White of the aversion of the French to courts and lawyers and of the Americans to the principles of civil law. He urged the judge to persevere in his arduous task amidst the antagonisms of ethnic conflict and prejudice. He then added this revealing passage: "The time was I believe when the Louisianians had formed an opinion, that the Executive of this Territory, was inimical to their best Interest, and designing men, had succeeded in impressing them with a further belief, that the Executive, harboured also some personal prejudices against them.

But these Impressions I trust are no longer entertained by the good and virtuous."[53] Claiborne was recalling the bitter early days of his service, the running battle he had fought from the very first with the hostile, suspicious, and resentful inhabitants aided and abetted by some notable Americans. Now serenity replaced rancor. The Louisianians had changed toward him as he had toward them. It was with deep sincerity that he confessed that "every sentiment of honor combines to render the General Interest of this Territory dear to my heart, and I should indeed be wanting in sensibility had not the many private virtues of the Louisianians recommended them to my sincere esteem."

There was a mellowness in these lines that had been absent in the past. The affinity of the governor and his people was a source of confidence, satisfaction, and strength. The nervousness and anxiety which had been so typical of Claiborne's earlier forays into political reportage were gone entirely, at least at this moment. He went on to say that it had been hinted to him "that a portion of my fellow Citizens (the native Americans) view me as opposed to their interests, and as desirous of giving a preponderance to what they term 'the french Influence'; Unjust, as is this imputation, it is nevertheless one, which I had anticipated would attach to my approbation of the Civil Code." He merely observed "that the adoption of this Code was recommended by the strongest considerations of Justice and policy."

"Justice and policy"—a curious juxtaposition, but one that comes naturally to the style of the seasoned public leader. For such had Claiborne become. He was no longer the detached novitiate of 1803, but the tested public man. Having weathered the storms of Burrism and Batturism, he could assume the habit of the legal statesman. The Digest represented the coming together of a number of public energies. It was a mark of the political maturity of William Claiborne that despite personal conviction and high public policy he allowed those elemental forces to merge.

VI

The enactment of a digest of civil law composed mostly of French, Spanish, and Roman sources—though interlarded with some local as well as a smattering of English materials—shows how deeply attached the old inhabitants of Louisiana were to their legal past, and how much they desired to preserve continuity with it.[54] In the light of this elementary fact, it is not surprising that Louisiana adopted a digest of law rather than a code of law.[55] A code, after all, represents a break with the past.

In abrogating antecedent law it wipes the slate clean. That is why, in modern times, codes have often been enacted in the wake of revolutionary upheaval. The enacted codes following the French Revolution, for example, completed the process of legal unification and modernization which was, in part, what the Revolution was about. The French codifiers of the Napoleonic period built into the structure of law the social transformations of the immediate past.[56]

In Louisiana, however, this is precisely what the ancients hoped to prevent. If anything, it was the Americans who desired a legal revolution to punctuate the political change that had just taken place. This is what lay behind the whole Jeffersonian effort to Americanize Louisiana legally and in every other way. Jefferson wanted to restructure society at its very core, in order to make it digestible by the larger national entity of which it was now a part. As Jefferson himself once put it, "in a whole composed of parts, no one part must carve for itself."[57] America was caught up in the process of nation building. To men for whom differences between Virginians and Bostonians appeared to be insurmountable barriers to union, the absorption of Louisiana seemed altogether preposterous.[58] The common law, therefore, was to be an instrument for cultural homogenization.

The great difficulty, however, was that the Americans had no neat package of law to substitute for the customary laws of Louisiana. There was no code of common law as such. Even Blackstone could no longer answer that need, for though it still served as school, library, and manual for the average law practitioner, the *Commentaries* reflected the law of England of 1700, and America needed a body of law better suited to a new time and an entirely different setting. The American Revolution had accelerated the movement for law reform and Americanization as a reaction to things English, but the process of redefinition still awaited completion. Given the eclectic, transitional, and untidy state of American common law, therefore, the Americans were ill equipped for the task of introducing their body of law by simple legislative enactment into the alien territory of Louisiana.[59] On the other hand, the Louisianians had available to them the French codes as formal models plus the body of Spanish law in its uncodified state—the *Partidas*, the *Fuero Real*, the Laws of Toro, the *Recopilaciones*—with which they were conversant. How much easier for them to reduce this body of law to a simple digest for their own convenience and especially for the education of their ill-informed and bewildered new governors.[60]

Thus the Digest of 1808 befitted the historical circumstances of early American Louisiana. It did not, however, establish a thoroughgoing civil law system. The Constitution and federal statutes were applied to Louisiana. There was little opposition to the introduction of American criminal law and criminal procedure. Procedural law, while unique, adopted many of the basic components of the American system: some of the common law forms of action, the adversary process itself, and the controlling importance of the judiciary in determining the meaning of the written law. Louisiana, like the rest of the American states, adopted the law merchant and thus rejected a commercial code that might have set it apart from the national economy upon which its prosperity was increasingly dependent.[61] The law of slavery, based on the French *Code Noir*, was unique in some respects, but statutory enactments would in time bring it into harmony with the slave codes in the other southern states.[62] The only real area of difference, then, was the private substantive law. The Digest of 1808, and the customary law upon which it was based, became the main pillar of the civil law in Louisiana, and in the absence of the other landmarks of a complete civil law system, it was to occupy an even more pivotal position in Louisiana life than civil codes of private law normally do in civil law communities.[63]

The Louisianians themselves appreciated how far they had fallen short of establishing a finished system. To be sure, the Digest was a watershed in the early history of the state. It tipped the scales in favor of the civil law tradition in the field of private law.[64] Even so, a legislative digest was not thought to be sufficient insurance for the future. Thus, in 1812, the new state constitution of Louisiana provided that "the General Assembly shall never adopt any system or code of laws by general reference to such a system or code of laws; but in all cases shall recite at length the several provisions of the laws it may enact"[65]—an oblique but unmistakable reference to the ongoing threat of common law reception by statutory enactment.

This constitutional provision of 1812, repeated in every subsequent Louisiana constitution, shows that Louisianians have viewed the legal conflict as far from settled. Because it is a civil law island in a sea of common law, the Louisiana bench and bar have remained alert to unwanted seepage and the erosion of their unique system of law. They have tried to select only those elements of American law which are not incompatible with local law and are, in themselves, desirable additions.[66] But the trend of modern legal systems, particularly when they coexist in contiguous geographic regions, is toward convergence. The growth in the common law world of the influence of the legal periodical and of "law school law"—what the civilians call doctrine—and the irresistible force of precedent in the civil law, which renders to case law an energy beyond its place in the traditional model, are two examples of this convergence.[67] To some extent common law America is less sensitive to these trends than is civil law Louisiana. The common law's pragmatic tradition outweighs commitments to systemic purity. But to the Louisiana civilian, the gradual erosion of the civil law and the accretion of foreign elements is, and should be, a matter of deep concern.[68]

Indeed, the consciousness of a persisting civil law—common law struggle in Louisiana has remained keen. It has led to the establishment of institutional safeguards designed to lighten the burden once shouldered by the Digest and the codal revisions which followed. The growth of Louisiana's law schools and the influence of their law reviews, as well as the establishment of the Louisiana State Law Institute, betoken a contemporary commitment to the preservation of the civil law not unlike that made in the halcyon days of the ancient Louisianians.[69] The deep and even passionate discussion of legal-historical issues which still animates scholarly debates in Louisiana is another sign of the vitality which Louisiana's special and complex legal history has produced.

VII

Summing up the turbulent era through which Louisiana had passed in the first years after its attachment to the American nation, Bernard Marigny, scion of a distinguished line of French Creoles dating back to Philippe de Marigny de Mandeville, a founder of New Orleans, highlighted the two transcending issues of the period—issues which went to the heart of the question whether the rights and interests of the original inhabitants of Louisiana were to be honored and preserved: the Batture of New Orleans and the clash of legal systems. Writing from Paris in 1822, just at the time when a comprehensive codification movement was underway in Louisiana, Marigny reflected upon the role he had played particularly in the great conflict of legal traditons:

> Called upon twelve years ago to take part in public affairs, I have supported and defended with all my ability and strength the rights and interests of the inhabitants of Louisiana of the same origin as myself. I . . . found myself in the opposing party, and I have never left it. If this system [of opposition] had not been carefully and constantly carried on by Messrs. Blanque, Thierry, and myself, the seat of government would

> long since have been transferred from New Orleans to Baton Rouge, and the civil laws, by which we are governed, annulled and replaced by the famous Common Law of England, a veritable *grimoire*, which, like the languages of Aesop, one can make another say whatever one wishes, to the great detriment of the unfortunate litigant.[70]

"A veritable *grimoire*" —a book of magic or an unintelligible scrawl: this was one Louisianian's vision of Anglo-American common law.

Louisiana's first digest, the precursor of its famous codes, was the product of a confrontation between competing cultures as much as it was the resolution of the particular problem of legal confusion. The Louisianians of the early nineteenth century defended much of their ancient legal heritage—as much as local political circumstances and national policy would allow. But viewed in broad historical perspective, the Digest of 1808 represented something more. It was, in fact, the political compromise on the basis of which the settled population of Lower Louisiana finally accepted permanent American rule. The Jefferson Administration faced the difficult and awkward problem of incorporating what was essentially a colonial possession into a federal union of self-governing and largely independent states. The alternatives were bleak: either Louisiana would remain an outright colony of the United States—an obvious breach of the terms of its acquisition and a repudiation of America's already established ideological opposition to colonialism—or an alien people used to authoritarian government, thought to be unlettered in representative institutions, steeped in a foreign culture, speaking a different language, and following strange legal customs and laws would have to be integrated into an increasingly homogeneous nation on equal terms.

Many of those who, like Thomas Jefferson, favored the acquisition of Louisiana were particularly troubled by these problems of legal and cultural diversity. At first, they believed that as a precondition for Louisiana's entry into the Union nothing less than a total cultural transformation would suffice. In essence, Jeffersonian policy aspired to nothing less. For a regime based upon the principles of strict construction and limited federal power, this was a remarkable doctrinal turnabout and a perversion of the essential meaning of republicanism. Such a solution, however, could only be the work of time. But Louisianians resisted Jeffersonian goals and gave the lie to many of the controlling assumptions of American policy. With remarkable speed, the old inhabitants of Lower Louisiana adopted the best of the American legal and political tradition, and then, when political circumstances were ripe, they acted in defiance of national policy. The redaction and enactment of the Louisiana Digest of 1808 manifested a political maturity and an instinct for self-goverment which was totally unexpected. In turn, Jeffersonian acceptance of the civil law in Louisiana represented a major concession in an otherwise heavy-handed effort to bring about some kind of adjustment between America and its first subject people.

Louisiana saw the exercise of American cultural and political imperialism, but it was also a kind of model of how that imperial thrust was once partially blunted. As a result of the Louisiana encounter, the new American nation was compelled to elevate the level of tolerance it was willing to display toward a foreign population caught in its midst, and in that way it too profited from the experience.

Notes

Selected Sources

Index

Notes

Chapter 1. *Jefferson's Louisiana: Land, People, Law*

1. Garrett Elliott Pendergrast, *A Physical and Topographical Sketch of the Mississippi Territory, Lower Louisiana and a Part of West Florida* [Philadelphia, 1803], p. 12; Major Amos Stoddard, *Sketches, Historical and Descriptive, of Louisiana* (Philadelphia, 1812), preface. On the purposes of Stoddard's *Sketches*, see C. A. Newton and J. M. Newton, " 'Not an Enemy of Cession Will Remain': Amos Stoddard's 1812 Assessment of Louisiana," *Louisiana Studies*, 5 (1966), 37-49.

2. Stoddard, *Sketches*, p. 151; [Jacob Wagner (comp.)], *An Account of Louisiana . . .* (Providence, 1803), p. 7. Average time was 8 to 10 days, but sometimes the trip took much longer. It all depended upon the wind direction and river current. Christian Schultz, another early reporter, said that the voyage could take anywhere from 5 to 30 days. He cited one example of a ship from Hamburg that required 76 days to sail from the Balize to New Orleans after an ocean voyage of only 65 days (*Travels on an Inland Voyage . . . performed in the years 1807 and 1808 . . .* , 2 vols. [New York, 1810], II, 209).

3. Alexander to Archibald Somerville, April 23, 1804, in Van Duzer Miscelleanous Papers, New York Historical Society.

4. Berquin-Duvallon, *Vue de la Colonie Espagnole du Mississippi ou des Provinces de la Louisiane . . . en l'Annee 1802* (Paris, 1803), trans. John Davis as *Travels in Louisiana and the Floridas* (New York, 1806), p. 19.

5. Alexander to Archibald Somerville, April 23, 1804, Van Duzer Miscellaneous Papers, New York Historical Society.

6. Berquin-Duvallon, *Travels*, p. 16; Henry M. Brackenridge, *Views of Louisiana . . . in 1811* (Baltimore, 1817), p. 311; John G. Clark, *New Orleans, 1718-1812: An Economic History* (Baton Rouge, Louisiana University Press, 1970), p. 52.

7. Berquin-Duvallon, *Travels*, p. 35; *Account of Louisiana*, p. 25; Anna Maria Peters to John Peters, March (?), 1807, Peters Family Letters, New York Public Library, Astor, Lenox and Tilden Foundations.

8. Christian Schultz, *Inland Voyage*, II, 176-177; F. M. Perrin du Lac, *Voyage dans les deux Louisianes . . . en 1801, 1802, et 1803* (Paris, 1805), trans. as *Travels through the Two Louisianas* (London, 1807), p. 90; John Duffey, "Pestilence in New Orleans," in *The Past as Prelude: New Orleans 1718-1968*, ed. Hodding Carter (New Orleans, Pelican Pub.,1968), pp. 88-115. Governor Claiborne estimated that one-third of the Americans who had recently come to New Orleans died in the

epidemic of 1804. Claiborne's first wife and daughter were among its victims.

9. Berquin-Duvallon, *Travels*, p.24. It was the custom for townspeople to use the river as a common dump for garbage and privy pots. This meant that at low water the beach or *batture* between the levee and the river became a swamp of pollution (Duffey, "Pestilence in New Orleans," pp. 101-102). Many, including Jefferson, attributed the unhealthfulness of New Orleans to the city's numerous public buildings and fortifications which impeded the free circulation of air, thus depriving the residents of the breezes by which the river regularly relieved their suburban and rural neighbors. The President proposed that cities like New Orleans be built or enlarged on a checkerboard pattern to secure open spaces so that "the atmosphere of such a town would be like that of the country, insusceptible of the miasmata which produce yellow fever" (Jefferson to C. F. C. De Volney, Feb. 8, 1805, in *The Writings of Thomas Jefferson*, ed. A. A. Lipscomb and A. E. Bergh (Memorial Ed., 20 vol., Washington, D.C., 1903-1905), XI, 66-67.

10. Schultz, *Inland Voyage*, p. 193; see also William Darby, *A Geographical Description of the State of Louisiana* (Philadelphia, 1816), p. 258.

11. Schultz, *Inland Voyage*, p. 181; Brackenridge, *Views of Louisiana*, p. 304; Berquin-Duvallon, *Travels*, p. 173.

12. The *arpent* was the standard measure of land in French Canada and Louisiana. It was slightly smaller than the acre, although the terms were often used interchangeably.

13. See illustration and explanation of this point in Fred B. Kniffen, *Louisiana: Its Land and People* (Baton Rouge, Louisiana State University Press, 1968), p. 128. On the effects of partible inheritance upon the standard lot see p. 122. The existence of double and triple lots is noted in *Account of Louisiana*, p. 43.

14. Victor Collot, *A Journey in North America* (3 vols., Paris, 1826; reprint, Florence, O. Lange, 1924), II, 168.

15. *Account of Louisiana*, p. 65; Darby, *Geographical Description*, pp. 173-222, *et passim*; *National Intelligencer*, Sept. 19, 1806; Stoddard, *Sketches*, p. 162.

16. William Darby, *The Emigrant's Guide to the Western and Southwestern States and Territories* . . . (New York, 1818), pp. 44-49; "Table of average distance from each county to New Orleans," Joseph Dubreuil de Villars Papers, Duke University; Kniffen, *Louisiana*, p. 142.

17. Kniffen, *Louisiana*, pp.142-144.

18. Magruder, *A Letter from Allan B. Magruder of Opelousas* . . . (New Orleans, 1808), pp. 5-11; B. Van Pradelles to Albert Gallatin, Jan. 9/16, 1806, Gallatin Papers, New York Historical Society; David Parmelee to Jefferson, Aug. 28, 1806, Jefferson Papers, Colonial Williamsburg Collection; Darby, *Emigrant's* Guide, p. 72; François D'Annemours, *Memoire sur le District de Ouachita dans la Province de la Louisiane* (1803), Madeira-Vaughan Collection, American Philosophical Society.

19. Jefferson to Timothy Bloodsworth, Jan. 29, 1804, in Jefferson, *Writings*, ed. Lipscomb and Bergh, X, 445.

20. *Account of Louisiana*, pp. 27-28; General Census (1807), Dubreuil Papers, Duke University; Jedediah Morse, *American Gazeteer* (3rd ed., Boston, 1810), appendix; Stoddard, *Sketches*, p. 151; Charles L. Dufour, "The People of New Orleans," in Carter, ed., *Past As Prelude*, p. 37. The 8,000 figure for 1803 is the most reliable, but there is good evidence that it is too high. A local census, commissioned by the city in 1805 and conducted by one Matthew Flanner, estimated the population to have been only 6,000 in 1803 (*New Orleans in 1805: A Directory and a Census* [New Orleans, 1936], p. 11). Use of this figure would serve to dramatize even more the rate of increase. Compared to other territories, however, the increase in Louisiana was modest. For example, the populations of Mississippi and Indiana between 1800 and 1810 grew 356 per cent and 334 per cent respectively. See Francis S. Philbrick, *The Rise of the West, 1754-1830* (New York, Harper and Row, 1965), p. 318.

21. Clark, *New Orleans*, pp. 275-276, 279, 317-318.

22. Berquin-Duvallon, *Travels*, p. 42; Schultz, *Inland Voyage*, p. 199; Kniffen, *Louisiana*, p. 127.

23. General Census (1807), Dubreuil Papers, Duke Univeristy; *New Orleans in 1805: A Directory and a Census*, p. 107; John S. Kendall, "New Orleans' 'Peculiar Institution'," *Louisiana Historical Quarterly*, 23 (1940), 864-886; James E. Winston, "The Free Negro in New Orleans, 1803-1860," *ibid.*, 21 (1938), 1075-1085; Annie Lee West Stahl, "The Free Negro in Ante-Bellum Louisiana," *ibid.*, 25 (1942), 301-396; Donald E. Everett, "Free Persons of Color in Colonial Louisiana," *Louisiana History*, 7 (1966), 21-50, and Donald E. Everett, "Emigres and Militiamen: Free Persons of Color in New Orleans, 1803-1815," *Journal of Negro History*, 38 (1953), 377-402.

24. The best discussion is Joseph G. Tregle, Jr., "Early New Orleans Society: A Reappraisal," *Journal of Southern History*, 18 (1952), 20-36. Tregle has exploded the myth that the Creoles were more refined and better educated than the "barbarous" Americans who descended upon Louisiana after 1803. Tregle's study is based upon materials of the 1820's and 1830's, but his conclusions hold for the first decades of the nineteenth century.

25. The most accurate and comprehensive tabulation of the eighteenth-century Acadian population of Louisiana can be found in Jacqueline Voorhies, *Some Late Eighteenth-Century Louisianians* (The University of Southwestern Louisiana History Series, Lafayette, Louisiana, 1973), pt. 3. See also, Kniffen, *Louisiana*, p. 127; Dufour, "People of New Orleans," pp. 33-35; Clark, *New Orleans*, pp. 185-187.

26. Tregle, "Early New Orleans Society," pp. 30-32.

27. Marcel Giraud, *Histoire de la Louisiane Française* (3 vols., Paris, Presses Universitaires de France, 1966), vol. III, pt. 2, chap. 7, pt. 3, chap. 3; J. Hanno Deiler, *The Settlement of the German Coast of Louisiana and the Creoles of German Descent* (Philadelphia, 1909; rep. Baltimore, Genealogical Pub. Co., 1970), pp. 116-127. Glenn R.

Conrad suggests that Deiler seriously overestimated the number of German immigrants who came to Louisiana in this period. See *Immigration and War: Louisiana, 1718-1721, from the Memoir of Charles le Gac*, trans. and ed., G. R. Conrad (USL History Series, Lafayette, Louisiana, 1970), pp. 40n, 51n, 56n; and *ibid.*, appendix A (p. 64), for a contemporary report on the composition of the immigrant population between 1717 and 1721. On this point see also René Le Conte, "The Germans in Louisiana in the Eighteenth Century," trans. G. R. Conrad, *Louisiana History*, 8 (1967), 67-84, which is the most concentrated treatment of German settlement in early Louisiana.

28. *Account of Louisiana*, pp. 18-19; Kniffen, *Louisiana*, pp. 129-130; Clark, *New Orleans*, p. 186.

29. There was, in fact, a "solid nucleus of an American elite" in New Orleans in the 1790's (Clark, *New Orleans*, pp. 350-351).

30. Thus, the population of Natchitoches, a settlement which remained predominantly French in this period, increased by only 400 (from 2,417 to 2,870) between 1807 and 1810, while Rapides, the nearest Red River community and largely American, increased by several thousand (from 2,473 to 4,573). See Morse, *Gazeteer*, appendix; General Census, Dubreuil Papers, Duke University; *Account of Louisiana*, pp. 23-24.

31. John G. Clark has noted this tendency of factional disputes to cut across ethnic lines (*New Orleans*, p. 277). Nevertheless, Clark does find a significant ethnic conflict in early nineteenth-century Louisiana. He speaks of "French" and "American" factions or parties in the territorial period (e.g., p. 347). William Darby spoke of the hatred between the two nations resident in Lower Louisiana. He placed most of the blame on the Americans (*Geographical Description*, p. 266). See also Lewis W. Newton, "Creoles and Anglo-Americans in Old Louisiana: A Study in Cultural Conflicts," *Southwestern Social Science Quarterly*, 14 (1933), 31-48.

32. For a more detailed discussion of the points sketched here see Kniffen, *Louisiana*, chap.23. Kniffen argues that the Anglo-American —French split has permanently affected the political life of the state and that traces of it are discernible even today. Anglo-American culture predominated in the north, the northwest, and the "Florida parishes" east of Baton Rouge. French Louisiana was the delta region, including the Atchafalaya Basin and the lower Mississippi. These zones of cultural as well as physical demarcation are still basic divisions in the complex geography of the state of Louisiana (see *ibid.*, map on p. 5, and pp. 7-9). In general Kniffen's geography is a fascinating work of central importance to an understanding of Louisiana history. For an interesting discussion of the French Creole's life style and his attitude toward Americans, see John Anthony Caruso, *The Mississippi Valley Frontier: The Age of French Exploration and Settlement* (New York, Bobbs Merrill, 1966), pp. 360-361, *et passim.*

33. Berquin-Duvallon, *Travels*, p. 48; Clark, *New Orleans*, p. 313.

34. Dufour, "People of New Orleans," p. 37; Schultz, *Inland Voyage*, p. 192; Berquin-Duvallon thought the English—not the

Americans—were the largest single group (*Travels*, p. 48). Vincent Nolte, an agent for certain European business interests who was resident in New Orleans in 1806 and 1807, estimated that the French (black and white) constituted three-fifths of the total number of inhabitants, the other two-fifths consisting of Spanish, Americans, and Germans (*Fifty Years in Both Hemispheres* . . . [New York, 1854], p. 86).

35. Gurley to Gideon Granger, July 14, 1804, Jefferson Papers, Library of Congress (LC). Gurley mistakenly estimated that the American and French populations of New Orleans were already equal in 1804.

36. For example, few Americans were available for militia duty at the time of the Battle of New Orleans in 1814-15. See Jane Lucas de Grummond, *The Baratarians and the Battle of New Orleans* (Baton Rouge, Louisiana State University Press, 1961), p. 11.

37. The architectural style of the Faubourg was decidedly different from that of the *Vieux Carré*. It was "a kind of Philadelphia suburb in the tropics" (James M. Fitch, "Creole Architecture 1718-1860: The Rise and Fall of a Great Traditon," in Carter,ed., *Past as Prelude*, p. 84).

38. Schultz, *Inland Voyage*, p. 196.

39. Anna Maria Peters, who arrived in the spring of 1807, wrote to her father in New York that she preferred to stay at home with her books and music rather than mingle with "the unpolished, and illiterate inhabitants, who have never left the woods of Louisiana." She enjoyed New Orleans only because of the "circle of Americans, who are extremely fond of giving their large and unceremonious parties." (Anna Maria Peters to John Peters, [n.d.] Peters Family Letters, New York Public Library, Astor, Lenox and Tilden Foundations).

40. Tregle, "Early New Orleans Society," pp. 29-30; Caruso, *Mississippi Valley Frontier*, p. 360; Clark, *New Orleans*, pp. 313-315; Jo Ann Carrigan, "Impact of Epidemic Yellow Fever on Life in Louisiana," *Louisiana History*, 4 (1963), 5-34, esp. 6-7. Interestingly enough, methods for treating the disease differed by ethnic group. The "French School" prescribed cold water baths; the Americans adopted more radical measures: bloodletting and mercury poisoning. See Duffy, "Pestilence in New Orleans," pp. 102-104.

41. Newton, "Creoles and Anglo-Americans," p. 33. For an analysis of how the French, through provisions of the first Louisiana constitution, attempted to forestall the inevitable political domination of Louisiana by incoming American settlers, see Joseph G. Tregle, Jr., "Political Reinforcement of Ethnic Dominance in Louisiana, 1812-1845," in *The Americanization of the Gulf Coast, 1803-1850*, ed. L. F. Ellsworth, Proceedings of the Gulf Coast History and Humanities Conference, Pensacola, Fla., 3 (1971), 78-87.

42. In using the term "legal tradition" rather than "legal system" I am following John Henry Merryman's *The Civil Law Tradition: An Introduction to the Legal Systems of Western Europe and Latin America* (Stanford, Stanford University Press, 1969). For his discussion of the difference between legal systems and a legal tradition, see pp. 1-2.

43. Throughout the text, the term "civil law" will be used to refer to

those legal systems which are fundamentally derived from Roman law and the Roman legal tradition.

44. English and America "common law" must be distinguished from the "common law of Europe" (*jus commun*) or the local custom of a particular region. Thus the French *droit commun* is not the equivalent of Anglo-American common law. A mid-nineteenth-century contrast of the two traditions can be found in the "Report on Civil and Common Law" prepared by the California Senate Committee on the Judiciary, Feb. 27, 1850, in 1 Calif. Reports 588 (1851), appendix. California was then confronted with what Louisiana had faced two generations before, and while the situations were not parallel, many of the same problems recurred (see *ibid*,. pp. 601-603).

45. New England opponents of the Louisiana cession, Federalist and Republican alike, played upon—but did not invent—this theme in their long but futile effort to obstruct American absorption of the new territory. In opposing the Louisiana Government Bill in February 1804, for example, William Eustis, moderate Massachusetts Republican, said that "the people of this country [i.e., Louisiana] differ materially from the citizens of the United States. I speak of the character of the people at the present time" (U.S. Congress, *Debates and Proceedings* [42 vols., Washington, D.C., 1834-1856], 8th Cong., 1st sess. [Feb. 28, 1804], p. 1058). And, in 1811, in the debate over statehood, Josiah Quincy, the Massachusetts Federalist, insisted that the people of Louisiana "may be girt upon us for a moment, but no real cement can grow from such an association" (*ibid.*, 11th Cong., 3rd sess., [Jan. 14, 1811], p. 536). Even Thomas Jefferson must have had doubts when he observed that "the Constitution had made no provision for our holding foreign territory, still less for incorpating foreign nations into our union" (Jefferson to John Breckinridge, Aug. 12, 1803, in Jefferson, *Writings*, ed. Lipscomb and Bergh, X, 411).

46. Louisiana, *Digest of the Civil Laws Now in Force in the Territory of Orleans with Alterations and Amendments Adapted to its Present System of Government* (New Orleans, 1808), Bk. 3, tit. 5, arts. 63-85, pp. 336-340. (Although the Digest of 1808 did alter the law which had been in force in Louisiana in 1803 in some particulars, it is still the most convenient source of Louisiana law as it existed at the time of the cession.) See Harriett S. Daggett, *The Community Property System of Louisiana* (Baton Rouge, Louisiana State University Press, 1945), chaps. 1-3 *et passim*; also, *idem*, "The Civil Law Concept of the Wife's Position in the Family," *Oregon Law Review*, 15 (1936), 291-305.

47. James Kent, *Commentaries on American Law* (12th ed., 4 vols.; Boston, Little Brown, 1884), II, 129ff.; Sir William Blackstone, *Commentaries on the Laws of England* (4 vols.; 1765-1769), I, 430. The extent to which American law mitigated the rigors of the English law of husband and wife is shown in Richard B. Morris, *Studies in the History of American Law: With Special Reference to the Seventeenth and Eighteenth Centuries* (New York, Columbia University Press, 1930), chap. 3; and Lawrence M. Friedman, *A History of American Law* (New York, Simon and Schuster, 1973), pp. 184-185. On the wife's legal

advantages in the civil law marriage regime and its superiority over the old common law dower, see Daggett, *Community Property System*, pp.33ff., 159, 178, 184, *et passim*. Also, *idem*, "General Principles of Succession on Death in Civil Law," *Tulane Law Review*, II (1937), 410.

48. Blackstone, *Commentaries*, I, 443.

49. Jean Brissaud, *A History of French Private Law*, trans. Rapelje Howell (Boston, Little Brown, 1912; reprint, 1968), pp. 213-215.

50. *The Laws of Las Siete Partidas which are still in force in the state of Louisiana*, trans. L. Moreau Lislet and Henry Carleton (2 vols., New Orleans, 1820), I, 553; Louisiana, *Digest* (1808), Bk. I, tit. 7, arts. 21-34, pp. 48-50; Bk. III, tit. 1, arts. 43-50, pp. 154-156; Robert A. Pascal, "Louisiana Succession and Related Laws and the Illegitimate: Thoughts Prompted by *Labine* v. *Vincent*, *Tulane Law Review*, 46 (1971), 167-183; Robert A. Pascal, "The Civil Law and Its Study," in *Continental and American Law: Insights and Contrasts*, seminar sponsored by Louisiana State University Law School, Rome, Italy, 1971 (published by LSU Law School and Development Fund of LSU Foundation), pp. 6-7; K. W. Ryan, *An Introduction to the Civil Law* (Brisbane, Law Book Co., 1962), p. 278. For some examples of the gradual mitigation of American law on illegitimates consult Kent, *Commentaries*, II, 209-217, and IV, 413-418.

51. Louisiana, *Digest* (1808), Bk. III, tit. 2, arts. 19-22, 126-130; pp. 212-214, 234-236; H. S. Daggett, "General Principles of Succession on Death in Civil Law," *Tulane Law Review*, 11 (1937), 399-411; Joseph Dainow, "The Early Sources of Forced Heirship: Its History in Texas and Louisiana," *Louisiana Law Review*, 4 (1941), 42-69; R. W. Lee, "The Civil Law and the Common Law: A World Survey," *Michigan Law Review*, 14 (1915), 89-101, at p. 98; Blackstone, *Commentaries*, II, 13-14, 503, 492-493, 496-497; Kent, *Commentaries*, IV, 519-520. But on this point see *ibid.*, pp. 525-527, for state statutes governing revocation of will which went far toward mitigation of the stricter rules of English law.

52. Pascal, "The Civil Law and Its Study," pp. 3-4.

53. On the divergences of early American law from English real property law, see Morris, *Studies in the History of American Law*, chap. 2; Marshall Harris, *Orgin of the Land Tenure System in the United States* (Ames, Iowa, Iowa State College Press, 1953), pp. 354-366, 405-411; and George L. Haskins, "The Beginnings of Partible Inheritance in the American Colonies," *Yale Law Journal*, 51 (1941-42), 1280-1315. In general, see Friedman, *History of American Law*, pp. 51-57.

54. Two generations after the Revolution James Kent would observe: "In passing from the subject of personal to that of real property, the student will immediately perceive that the latter is governed by rules of distinct and peculiar character. The law concerning real property forms a technical and very artificial system; and though it has felt the influence of the free and commercial spirit of modern ages, it is still very much under the control of principles derived from the feudal policy. We have either never introduced into the

jurisprudence of this country, or we have, in the course of improvements upon our municipal law, abolished all the essential badges of the law of feuds; but the deep traces of that policy are visible in every part of the doctrine of real estates, and the technical language, and many of the technical rules and fictions of that system, are still retained" (*Commentaries*, II, 533). In general, see James Sullivan, *History of Land Titles in Massachusetts* (Boston, 1801).

55. Henry A. Bullard, "Discourse Delivered before the Historical Society of Louisiana," Jan. 13, 1836, in B. F. French, comp., *Historical Collections of Louisiana* (5 vols., New York, 1846-1853), I, 15-16; Stoddard, *Sketches*, p. 270.

56. Letter of Charles Watts to William Sampson [n.d.], in *Sampson's Discourse and Correspondence with Various Learned Jurists upon the History of the Law* . . . (Washington, 1826), pp. 76-77.

57. Ryan, *Introduction to the Civil Law*, pp. 156-160; Phaner J. Eder, *A Comparative Survey of Anglo-American and Latin American Law* (New York, New York University Press, 1950), chap. 5.

58. Friedman, *History of American Law*, pp. 210-212, 221-224.

59. Louisiana, *Digest* (1808), Bk. III, tit. 2, art. 40, p. 216.

60. Eugene A. Nabors, "Restrictions Upon the Ownership of Property in Louisiana: Trusts, Fidei Commissa and Substitutions," *Tulane Law Review*, 4 (1929), 1-17; Robert A. Pascal, "Some ABC's about Trusts and Us," *Louisiana Law Review*, 13 (1953), 555-568, *esp.* 556-557; and Robert A. Pascal, "The Trust Concept and Substitution," *Louisiana Law Review*, 19 (1959), 273-286.

61. Louisiana, *Digest* (1808), Bk. III, tit. 3, arts. 31-33, p. 264; George M. Snellings, Jr., "Cause and Consideration in Louisiana," *Tulane Law Review*, 8 (1934), 178-214; Eder, *Comparative Survey*, pp. 131-132; Pascal, "The Civil Law and Its Study," p.5.

62. Blackstone, *Commentaries*, II, 447-448, 452; III, 165; Kent, *Commentaries*, II, 478-482; Friedman, *History of American Law*, pp. 233-235; Louisiana, *Digest* (1808), Bk. III, tit. 6, arts. 65-81, 109-117, pp. 356-360, 364-366; 1 Calif. Reports 595 (1851), appendix.

63. Louisiana, *Digest* (1808), Bk. 1, tit. 8, arts. 11-31, 51-77, pp. 60-72; Kent, *Commentaries*, II, 225-231; Lee, "The Civil Law and the Common Law," pp. 94-95.

64. Louisiana, *Digest* (1808), Bk. III, tit. 18, arts. 1-21, pp. 446-448; *Laws of Las Siete Partidas*, trans. Moreau Lislet and Carleton, II, 888-892; Kent, *Commentaries*, II, 577-586. In general the law of pledge was much better developed in civil law than in common law in this period. See Henry Denis, "The Analogies and Differences of the Civil and the Common Law," *American Law Review*, 33 (1899), 28-41.

65. Louisiana, *Digest* (1808), Bk. III, tit. 3, arts. 217-236, pp. 304-308, *et passim; Laws of Las Siete Partidas*, trans. Moreau Lislet and Carleton, I, 244-257; Louis Baudouin, "Le Notariat," *Revue du Notariat*, 67 (1964), 167-191; Edgar Grima, "The Notarial System of Louisiana," *Louisiana Historical Quarterly*, 10 (1927), 76-81.

66. William Geldart, *Elements of English Law* (7th ed., London, Oxford University Press, 1966), pp. 2-9; Morton J. Horwitz,

"The Emergence of an Instrumental Conception of American Law, 1780-1820," in *Perspectives in American History*, ed. D. Fleming and B. Bailyn, 5 (1971), 287-326; but see J. Willard Hurst, *The Growth of American Law: The Law Makers* (Boston, Little Brown, 1950), chaps. 2, 4. For a classic formulation of the role of courts in the common law system, see Oliver Wendell Holmes, Jr., "The Path of the Law," in *Collected Legal Papers* (New York, Harcourt, Brace and Howe, 1920), pp. 167-202, esp. 167-168, 173.

67. Pascal, "The Civil Law and Its Study," pp.7-9.

68. For the role of equity in the growth of English law, see S. F. C. Milsom, *Historical Foundations of the Common Law* (London, Butterworths, 1969), pp. 74-87; and René David and John E. C. Brierley, *Major Legal Systems in the World Today: An Introduction to the Comparative Study of Law* (New York, The Free Press, 1968), pp. 273-279.

69. On the importance of procedure in the common law tradition, see David and Brierley, *Major Legal Systems*, pp. 270-271. For the early development of the jury, see Sir Frederick Pollock and Frederic W. Maitland, *The History of English Law before the Time of Edward I* (2 vols., 2nd ed.; London, Cambridge University Press, 1968), II, 598-673. For the place of procedure in the development of the modern civil law, see John H. Merryman, *The Civil Law Tradition: An Introduction to the Legal Systems of Western Europe and Latin America* (Stanford, Stanford University Press, 1969), chap. 16.

70. Judicial administration as it existed under the Spanish is described in *Account of Louisiana*, pp. 46-54. For analysis of early Louisiana civil procedure consult H. P. Dart, "The Legal Institutions of Louisiana," *Louisiana Historical Quarterly*, 2 (1919), 72-103; and, *idem*, "Courts and Law in Colonial Louisiana," *Reports of the Louisiana Bar Association*, 22 (1921), 17-63. A legislative attempt, in 1806, to declare Spanish law in force by general reference specifically provided for the adoption of trial by jury and the writ of habeas corpus. See Elizabeth G. Brown, "Legal Systems in Conflict: Orleans Territory, 1804-1812," *American Journal of Legal History*, 1 (1957), 35-75, at 46-48. The objection to the use of juries in civil causes is noted in Stoddard, *Sketches*, p. 281. Suspicion of the "prodigious number of lawyers" who had suddenly descended upon Lower Louisiana is reflected in [Pierre Derbigny], *Esquisse de la Situation Politique et Civile de la Louisiane* . . . (New Orleans, 1804), pp. 34-35; and, *Instructions from the Inhabitants of the Territory of Orleans to Their Representatives in the Legislature* [New Orleans, 1805], p. 1, *et passim*.

71. See below, chaps. 5-6, *passim*.

72. The Louisiana land claims question is not analyzed in the text, partly because the subject has been treated in depth in numerous published works. The most recent study of this complex problem is Malcolm J. Rohrbough's *The Land Office Business: The Settlement and Administration of American Public Lands, 1789-1837* (New York, Oxford University Press, 1968), esp. pp. 38-50, 161-164. Of particular importance is the work of Harry L. Coles, "The Applicability of the

Public Land System to Louisiana," *Mississippi Valley Historical Review*, 44 (1956), 39-58, and "The Confirmation of Foreign Land Titles in Louisiana," *Louisiana Historical Quarterly*, 38 (1955), 1-22. Also useful are the related studies of C. Richard Arena, "Landholding and Political Power in Spanish Louisiana," *Louisiana Historical Quarterly*, 38 (1955), 23-39; Leslie Moses, "The History of Land Titles in Louisiana," *Southwestern Law Journal*, 7 (1953), 64-75; and Francis P. Burns, "The Spanish Land Laws of Louisiana," *Louisiana Historical Quarterly*, 11 (1928), 557-581.

73. See below, chap. 4.

Chapter 2. William C. C. Claiborne and the Politics of Territorial Government

1. There are numerous books detailing the complex negotiations between the U.S. and France which led to the purchase of Louisiana. The standard accounts are E. W. Lyon, *Louisiana in French Diplomacy, 1759-1804* (Norman, University of Oklahoma Press, 1934), and A. P. Whitaker, *The Mississippi Question, 1795-1803: A Study in Trade, Politics, and Diplomacy* (Gloucester, Mass., Peter Smith, 1934). The best discussion and analysis of the relevant constitutional issues and the debates in Congress is Everett S. Brown, *The Constitutional History of the Louisiana Purchase, 1803-1812*, University of California Publications in History, vol. X (Berkeley, 1920). Also useful in this connection is Thomas J. Farnham, "The Federal-State Issue and the Louisiana Purchase," *Louisiana History*, 6 (1965), 5-25. For an up-to-date discussion of the main issues surrounding the Purchase which contains an abundance of bibliographical material, see Marshall Smelser, *The Democratic-Republic, 1801—1815*, The New American Nation Series (New York, Harper and Row, 1968), chap. 5.

2. As one correspondent explained, " . . . it will be best for us to have no more Territory beyond the Mississippi than what is necessary to secure the Navigation; now *to ascertain, extend, establish, and maintain the Frontiers* . . . [of] Louisiana, would be *expensive, troublesome, dangerous and consequently impolitic in the highest degree.* —But to obtain east and west Florida, *would be the reverse*" [original italics]. Thomas M. Potter to Jefferson, Sept. 17, 1804, in Jefferson Papers, Library of Congress (LC). See also James Monroe to James Madison, May 18, 1803, in *The Writings of James Monroe*, ed. S. M. Hamilton (7 vols., New York, 1898, reprint, 1969), IV, 25-26. Both Jefferson and Madison specifically rejected the idea of exchanging Louisiana, or any portion of it, for West Florida because they both believed that American acquisition of this key area was only a matter of time. See Jefferson to John Dickinson, Aug. 9, 1803, in *The Writings of Thomas Jefferson*, ed. P. L. Ford (10 vols., New York, 1892-1899), VIII, 261-263; Madison to Monroe, July 29, 1803, in *The Writings of James Madison*, ed. Gaillard Hunt (9 vols., New York, Putnam's Sons, 1900-1910), VII, 57-58. On this point, also consult Francis S. Philbrick,

The Rise of the West, 1754-1830 (New York, Harper and Row, 1965), pp. 217-218, 233. On the "essential unity of the region" (i.e., New Orleans and West Florida) see Isaac Joslin Cox, *The West Florida Controversy, 1798-1813: A Study in American Diplomacy* (Baltimore, 1918; reprint, Gloucester, Mass., Peter Smith, 1967), pp. 1-6.

3. Jefferson to Robert R. Livingston, April 18, 1802, in *The Writings of Thomas Jefferson*, ed. A. A. Lipscomb and A. E. Bergh (Memorial Ed., 20 vols., Washington, D.C., 1903-1905), X, 314-315; Jefferson to Monroe, Jan. 13, 1803, *ibid.*, p.344; Jefferson to William C. C. Claiborne, May 24, 1803, *ibid.*, p.391; Madison to Livingston and Monroe, March 2, 1803, in Madison, *Writings*, ed., Hunt, VII, 9; Livingston to Madison, April 11, 1803, quoted in Henry Adams, *History of the United States of America during the First Administration of Thomas Jefferson* (2 vols., New York, 1889), II, 27; Monroe to Madison, May 18, 1803, in Monroe, *Writings*, ed. Hamilton, IV, 26. In general, see Adams, *History of the United States*, vol. II, chaps. 3, 12, 13; and Dumas Malone, *Jefferson the President: First Term, 1801-1805* (Boston, Little Brown, 1970), pp. 303-309, 342-347, *et passim*. In the early days of the Jefferson Administration Albert Gallatin considered West Florida even more vital than New Orleans itself: see Gallatin to Madison, Feb. 7, 1803, in *Letters and Other Writings of James Madison* (4 vols., Philadelphia, 1865), II, 179-180.

4. Kenneth Drude, "Fort Baton Rouge," *Louisiana Studies*, 7 (1968), 259-269.

5. William Darby, *A Geographical Description of the State of Louisiana* (Philadelphia, 1816), p. 188; Charles Gayarré, *History of Louisiana* (4 vols., New Orleans, 1885), IV, 404. Wilburt S. Brown, a military historian, considers the Rigolets to have been "the most strategic spot in Louisiana" (*The Amphibious Campaign for West Florida and Louisiana, 1814-1815: A Critical Review of Strategy and Tactics at New Orleans*, [University, Ala., University of Alabama Press, 1969], p. 65).

6. Richard P. Weinert, "The Neglected Key to the Gulf Coast," *Journal of Mississippi History*, 31 (1969), 269-301.

7. The regular mail to New Orleans usually went by way of Fort Stoddert (on the Tombigbee River) and Mobile Bay, a route which depended on Spanish goodwill. See the Postmaster General's report on the best routes to New Orleans, Gideon Granger to Jefferson, Feb. 6, 1805, Jefferson Papers, LC; and Cox, *West Florida Controversy*, pp. 171-172. In short, as Cox put it, "West Florida was necessary for the defense of New Orleans" (*ibid.*, p. 101).

8. Wilkinson to Henry Dearborn, Jan. 11, 1804, in Clarence E. Carter, ed., *The Territorial Papers of the United States* (26 vols., Washington, D.C., Government Printing Office, 1934-1962), IX, 159.

9. Andrew Jackson's strategic problem, only ten years later, was far different from Wilkinson's. By 1814, the only important military position along the various approaches to New Orleans not in American hands was Ship Island. The resulting tactical dilemmas facing the British are discussed in Hugh F. Rankin, "The British at New Orleans: Strategy or Blunder?" *Louisiana Studies*, 4 (1965), 179-186, and John K.

Mahan, "British Command Decisions Relative to the Battle of New Orleans," *Louisiana History*, 6 (1965), 53-76. British preference for the route of advance they eventually adopted was apparently longstanding. See Joseph G. Tregle, Jr., "British Spy along the Mississippi: Thomas Hutchins and the Defense of New Orleans, 1773," *Louisiana History*, 8 (1967), 313-327. For the strategic situation as Jackson saw it, see Brown, *Amphibious Campaign*, pp. 64-69.

10. For a detailed accounting of the numbers of troops in Upper and Lower Louisiana at the end of 1804 see the report sent by Secretary of War Dearborn to Jefferson, Nov. 29, 1804, in Jefferson Papers, LC. Gallatin repeatedly urged the building up of forts St. John and Plaquemines. See Gallatin to Jefferson, Nov. 16, 1806, and July 25, 1807, in *The Writings of Albert Gallatin*, ed. Henry Adams (3 vols., Philadelphia, 1879), I, 317, 344. On gunboat deployment, Jefferson to Dearborn, April 26, 1806, and Jefferson to Claiborne, April 27, 1806, in Jefferson Papers, LC. During Jefferson's presidency twenty gunboats were stationed on the Mississippi at New Orleans (Brown, *Amphibious Campaign*, p. 72; Dumas Malone, *Jefferson the President: Second Term, 1805-1809* [Boston, Little Brown, 1974], p. 502). On the Carondelet Canal, see Jefferon's Special Message to Congress, Jan. 6, 1809, in *Writings*, ed. Lipscomb and Bergh, III, 487-488.

11. See below, Chap. 6, sec. VI.

12. Before 1822 other territorial governors were paid only $2,000 per annum (Jack C. Eblen, *The First and Second United States Empires: Governors and Territorial Government, 1784-1912* [Pittsburgh, University of Pittsburgh Press, 1968], p. 311).

13. On Claiborne's early career see Joseph T. Hatfield, "William C. C. Claiborne, Congress and Republicanism, 1797-1804," *Tennessee Historical Quarterly*, 24 (1965), 156-180. For a brief sketch of his public life, See John D. Winters, "William C. C. Claiborne: 'Profile of a Democrat,' " *Louisiana History*, 10 (1969), 189-209.

14. Walter Prichard, "Selecting a Governor for the Territory of Orleans," *Louisiana Historical Quarterly*, 31 (1948), 269-393.

15. The territorial governors have even been compared to intelligence officers for the federal government. See Eblen, *First and Second Empires*, p. 201.

16. There were, as Eblen points out, modular differences in the office of the American territorial governor and the Britih colonial governors. For example, the salary of the territorial governors was fixed and appropriated by Congress—not, as in some of the original thirteen colonies, by the local assembly. Nevertheless, though the territorial governor's powers were somewhat greater than those of his British colonial counterpart, their experience proved to be very similar. In both cases extensive executive powers were whittled away by local political forces. While the territory of Orleans was an atypical case, in important respects it was illustrative of many of the points Eblen has made in his comprehensive analysis. On these points and those in the text, see *ibid.*, pp. 49-51, 201, 300-301. On the experience of the British colonial governors in pre-Revolutionary America see Bernard Bailyn, *The Origins of American Politics* (New York, Knopf, 1968), chap. 2.

17. Dr. O. H. Spencer to Nathaniel Evans, [Dec. 20, 1803], Nathaniel Evans Papers, Louisiana State University, Baton Rouge, Louisiana.

18. Briggs to Jefferson, Jan. 2, 1804, in *Territorial Papers*, ed. Carter, IX, 147.

19. Claiborne to Madison, Jan. 10, 1804, in *Official Letter Books of W. C. C. Claiborne, 1801-1816*, ed. Dunbar Rowland (6 vols., Jackson, Miss., 1917), I, 331.

20. Claiborne to Madison, Jan. 31, 1804, *ibid.*, p. 355.

21. Claiborne and Wilkinson to Madison, Feb. 7, 1804, in Carter, ed., *Territorial Papers*, IX, 177; deposition of George Morgan, Jan. 28, 1804, *ibid.*, p. 180; Boré to Jefferson, Feb. 10, 1804, *ibid.*, p. 184. The city council acted to contain future disturbances. On Jan. 25 it established regulations governing the conduct of public dances. See Records of the City Council, vol. I, no. 1, pp. 26-28, in New Orleans Public Library.

22. The problem of the public festivities was the most dramatic incidence of ethnic conflict, but others occurred. For example, in July the Americans objected violently to French observance of Bastille Day (see Claiborne to Madison, July 16, 1804, *Letter Books*, II, 249). Another outbreak, triggered by a personal feud, took place in October (Claiborne to Madison, Oct. 19, 1804, *ibid.*, 367, and Captain Sterrett to Nathaniel Evans, Oct. 22, 1804, Nathaniel Evans Papers, LSU). James Sterrett was a captain of troops stationed in New Orleans. He wrote frequently to Evans, postmaster, planter, and merchant at Fort Adams in the Mississippi territory. His most interesting letters reflect the ethnic conflict between the French and the Americans. Some are particularly colorful. June 23, 1804: "A few days ago a Company of Mulatoes paraded at the Governor's to receive a stand of Colours that His Excellency was pleased to present them with—His guard were placed round the Square to keep off the mob and one of Michlenberg's men struck a French man (that crowded on him) with his gun. The French man enter'd a Complaint and this day we are to try the Soldier—the other Soldiers Swear hard in favor of their mess mate—and the French Men Swear equally hard against him—some of those little *Frog eaters* will get themselves into trouble, I foresee." Nov. 26, 1804: "The people here are not very tranquil—we had a hell of a dust the other evening about arresting and Confining a Spanish Captain—the story is too long to tell. You'l See it all in the news papers—our troops were under arms and things looked for a few Minutes a little Squally—all things now go on smoothly." Dec. 17, 1804: "Nothing very important here. Now and then a battle—a few days ago Mr. Abner L. Duncan had a dispute with a French att.y. The dispute became warm [.] Mr. D. took the French-mans Stick from him and was So *impolite* as to knock him down—The French-man is no less a personage than Chevalier De Moyet— he came from France in the *suite* of Mon.sr Lussatt [Laussatt] the Colonial prefect, and did think on this Occasion that his rank etc etc. was too great to risque a Single Combat with Mr. D. and ran (bleeding in all his glory) to Judge Prevost and made his complaint [.] The Judge of Course had to call up Mr. D. for insulting the Majesty of the law and now the business is before court—So we fight our battles."

Obviously Sterrett was not an impartial observer. His letters betray the decided anti-French bias which was prevalent among Americans in New Orleans at this time.

23. Claiborne to Madison, Jan. 2, 1804, *Letter Books*, I, 328. The belief that the French in the northwest as well as in the southwest were unprepapred for self-government was widespread in this period. See Eblen, *First and Second Empires*, p. 55.

24. Claiborne to Madison, April 14, 1804, *Territorial Papers*, ed. Carter, IX, 220. Claiborne expected the contents of his letter to be made known to Congress, however. See Claiborne to Jefferson, Aug. 30, 1804, *ibid.*, 288.

25. Letter to an unknown correspondent (English translation in typescript), June 2, 1804 (p. 7), Joseph Dubreuil de Villars Papers, Duke University.

26. *Ibid.*, p. 5.

27. Francis Newton Thorpe, comp., *The Federal and State Constitutions, Colonial Charters and Other Organic Laws of the . . . United States of America* (7 vols., Washington, D.C., Government Printing Office, 1909), III, 1364-71.

28. The first organic law for Orleans represented a departure from the traditional pattern of territorial government. In effect, the system it established was midway between the first or "district stage" and the second stage of territorial administration. See Eblen, *First and Second Empires*, pp. 145-147.

29. Thorpe, comp., *Federal and State Constitutions*, III, 1360.

30. This was corrected in the second organic law of March 2, 1805, *ibid.*, p. 1372.

31. Act of March 26, 1804, sec. 4, *ibid.*, p. 1365.

32. Sec. 10, *ibid.*, p. 1368.

33. Historial experience justified this view. A primary cause of economic failure in French Louisiana, prior to 1763, was the decline in Crown support for supplying the colony with an adequate number of slaves. See John G. Clark, *New Orleans, 1718-1812: An Economic History* (Baton Rouge, Louisiana State University Press, 1970), pp. 128-129, 134-135.

34. Claiborne to Madison, March 10/16, 1804, *Letter Books*, II, 25, 42.

35. This is the only mention of Tupper. He apparently played a minor part in the developing opposition to Claiborne.

36. Claiborne to Madison, March 10, 1804, *Letter Books*, II, 26.

37. Claiborne to Madison, March 16, 1804, *ibid.*, p. 46.

38. On May 16, 1804, the mayor of New Orleans, Etienne Boré, in an address to the municipal council, called for a formal protest to Congress (see City Council Records, vol. I, no. 1, p. 94, New Orleans Public Library). Joseph Dubreuil outlined the principal purposes of the memorial: "1st . . . the non-division of the ceded Territory; 2nd . . . the immediate establishment of the said Territory into a free State." Dubreuil's observations are of added interest, because they reveal that,

contrary to the frequent assumption made by many Americans, the Louisianians fully comprehended the workings of a representative system of government. He wrote, "Finally, the Deputies [bearing the memorial to Congress] will be specially instructed to send copies of this memoir to all the legislative bodies of individual States, and to all the printing houses and journalists who have the best reputation and who are most widely known. By this means we would be sure to have as many advocates and supporters with Congress as there may be worthy citizens all over the United States.

"This last step, my dear fellow, is perfectly well planned. In absolute governments, the oppression of an individual is really a special evil about which nobody worries, because from the very nature of things, everyman is left alone and is obliged to fight things out for himself, but under Democratic Constitutions the oppression of one individual is necessarily a general evil, because all rights and liberties included therein are in a real and imminent danger, the minute the public authority dares to violate a single one of the rights of even the most obscure of their citizens."—Letter of June 2, 1804, Dubreuil Papers, Duke University.

39. On the intricate history of the Baron de Bastrop land grant, see J. O. Mitchell and R. D. Calhoun, "The Marquis de Maison Rouge, the Baron de Bastrop, and Col. Abraham Morhouse: Three Ouachita Valley Soldiers of Fortune. The Maison Rouge and Bastrop Spanish Land 'Grant'," *Louisiana Historical Quarterly*, 20 (1937), 289-462.

40. Edward Livingston to Thomas Chase, April 18, 1804, John M. McCalla Papers, Duke University; and E. Livingston to ?, May 13, 1804, Simon Gratz Papers, Historical Society of Pennsylvania.

41. See Part One, "Papers Relating to the Foundations of the Territory of Orleans, 1803," in *Territorial Papers*, ed. Carter, IX, 3-139, for communications between Clark and Madison, and Clark and Claiborne, during the months preceding the transfer. "He pants for power, and is mortified by disappointment," was one characterization of Daniel Clark (*ibid.*, p. 255.). For Clark's business activities, see Clark, *New Orleans*, p. 272.

42. Claiborne to Jefferson, Oct. 13, 1804, *Territorial Papers*, ed. Carter, IX, 310; Claiborne to Madison, July 1, 1804, *Letter Books*, II, 233; Claiborne to Madison, July 13, 1804, *Territorial Papers*, ed. Carter, IX, 261.

43. Claiborne to Madison, June 22, 1804, *Letter Books*, II, 217.

44. Claiborne to Jefferson, July 1, 1804, *Territorial Papers*, ed. Carter, IX, 246.

45. Claiborne's assessment of the memorial was summarized in a November letter: "Whatever may be the fate of the Memorial to Congress," he wrote Madison, "you need not apprehend any disturbances in this quarter. I believe myself a rejection of the Memorial would only be regretted by a few Citizens of New Orleans & its vicinity—unless as it respects the African Trade, & on that subject, the people generally, seem greatly interested" (Nov. 5, 1804, *Territorial Papers*, ed. Carter,

IX, 320). The clearest explanation available to the Administration was that of John Gurley, the land registrar (Gurley to Gideon Granger, July 14, 1804, *ibid.*, 262.).

46. For further discussion of the contents of the memorial, see below, pp. chap. 5, sec. VI.

47. Jefferson to Claiborne, April 17, 1804, *Territorial Papers*, ed. Carter, IX, 225.

48. Claiborne to Jefferson, May 29, 1804, *Letter Books*, II, 175-176.

49. In February 1804 Claiborne had delegated Watkins to visit all of the outlying parishes in order to appoint civil commandants where none existed and to inform those in being to continue. Watkins was instructed to quiet disturbances occasioned by the change in central authority and to reassure the populace of the permanence of American tenure in Louisiana (Claiborne to Watkins, Feb. 9, 1804, and Claiborne to Madison, March 1, 1804, in Territorial Papers, Orleans Series, 1764-1813, National Archives). Watkins also sounded out sentiment on various matters of public concern, in particular the desire of the rural planters to continue slave importations. See his report, *ibid.*, dated [erroneously] Feb. 2, 1804.

50. Jefferson to Claiborne, July 7, 1804, Jefferson Papers, LC.

51. This observation confirms Eblen's view as to the status of parties in the territories (*First and Second Empires*, p. 56).

52. Wilkinson to Jefferson, *Territorial Papers*, ed. Carter, IX, 248-258. This list was rich in detail and much more extensive than Claiborne's would be.

53. Joseph Briggs to Jefferson, Aug. 17, 1804, *ibid.*, p. 276 (the list was enclosed; see pp. 277-278); Claiborne to Jefferson, Aug. 30, 1804, *ibid.*, p. 284.

54. Jefferson to Claiborne, Aug. 30, 1804, *ibid.*, 282. Jefferson was less than candid. Numerous other candidates for the governorship were under consideration. Claiborne was by no means his second choice after Lafayette, but none of the preferred candidates was able to serve. See Prichard, "Selecting a Governor for the Territory of Orleans," *passim*.

55. Dickerson never took office. Jefferson reappointed Kirby to the governorship of the Mississippi territory because he lacked knowledge of French (Jefferson to Kirby, Dec. 1, 1804, Jefferson Papers, LC). He asked James Brown to occupy the post on the Superior Court (Jefferson to Brown, Dec. 1, 1804, *Territorial Papers*, ed. Carter, IX, 341). In Brown's place as territorial secretary he appointed John Graham (Jefferson to Graham, Dec. 1, 1804, *ibid.*, p. 342.) Kirby died soon after his arrival at Fort Stoddert and Brown declined to serve on the court, but Graham did become territorial secretary.

56. Boré had resigned as mayor of New Orleans in June.

57. Jefferson summarized his Orleans appointments in a letter to Dearborn on Sept. 6, 1804. See *Territorial Papers*, ed. Carter, IX, 291.

58. Claiborne to Jefferson, Oct. 5, 1804, *ibid.*, 307. Monroe's suitability was perfectly well known to the President. Unfortunately, Jefferson could not persuade him to accept the job.

59. Jones to Claiborne, Oct. 8, 1804, *Letter Books*, II, 350; Claiborne to Madison, Oct. 8, 1804, *ibid.*, p. 349.

60. The *Telegraphe* published it first on Oct. 10. The *Union* followed on Oct. 15. Even the *Mississippi Herald* of Natchez reprinted it on Oct. 26. See also, Claiborne to Madison, Oct. 13, 1804, *Territorial Papers,* ed. Carter, IX, 310.

61. A point made by one FLAGELLUS in the *Union,* Oct. 20, 1804.

62. Letter to the *Union* by FAIR PLAY, Oct. 15, 1804.

63. In addition to the critical pieces cited above by FLAGELLUS and FAIR PLAY there was one by A LOUISIANIAN in the *Union* on Oct. 15, and another by LAELIUS, the pseudonym of James Workman, reprinted from the *Telegraphe* of Oct. 13 in the *Mississippi Herald* on Oct. 26.

64. Claiborne to Madison, Oct. 22, 1804, *Letter Books,* II, 272; Robert Dow to Claiborne, Oct. 10, 1804, *ibid.,* p. 374.

65. See "List of Councillors," *ibid.,* p. 375.

66. Claiborne to Madison, Nov. 5, 1804, *ibid.,* p. 390.

67. Claiborne to Jefferson, Dec. 2, 1804, *Territorial Papers,* ed. Carter, IX, 344; Claiborne to Jefferson, Dec. 8, 1804, *ibid.,* p. 347.

68. Claiborne to Jefferson, *ibid.,* p. 347.

69. The only source for his speech is Gayarré, *History of Louisiana,* IV, 34-35.

70. *A Speech by Mr. Poydras, President of the legislative council of Orleans, after the governor's address had been delivered, on the 4th of December, 1804* [n.p., n.d.].

71. Sterrett to Evans, Dec. 10, 1804, Evans Papers, LSU.

72. [Pierre Derbigny], *Esquisse de la Situation Politique et Civile de la Louisiane, depuis le 30 novembre, 1803, jusqu'au 1er octobre 1804. Par un Lousianais* (New Orleans, 1804).

73. Claiborne to Madison, Oct. 16/27, 1804, *Letter Books,* II, 352, 377.

74. Only one office under presidential patronage (excepting the council itself) was allotted to an old inhabitant. All the rest were given to Americans, and Jefferson's selection of men from many states reflected his attempt to use the territory to satisfy national political obligations. Interesting scraps, jottings, and notes in the Jefferson Papers, Library of Congress, for the end of the year 1804 reveal how important a wide geographic distribution was in the President's patronage calculations. There was widespread opposition to "imported" appointees in all of the territories in this period. In Orleans, of course, the ethnic difference aggravated such resentments. See Eblen, *First and Second Empires,* pp. 123-124.

75. Unfortunately few numbers of the *Telegraphe* are extant.

76. John Breckinridge to John Boyle, Sept. 6, 1804, John Breckinridge Papers, LC.

77. Bradford to Brown, Sept. 10, 1804, James Brown Papers, LC.

78. Claiborne to Jefferson, Dec. 21, 1804, *Territorial Papers,* ed. Carter, IX, 358; Claiborne to Robert Smith, Nov. 18, 1809, *Letter Books,* V, 15. Although there never was a "Federal party" as such in the territory, opposition of any kind was looked upon as having a Federalist motivation. Bradford was free of that charge because his Republican credentials were well established by his associations with the Browns in

Kentucky. In addition to the six major papers that I have discussed there were a few fugitive journals that appeared briefly. For the period prior to 1809 these were the *Lanterne Magique* (1808-1809), the *Echo du Commerce* (1808-1809), and the *Misisipi* (1809-1810). For a brief survey of the French press in this period, see Samuel J. Marino, "Early French-Language Newspapers in New Orleans," *Louisiana History*, 7 (1966), 309-321.

79. Granger to Edward Livingston, Nov. 5, 1804, *Territorial Papers*, ed. Carter, IX, 321. To remedy this, Granger devised a scheme whereby newspapers and letters were to be sent in separate portmanteaus (Granger to Claiborne, Dec. 20, 1804, *ibid.*, p. 357).

80. Claiborne to Poydras, Aug. 6, 1804, *Letter Books*, II, 295.

81. Claiborne to Madison, Oct. 22, 1804, *Territorial Papers*, ed. Carter, IX, 313.

82. *Union*, Oct. 10/15/20; Nov. 10/14, 1804.

83. Claiborne to Madison, Jan. 19, 1805, *Territorial Papers*, ed. Carter, IX, 371.

84. Certificate of John Kidder, Jan. 18, 1805, *ibid.*, 376.

85. These eighteenth-century conventions probably lasted longer in the territories than in the politically more mature parts of the country. For discussion of the content of this negative ideology toward party and faction see Richard Hofstadter, *The Idea of a Party System: The Rise of Legitimate Opposition in the United States, 1780-1840* (Berkeley, University of California Press, 1969) chap. 1; see also Bailyn, *Origins of American Politics*, chap. 1, esp. pp. 36-37.

86. Claiborne to Jefferson, Jan. 10, 1805, *Territorial Papers*, ed. Carter, IX, 367.

87. Orleans Territory, Legislative Council, *Acts Passed*, 1st and 2nd sessions (New Orleans, 1805).

88. Briggs to Jefferson, Feb. 9, 1805, Jefferson Papers, LC; Claiborne named Edward Livingston as the author in a letter to Madison on February 15, 1805. See *Territorial Papers*, ed. Carter, IX, 396.

89. "The Public Accuser, No. 1," *Orleans Gazette*, Jan. 10, 1805.

90. "The Public Accuser, No. 2," *ibid.*, Jan. 19, 1805. Other Documents relating to this affair are: Claiborne to Peter Pedesclaux, notary public, June 16, 1804, *Letter Books*, II, 219; Claiborne to Casa Calvo, Sept. 5, 1804, *ibid.*, p. 320; Claiborne to Madison, Jan. 19, 1805, *Territorial Papers*, ed. Carter, IX, 371.

91. Claiborne to Madison, *Territorial Papers*, ed. Carter, IX, 371.

92. A second letter to Madison on the Hulin-Villamil matter was sent on Feb. 21, 1805 (*ibid.*, p. 395).

93. *Orleans Gazette*, Jan. 26, 1805.

94. It was not uncommon for publishers to permit their journals to be used to voice views opposing their own. In New Orleans, with its relatively small population, the newspapers had to compete for subscriptions. The papers advertised themselves as open to the expression of opinion of every hue. It was a major selling point. Kerr appeared in the *Orleans Gazette* under the pseudonym of Curtius. He wrote a series of articles in answer to the Public Accuser, but only one is extant, that of Jan. 19, 1805. It was a weak ad hominem counterattack. James Work-

man wrote as LAELIUS. For an analysis of this piece, see below, chap. 5. A series in answer to LAELIUS by a "Louisianian" appeared in the *Louisiana Gazette* on Jan. 11/15/22/29, 1805.

95. Sterrett to Evans, Jan. 14, 1805, Evans Papers, LSU.

96. Claiborne to Madison, Jan. 26, 1805, *Territorial Papers,* ed. Carter, IX, 380.

97. Claiborne to Jefferson, Jan. 29, 1805, *ibid.*, p. 386. Another series of critical letters by "Gilbert Hurlstone" appeared in the *Orleans Gazette* on Feb. 7, 1805. See also Claiborne to John Sibley, April 8, 1805, *Territorial Papers,* ed. Carter, IX, 433. In addition to attacks on and defenses of the governor the papers engaged in lively intramural combat of their own. The *Orleans Gazette* and the *Telegraphe* were the principals in this little war. See the *Gazette* for Feb. 5, 1805, and July 17, 1805.

98. Sterrett to Evans, Feb. 25, 1805, Evans Papers, LSU.

99. Briggs to Jefferson, Feb. 9, 1805, Jefferson Papers, LC.

100. Claiborne to Jefferson, Feb. 17, 1805, *Territorial Papers,* ed. Carter, IX, 393. Three other duels were reported by Sterrett on Feb. 25. The tendency to personalize public debate was apparently irresistible, particularly in a period when politics lacked structure. The use of this primitive method for settling political disputes was symptomatic of the low state of political development in these early years of the territory. Claiborne himself would resort to private combat against Daniel Clark in June 1807. The location of his wounds was a source of amusement to Jefferson, however discomfiting they were to the zealous governor while he convalesced during the hottest season of the year.

101. Jefferson to Claiborne, March 14, 1805, *Territorial Papers,* ed. Carter, IX, 416.

102. Madison to Jefferson, March 17, 1805, Jefferson Papers, LC.

103. Jefferson to Madison, March 23, 1805, *Territorial Papers,* ed. Carter, IX, 416n.

104. The pastoral letter was dated March 27, 1805. Claiborne enclosed it in a note to Madison, March 31, 1805. Both documents are in the Territorial Papers, Orleans Series, National Archives.

105. Bellechasse's reply was enclosed by Claiborne in a letter to Madison, April 1, 1805, *ibid.*

106. Claiborne to Madison, March 18/26, 1805, *Territorial Papers,* ed. Carter, IX, 420, 425.

107. Claiborne to Madison, June 6, 1805, *Letter Books,* III, 80.

108. Claiborne to Madison, March 24, 1805, Territorial Papers, Orleans Series, National Archives.

109. *Ibid.*

110. Walsh to Claiborne, July 11, 1805, *Letter Books,* II, 121.

111. Claiborne to Walsh, July 12, 1805, *ibid.*, p. 122.

112. Claiborne to Dearborn, Oct. 8/10, 1806, *Letter Books,* IV, 25-26, 28.

113. *Orleans Gazette,* May 23, 1805.

114. As part of this effort a letter was sent on Aug. 13, 1805, to Rev. John H. Hobart in New York in which Hobart was asked to recommend a man who "shall be of the Episcopalian denomination; but it is to be

recollected that his supporters are not only of his own persuasion, but also Presbyterians, Catholics, etc. etc. etc." (Protestant Episcopal Church Archives, Church Historial Society Papers, Austin, Texas). That Catholics as well as Protestants were to participate in the Protestant service shows that the ethnic-linguistic division in Louisiana was at least as important as religious differences. English-speaking Catholics in New Orleans were dissatisfied because sermons were delivered in French.

115. *Orleans Gazette*, Nov. 20, 1805. A poem by DAMON honoring the arrival of the Reverend Chase was composed for delivery on Nov. 17 and subsequently published. It reflected an abiding Protestant hostility toward Catholics and the Catholic faith. Verse writing seemed to be the order of the day. One Joshua R. Toumlin wrote to Jefferson that it was "a matter of unspeakable joy to a number of the inhabitants and more particularly so to J.R.T. who has been deeply lamenting the situation of Orleans with respect to the gloomy state of religion, together with the superstition and idolatry of the island in general . . ."— further evidence of hostility toward the Catholics. Since Toumlin "moves in an humble sphere, he can not expect the President of the U.S. will condescend to notice him or his writing." In that, at least, he was correct. Toumlin to Jefferson, Nov. 28, 1805, Jefferson Papers, LC.

116. Claiborne's papers reflect no attention to this particular problem. This, in itself, is evidence. Claiborne interested himelf in the most minute details of territorial administration. He was close to every issue that arose. His executive journal is not complete, but it is fair to surmise that the absence of a single reference to the Protestant question reveals deliberate disinterest.

117. Claiborne emphasized "party Spirit" as the chief impediment to good government in his speech proroguing the legislative council on July 3, 1805 (*Letter Books*, III, 108; Claiborne to Madison, July 6, 1805, *ibid.*, p. 115).

118. Claiborne to John Alexander, May 7, 1805, *ibid.*, p. 42.

119. Act of March 2, 1805, Thorpe, comp., *Federal and State Constitutions*, III, 1371-1373.

120. James Brown to John Breckinridge, Oct. 31, 1805, Breckinridge Papers, LC.

121. The ten nominees were Joseph de Ville Bellechasse, John Gurley, Pierre Derbigny, John Baptist MaCarty, Jean Noël Destréhan, Pierre Sauvé, Dominique Bouligny, Joseph Villars, and Evan Jones. Of these Jefferson chose Gurley, MaCarty, Destréhan, Bellechasse, and Sauvé. The Senate rejected Gurley. Julien Poydras was eventually appointed to fill the fifth vacancy. Destréhan to Jefferson, Nov. 11, 1805, and Claiborne to Jefferson, Nov. 13, 1805, *Territorial Papers*, ed. Carter, IX, 523-526; Jefferson to Claiborne, Feb. 10, 1806, *ibid.*, p. 580; Claiborne to Jefferson, Feb. 20, 1806, *ibid.*, p. 604; Watkins to Jefferson, April 4, 1806, *ibid.*, pp. 622-623; Claiborne to Jefferson, April 3, 1806, *Letter Books*, III, 283-284; Claiborne to Poydras, June 13, 1806, *ibid.*, pp. 326-327.

122. March 24, 1806, *Letter Books*, III, 274.

123. Claiborne to Jefferson, April 10, 1806, *ibid.*, p. 288.

124. Message to the legislature, May 6, 1806, *ibid.*, p. 296; Claiborne to Madison, May 8, 1806, *ibid.*, p. 297.

125. Veto message, May 26, 1806, *ibid.*, p. 313; Claiborne to Madison, May 22/26, 1806, *ibid.*, pp. 305, 309, 313; Claiborne to Dearborn, May 31, 1806, *ibid.*, p. 320.

126. Claiborne to Jefferson, May 21, June 21, 1806, *ibid.*, pp. 303, 339; Claiborne to John Graham, June 22, 1806, *ibid.*, p. 340; Claiborne to Jefferson, July 9, 1806, *Territorial Papers*, ed. Carter, IX, 670; Claiborne to Gallatin, Nov. 10, 1806, *ibid.*, p. 685. The power and importance of the territorial delegate as a rival to the territorial governor is stressed by Eblen, *First and Second Empires*, p. 161.

127. For a more detailed treatment of this first clash over the legal question, see below chap. 6, sec. IV.

128. This double-jointedness of the territorial governor's role was also a problem for the British colonial governors who had to function successfully in two "polycentric systems of politics"—the imperial and the colonial. See Stanley N. Katz, *Newcastle's New York: Anglo-American Politics, 1732-1753* (Cambridge, Harvard University Press, 1968), esp. pp. 55-58. I am indebted to Professor Katz for helping to clarify my thinking on this as on many other points.

129. Eblen, *First and Second Empires*, pp. 41-42.

130. On the precarious position of the territorial governor as the liaison between federal and territorial government, attempting to steer between national policy and local needs, see *ibid.*, p. 201. There were more than two conflicting authorities with which the governor had to contend. Besides the federal-territorial conflict there was the territorial-local problem (*ibid.*, p. 14). John G. Clark has shown how the overlapping of multiple jurisdictions in Orleans—national, territorial, parish, and municipal—caused serious problems for the New Orleans city council (*New Orleans*, p. 280 *et. seq.*). More than any other official, however, the territorial governor was caught between these frequently warring governmental bodies and their supporting political constituencies.

131. Personal factors must have played some part in Claiborne's metamorphosis. Both his second and third wives were French. Isaac J. Cox suggests the importance of this factor in his article on Claiborne in the *Dictionary of American Biography*. However, it is always hard to assess the relative weight to be given to personal and public policy motivations in these matters. Many forces converged here. None alone was decisive. Claiborne's personal connections and his public position on major issues were, in the end, mutually reinforcing.

Chapter 3. Burr's Conspiracy and the Orleans Territory

1. The historical treatment of the Burr conspiracy has tended to be polarized between accusers and defenders of the two principal characters—Burr and Wilkinson—in what has come down as a fantastic *opera bouffe*. Walter F. McCaleb has been Burr's most consistent advocate (*The Aaron Burr Conspiracy; and, A New Light on Aaron*

Burr [New York, Argosy, 1966]), while Thomas P. Abernethy is the leading anti-Burr authority (*The Burr Conspiracy* [New York, Oxford University Press, 1954] There are numerous lesser works, most of which are one-sided, either for or against Wilkinson or Burr. Some were evaluated by Julius Pratt in "Aaron Burr and the Historians," *New York History*, 26 (1945), 447-470. A more balanced analysis than most is H. S. Parmet and M. B. Hecht, *Aaron Burr: Portrait of an Ambitious Man* (New York, Macmillan, 1967), esp. chaps. 16-19. The most recent extended treatment of the subject can be found in Dumas Malone, *Jefferson the President: Second Term, 1805-1809* (Boston, Little Brown, 1974), chaps. 13-20. Francis S. Philbrick has challenged the established historiography on the conspiracy in his stimulating chapter in *The Rise of the West, 1754-1830* (New York, Harper and Row, 1965); see chap. 9. Philbrick interprets the "supposed conspiracy" as largely an invention of historians. His interesting but somewhat overargued analysis is designed to discredit the notion of early western secessionist sentiment of which Burr's conspiracy was, for antiwestern historians, the best example. On the Burr trial, a field in itself, see Richard B. Morris, *Fair Trial: Fourteen Who Stood Accused from Anne Hutchinson to Alger Hiss* (New York, Knopf, 1953), chap. 5, and the older more extensive discussion in Albert J. Beveridge, *The Life of John Marshall* (4 vols., Boston, Houghton Mifflin, 1916-1919), III, 274-529. The trial record is in David Robertson's *Report of the Trials of Colonel Aaron Burr* . . . (2 vols., Philadelphia, 1808).

2. Philbrick (*Rise of the West*, p. 236) has rightly asserted that the Burr conspiracy did not warrant the historical attention it has received. This is true insofar as national history is concerned, but not true for local Louisiana history, on which its effects have been largely unexplored. Whether or not it was a "conspiracy" is somewhat beside the point of this chapter. Most of the principals whose actions are analyzed in these pages perceived it as an illegal enterprise conspiratorial in nature, which is the way Jefferson described it in his Nov. 27 proclamation (James D. Richardson, ed., *A Compilation of the Messages and Papers of the Presidents, 1789-1897* [10 vols., Washington, D.C., 1896-1899] , I, 404-405).

3. One William Cooke had informed Madison as early as October 1804 "that there is brewing a most Formidable and Treasonable Conspiracy against Louisiana" (Clarence E. Carter, ed., *The Territorial Papers of the United States* [26 vols., Washington, D.C., Government Printing Office, 1934-1962], IX, 309). Jefferson himself had received warnings since December 1805 (Thomas P. Abernethy, *The South in the New Nation, 1789-1819* [Baton Rouge, Louisiana State University Press, 1961] p. 285). Daveiss kept up a steady stream of letters to Jefferson throughout 1806 and was thoroughly nonplussed by Jefferson's imperturbability. The President explained that this was because he wanted to keep their little secret confidential until the moment was right to strike (Jefferson to Daveiss, Sept. 12, 1806, Jefferson Papers, LC). Daveiss later published a pamphlet in which he indicted Jefferson for his lackluster reaction to the Burr threat. In it he

included all of his letters to Jefferson during 1806 when the conspiracy was gaining momentum. Daveiss, a brother-in-law of John Marshall, was using this to build western Federalism. His disclosures placed the President in an awkward position. If Jefferson gave them credence, then he was abandoning his Republican supporters in the southwest upon the word of a Federalist. If he did nothing, then he was liable to the charge, implicit in Daveiss's pamphlet, that the President was sacrificing the national interest for political gain. In the end, the fact that the Burr conspiracy implicated so many of the President's partisans but damaged Republicanism only slightly was due to Jefferson's deft handling of the problem. In addition, Wilkinson deflected a goodly portion of the criticism. See Joseph Hamilton Daveiss, "View of the President's Conduct Concerning the Conspiracy of 1806," reprinted in *Quarterly Publications of the Historical and Philosophical Society of Ohio*, 12 (1917), nos. 2 and 3. For discussion of Daveiss's warnings, consult Malone, *Jefferson the President: Second Term*, pp. 223-225, 237-238.

4. Claiborne to Jefferson, Nov. 5, 1806, in *Official Letter Books of W. C. C. Claiborne, 1801-1816*, ed. Dunbar Rowland (6 vols., Jackson, Miss., 1917), IV, 33.

5. Claiborne to Mead, Nov. 18, 1806, *ibid.*, p. 35.

6. Claiborne to Madison, Nov. 18, 1806, *ibid.*, p. 36.

7. Claiborne to Jefferson, Nov. 12, 1806, *Territorial Papers*, ed. Carter, IX, 687.

8. Mead to Claiborne, Nov. 23, 1806, Territorial Papers, Orleans Series, National Archives.

9. Jackson to Claiborne, Nov. 12, 1806, *Letter Books*, IV, 53-54.

10. Claiborne to Madison, Nov. 25, 1806, *ibid.*, p. 37.

11. Claiborne to Capt. Shaw, Dec. 1, 1806, *ibid.*, p. 38; Claiborne to Madison, Dec. 4/9, 1806, *ibid*, pp. 41, 52.

12. Claiborne to Madison, Dec. 5, 1806, *ibid.*, p. 43.

13. The famous cipher leter to Wilkinson can be found in the Burr Conspiracy Letters (pp. 62-63), LC, and is reprinted in Henry Adams, *History of the United States of America during the Second Administration of Thomas Jefferson* (2 vols., New York, Scribner's, 1921), I, 252-254.

14. The Mexican Association was the group referred to by John Graham, the territorial secretary, in a letter to Madison on Jan. 2, 1805 (*Territorial Papers*, ed. Carter, IX, 552), a letter in which the military needs of Orleans were outlined. This would confirm the existence of the Association prior to Burr's visit in June of that year. Graham explained that is was a private militia force formed for purely defensive purposes. On this point see Charles Gayarre', *History of Louisiana* (4 vols., New Orleans, 1885), IV, 124.

15. Adams, *History of the U.S.*, I, 223-224; Abernethy, *Burr Conspiracy*, pp. 25, 26, 30, 269-270.

16. Statement of Claiborne and Shaw, Dec. 3, 1806, and Claiborne to Madison, Dec. 4, 1806, *Letter Books*, IV, 40; Claiborne to the governors of Kentucky, Tennessee, Ohio, and Indiana, Dec. 5, 1806, *ibid.*, p. 42.

17. See a letter of Wilkinson dated Dec. 6, 1806, Burr Conspiracy Letters, LC. Samuel Brown later denied these allegations (Brown to Jefferson, June 3, 1808, in *Register of the Kentucky State Historical Society*, 35 [1937], 106-110).

18. Wilkinson to Jefferson, Nov. 12, 1806, quoted in Wilkinson's *Burr's Conspiracy exposed; and General Wilkinson Vindicated against the Slanders of His Enemies on That Important Occasion* (Washington City, 1811), appendix, p. 79; and, memorandum of Wilkinson of a conversation with Dr. Watkins, Nov. 1806, *ibid.*, p. 125; also Wilkinson to Claiborne, Nov. 12, 1806, *Letter Books*, IV, 55.

19. Sterrett to Evans, Dec. 19, 1806, Nathaniel Evans Papers, Louisiana State University. Sterrett reported that "business of almost every kind is forgotten in the preparations for the reception of Mr. Burr."

20. Wilkinson justified his conduct in a public deposition but refused to submit to a judicial hearing. See deposition of James Wilkinson, Dec. 26, 1806, *Letter Books*, IV, 149-155.

21. Presentment of the Grand Jury, Jan. 12, 1807, *ibid.*, pp. 170-171; Wilkinson to Claiborne, Jan. 14, 1807, *ibid.*, pp. 94-95.

22. The most detailed contemporary account of Wilkinson's "reign of terror" is [Edward Livingston's] *Faithful Picture of the Political Situation of New Orleans at the Close of the Last and the Beginning of the Present Year—1807* (Boston, 1808). Other contemporary evidence is Claiborne to Madison, Jan. 15, 1807, *Letter Books*,IV, 95; *Louisiana Gazette*, Dec. 19, 1806. James Sterrett named a number of military officers who might have been implicated. "The boys had better keep a bright look out," he wrote Nathaniel Evans on Jan. 16, 1807 (Evans Papers, LSU). Useful summaries can be found in Abernethy, *Burr Conspiracy*, chap. 11, and McCaleb, *Aaron Burr Conspiracy*, chap. 8.

23. Claiborne to Madison, Jan. 15, 1807, *Letter Books*, IV, 95-97.

24. *Louisiana Gazette*, Jan. 6, 1807.

25. Wilkinson to Claiborne, Dec. 6/7/15, 1806, *Letter Books*, IV, 46, 49, 58; Claiborne to Wilkinson, Dec. 8/17, 1806, *ibid.*, pp. 49, 63; Claiborne to Madison, Dec. 9, 1806, *ibid.*, p. 50.

26. *Louisiana Gazette*, Dec. 16, 1806; *Territorial Papers*, ed. Carter, IX, 694-695.

27. Instead he penned a tepid rebuke to the general just to cover himself (Claiborne to Wilkinson, Dec. 25, 1806, *Letter Books*, IV, 69). Claiborne dissimulated with Cowles Mead, claiming that he was ready to support the judiciary if called upon. He *was* called upon, but *was not* ready (Claiborne to Mead, Jan. 2, 1807, *ibid.*, pp. 76-77). Mead continued to suspect Wilkinson's good faith (Mead to Claiborne, Dec. 14, 1806, *ibid.*, pp. 65-66).

28. Livingston detailed Wilkinson's accusations against him in the public press and defended himself with his usual thoroughness (*Mississippi Herald*, Jan. 18, 1807). Bradford was intimidated and moderated his criticism for some time after his confinement. He noted "the mortifying silence and submission to which I am doomed" (*Mississippi Herald*, March 18, 1807). Livingston also commented upon

the intimidation suffered by the press at Wilkinson's hands, Bradford most of all (*Faithful Picture*, pp. 26-27).

29. Wilkinson to Jefferson, Dec. 9, 1806, Daniel Parker Papers, Historical Society of Pennsylvania; Claiborne to Madison, Dec. 9, 1806, *Letter Books*, IV, 50; Wilkinson to Clark, Dec. 10, 1806, Gilpin Family Papers, Historical Society of Pennsylvania. Claiborne wrote Madison on Jan. 29, 1807 (*Letter Books*, IV, 114-115): "[W]e however are assured of the fidelity of the Ancient Louisianians to th U. States & of their attachment to the General Government. For myself I do believe that this declaration is correct so far as relates to a majority of the ancient Louisianians, & (Perhaps) the whole, so far as to exempt them from all participation in Burr's Conspiracy: but of that portion of our society whose native language is English, I cannot speak so favorably; of the patriotism of many, I have had abundant proofs; but there are others,(& the number I fear not inconsiderable) who I verily believe, would most cordially have supported the views of Burr."

30. Even Livingston noted the surprise which greeted Kerr's arrest. "This gentleman had been for several years in the habits of friendship with Governor Claiborne," he wrote later, "and was generally believed to have been high in his confidence, and very serviceable to his government" (*Faithful Picture*, pp. 32-33).

31. That Claiborne had earlier been Workman's political benefactor was duly noted in the letter of LIBERTAS in the *Louisiana Gazette*, April 14, 1807.

32. Speech to the Assembly, Jan. 13, 1807, *Letter Books*, IV, 87-94.

33. Replies from the council and the House, Jan. 22/26, 1807, *ibid.*, pp. 110-114.

34. Claiborne's message, Feb. 10, 1807, *ibid.*, pp. 117-119; Adams, *History of the U.S.*, I, 338-339. Edward Livingston attributed the failure of the legislature to suspend habeas corpus to James Brown, who advised against it. William B. Giles, Jefferson's legislative whip, was attempting to get a habeas corpus suspension through Congress. Joseph Alston, son-in-law of Aaron Burr, published a pamphlet in which he condemned Wilkinson's actions, minimized the emergency, and concluded that a suspension of the writ by Congress was unwarranted. See Agrestis, *A Short Review of the Late Proceedings at New Orleans and Some Remarks upon the Bill, for Suspending the Privilege of the Writ of Habeas Corpus* . . . (South Carolina, 1807).

35. *Territorial Papers*, ed. Carter, IX, 707-708; Claiborne to Madison, Feb. 20, 1807, *Letter Books*, IV, 121.

36. In the early nineteenth century the word "political" meant having a divisive nature. For example, in Orleans it was normally employed to describe sentiment favoring a retrocession to either Spain or France. The Livingston and Kerr defense of the Mexican Association, therefore, represented a departure from conventional usage and was an effort to show that "politics" was not akin to treason and that "political societies" had a place and a function. The quotations are taken from *The Trials of the Honorable James Workman and Col. Lewis Kerr* . . . (New Orleans, 1807), pp. 119, 164. This publication was not a complete

record of the trial. The prosecution's arguments were excluded almost entirely. The pamphlet was designed to furnish more support for "Workman and Company" in the warming battle with Claiborne. In addition, while both men were acquitted, their reputations were badly smudged, and they wished to do something to refurbish them.

37. Wilkinson impugned the jury in the trial of Kerr (Wilkinson to Jefferson, April 15, 1807, Burr Conspiracy Letters, LC). Philip Reibelt shared Wilkinson's views of the trials. He called them "a farce" (Reibelt to Jefferson, March 8, 1807, Jefferson Papers, LC). The letters of Reibelt to Jefferson (May 1806 to December 1808, *ibid.*) constitute an interesting body of reportage of Wilkinson's activities in New Orleans. Reibelt was seeking appointive office, and he tried to win the President's favor by showing him what an acute observer he was of public events. Reibelt stressed the need for vigorous support of Wilkinson, dismissed Claiborne as totally incompetent, and denounced the bench and the bar which he believed to be bent upon defeating Wilkinson's measures. Unfortunately, Reibelt was so busy ingratiating himself with the general that he failed to report to Natchitoches in time to begin his official duties there as parish judge and factor. As a result, he was fired even before he arrived. Subsequently he was made a justice of the peace in the Rapides district, but the universal criticism of his performance there made it impossible for either Claiborne or Jefferson to sustain him in office (Dr. John Sibley to Dearborn, Aug. 7, 1808, in "Dr. John Sibley and the Louisiana—Texas Frontier, 1803-1814," ed. Julia K. Garrett, *Southwestern Historical Quarterly*, 46 (1942-43), 272-277). Reibelt put the blame for his penury at the door of Daniel Clark and tried to get a reappointment by associating himself with the great triumvirate of Jefferson, Wilkinson, and Claiborne, but this tactic failed.

38. The draft memorial with documents appended is in the Joseph Dubreuil de Villars Papers, Duke University, in a five-page memorandum. See also, *Debate in the House of Representatives of the Territory of Orleans on a Memorial to Congress Respecting the Illegal Conduct of General Wilkinson* (New Orleans, 1807).

39. Lvingston's authorship is noted on page 3 of the Library of Congress copy. The marginal notes, for the benefit of Jefferson, to whom he sent a copy of the *Debate*, are in Claiborne's hand. His major point (p. 7) was that any attempt on his part to challenge Wilkinson would have caused a civil war.

40. *Ibid., passim.* Watkins's remarks were carried by the *Louisiana Gazette* during March and April 1807.

41. This material was published in pamphlet form also. See James Workman, *A Letter to the Respectable Citizens, Inhabitants of the County of Orleans Together with Several Letters to Governor Claiborne* (New Orleans, 1807). The letters of Workman were also carried by the *Louisiana Gazette*. Jefferson received a copy. He was fully in accord with Claiborne and Wilkinson on Workman's conduct. Jefferson had little sympathy for judges and was quick to perceive political motives in their actions. He wrote Joseph C. Cabell, one of his close correspondents in Virginia, upon receipt of the pamphlet: "Of the author he knew nothing personally; but being known to be one of the

Mexican league, his availing himself of his office as judge to liberate his accomplices is not in his favor. This insurrection will probably show that the fault in our constitution is not that the Executive has too little power, but that the Judiciary either has too much or holds it under too little responsibility" (March 18, 1807, Jefferson Papers, University of Virginia Collection).

42. Wilkinson pleaded with the President that he "not be left alone to buffet a combination of the Bar and Bench, the mass of American Commerce, and every man in office here, federal or territorial, excepting Governor Claiborne" (Feb. 13, 1807, Burr Conspiracy Letters, LC).

43. The Richmond grand jury barely missed indicting Wilkinson. Randolph said that "the mammoth of iniquity escaped." George Hay, the U.S. attorney for Virginia, believed in Wilkinson's guilt (Abernethy, *South in the New Nation*, p. 294). Burr's defense alleged that Wilkinson, not Burr, was the guilty party (Morris, *Fair Trial*, p. 136).

44. This was partly true in Orleans as well. Claiborne wrote Madison that "there are some citizens who seem to view [Wilkinson's] Conduct as more censurable than that of Cole: Burr's whose traitorous designs Wilkinson has opposed, and . . . defeated" (Feb. 6, 1807, Burr Conspiracy Letters, LC).

45. Jefferson's consistent defense of Wilkinson is hard to explain. See Abernethy, *South in the New Nation*, pp. 287, 295; and Malone, *Jefferson the President: Second Term*, pp. 276-280.

46. "Extract of a letter from a respectable gentleman in New Orleans," dated March 1807 in *National Intelligencer*, April 6, 1807.

47. The addresses thanked Wilkinson and Claiborne for dissipating the dangers which menaced New Orleans and congratulated them for their success in exposing "the wicked plot." They acknowledged that extraordinary measures had been taken but justified these as appropriate to the threat. The addresses were dated March 23, 1807, and a copy, with signatures appended, was published by the *National Intelligencer*, April 6, 1807.

48. Wilkinson suggested "the necessity of a radical change of officers, in every department general and local" in February (Wilkinson to Jefferson, Feb. 13, 1807, Burr Conspiracy Letters, LC). He excepted only Claiborne and several others.

49. *Faithful Picture*, p. 48. Livingston's pamphlet, which was published soon after the defeat of his memorial, was composed as a position paper for the Watkins-Workman group.

50. "Extract," *National Intelligencer*, April 6, 1807.

51. Claiborne to Watkins, March 7, 1807, in American Documents (a manuscript volume), New Orleans Public Library; Claiborne to Madison, March 27, 1807, *Territorial Papers*, ed. Carter, IX, 723-724. Philip Reibelt had doubted that Claiborne would have the courage to purge Watkins (Reibelt to Jefferson, Feb. 27, 1807, Jefferson Papers, LC). Then he criticized the replacement. Mather, he thought, was too fond of drink (Reibelt to Jefferson, March 3, 1807, *ibid.*).

52. Claiborne to Madison, May 3, 1807, *Territorial Papers,* Carter, ed. IX, 731; also, Claiborne to Madison, Feb. 20, 1807, Burr Conspiracy Letters, LC; *Louisiana Gazette,* May 19, 1807.

53. Wilkinson specifically recommended his removal (Wilkinson to Jefferson, March 20, 1807, Burr Conspiracy Letters, LC), but it was not until the end of 1808 that this occurred.

54. March 20, 1807, Evans Papers, LSU.

55. Edward Livingston to Robert R. Livingston, Jan. 30, 1807, Robert R. Livingston Papers, New York Historical Society.

56. *Faithful Picture,* pp. 36-37.

57. Livingston to Robert R. Livingston, Jan. 30, 1807, Robert R. Livingston Papers, New York Historical Society.

58. Graham to Madison, March 5, 1807, Burr Conspiracy Letters, LC.

59. Wilkinson to Clark, March 20, 1807, Gilpin Family Papers, Historical Society of Pennsylvania.

60. Claiborne to Madison, March 27, 1807, *Territorial Papers,* ed. Carter, IX, 723.

61. Claiborne to Jefferson, May 3, 1807, *ibid.,* pp. 729-731. Cowles Mead, secretary of the Mississippi territory, had been acting governor there in Novermber and December, just when the conspiracy was breaking.

62. Claiborne to Jefferson, May 19/20, 1807, *Territorial Papers,* ed. Carter, IX, 734-737. Neither man served. The appointment went to Thomas Bolling Robertson of Virginia (Jefferson to Robertson, Aug. 17, 1807, Jefferson Papers, Colonial Williamsburg Collection; also, *Territorial Papers,* ed. Carter, IX, 761).

63. But Wilkinson still had contempt for Claiborne. His favorite characterization of the governor was "cet Bete" (Wilkinson to Clark, Jan. 8, 1808, Gilpin Family Papers, Historical Society of Pennsylvania).

64. Claiborne to Jefferson, June 28, 1807, *Territorial Papers,* ed. Carter, IX, 745.

65. Claiborne to Madison, Aug. 24, 1807, *Letter Books,* IV, 134-135. The Americans did, of course, rally to a man behind the flag in the Chesapeake Affair. See, *Louisiana Gazette,* Aug. 11, 1807.

66. Claiborne to Madison, Oct. 5, 1807, *Territorial Papers,* ed. Carter, IX, 766.

67. Elizabeth Trist to Jefferson, Oct. 27, 1807, Nicholas P. Trist Papers, Southern Historical Collection, University of North Carolina.

68. Wilkinson to Jefferson, April 9, 1807, Burr Conspiracy Letters, LC; Claiborne to Jefferson, June 1, 1807, *Territorial Papers,* ed. Carter, IX, 742-743; Sterrett to Evans, Aug. 21, 1807, Evans Papers, LSU.

69. Claiborne to Jefferson, May 3, 1807, *Territorial Papers,* ed. Carter, IX, 731.

70. Claiborne to Jefferson, June 1, 1807, *ibid.,* pp. 742-743.

71. Wilkinson helped him in this. Wilkinson to Clark (extract), July 10, 1807, Wilkinson vs. Clark file, Gilpin Family Papers, Historical Society of Pennsylvania.

72. Clark busied himself negotiating with Jefferson and Gallatin over the disposition of public buildings and commons lots. He had been in-

structed by the municipality of New Orleans to attempt to gain possession of these properties either for the city or the territory. His exertions towards this end were admirable, but they did not dispel the bitterness that his own refusal to compromise with the city on a similar matter engendered (see below). See the letters of Daniel Clark written to the municipality from Washington (1806-1808) in American Documents, a manuscript volume of miscellaneous letters (1804-1814), Louisiana Room, New Orleans Public Library.

73. John Graham to Madison, March 18, 1807, Burr Conspiracy Letters, LC; Graham to Clark, May 13, 1807, Wilkinson vs. Clark File, Gilpin Family Papers, Historical Society of Pennsylvania.

74. U.S. Cong., *Debates and Proceedings* (42 vols.; Washington, D.C., 1834-1856), 9th Cong., 2nd sess. (Dec. 24, 1806), p. 215.

75. Claiborne to Clark, May 23, 1807, *Territorial Papers*, ed. Carter, IX, 738.

76. Claiborne to Jefferson, June 17/28, 1807, *ibid.*, pp. 743, 745-746; Jefferson to Benjamin Morgan, July 18, 1807, Jefferson Papers, LC; *Louisiana Gazette*, May 29, June 2, 1807.

77. Meloncy C. Soniat, "The Faubourgs Forming the Upper Sections of the City of New Orleans," *Louisiana Historical Quarterly*, 20 (1937), 192-211.

78. The matter of the New Orleans ropewalk was before the city council from July 1805 until September 1808. See Records of the City Council, July 20, 1805 (vol. I, no. 2, pp. 69-70); July 27, 1805 (*ibid.*, 76); June 6, 1806 (vol. I, no. 3, pp. 73-74); June 11, 1806 (*ibid.*, 75); June 18, 1806 (*ibid.*, 76-77); June 25, 1806 (*ibid.*, 81); Aug. 20, 1806 (*ibid.*, 106); Oct. 8, 1806 (*ibid.*, 122-124); Oct. 9, 1806 (*ibid.*, 125-126); March 18, 1807 (*ibid.*, 169-170); Aug. 10, 1808 (vol. II, no. 1, 238-239); Sept. 28, 1808 (*ibid.*, 274). On June 4, 1806, a fire started in the ropewalk. The entire structure burned to the ground. Had the wind changed, the whole city might have been consumed in a holocaust. (A similar tragedy had occurred twenty years before.) The city council met in extraordinary session and tried to persuade Clark to relinquish his title to the lots, but he refused. Then, in defiance of the public, the ropewalk was rebuilt. James Sterrett described the fire on June 4 (Sterrett to Evans, June 5, 1806, Evans Papers, LSU).

79. See below, chap. 4.

80. Even in Washington, Clark's reputation was not good. Gallatin thought that intimacy with Clark was a minus in a candidate for appointment (Gallatin to Jefferson, March 12, 1807, *Territorial Papers*, ed. Carter, IX, 718).

81. U.S. Congress, *Debates and Proceedings*, 10th Cong., 1st sess. (Dec. 31, 1807), pp. 1257-69.

82. Abernethy, *Burr Conspiracy*, p. 267, *et passim*. Wilkinson's vindication by the court did not satisfy Clark. He took his evidence before the proverbial bar of public opinion and published, one year later, his *Proofs of the Corruption of General James Wilkinson and of his Connexion with Aaron Burr* (Philadelphia, 1809).

83. Abernethy (*Burr Conspiracy*, p. 264) offers no convincing ex-

planation why Clark turned on Wilkinson. He does suggest that Wilkinson provoked him into it by careless remarks to third parties. Personal grievances also may have played a role in turning Clark against him. See J. F. H. Claiborne, *Mississippi as a Province, Territory and State with Biographical Notices of Eminent Citizens* (Jackson, Miss., 1880), p. 247.

84. John Graham reported the trial from Richmond to James Brown. Referring to Marshall's opinion he wrote, "This as you will see has put an end to all the Trials for Treason in this court and will probably have the same effect on those for misdemeanor" (Sept. 8, 1807, James Brown Papers, LC). Graham expected Burr's acquittal to deepen divisions in Orleans. Clark's decision to denounce Wilkinson accomplished precisely that.

85. Some believed that Jefferson would abandon Wilkinson after Burr's acquittal. James Sterrett wrote, "Some of Wilkinson's honest dupes made *long faces* about the acquittal of *Burr*—some of the knowing ones think that *Tommy* will let this great military chieftain down—" (Sterrett to Evans, Oct. 4, 1807, Evans Papers, LSU).

86. Notice of *La Lanterne Magique* appeared in *The Mississippian* of Natchez of Jan. 19, 1808. The paper, it said, possessed "grub street humour" and its purpose was "the abuse of the administration and government of the union." The editor was thought to be "an honorable member of the Burr brotherhood." Claiborne mentioned it in letters to the Secretary of State, March 17, 1808 (*Letter Books*, IV, 167) and Feb. 13, Nov. 18, 1809 (*ibid.*, IV, 317, and V, 16). James Brown was one of its subscribers (receipt from Thomas Ravenscraft for $1.00 in payment for four numbers of the journal, James Brown Papers, LC), despite John Graham's warning that he steer clear of factional politics by supporting the local government "against those who from wicked motives wish to assail it . . . Suffer not designing men to shield themselves under your good name" (Graham to Brown, Sept. 8, 1807, *ibid.*). Frequent references to the *Lanterne Magique* appeared in the New Orleans press throughout 1808 (*Louisiana Gazette*, March 15, July 1; *Courier*, March 2/27/28, July 4/13, Sept. 9). See also Clarence S. Brigham, *History and Bibliography of American Newspapers, 1690-1820* (2 vols., Worcester, Mass., American Antiquarian Society, 1947), I, 186.

87. *Orleans Gazette*, Aug. 31, 1807.

88. *Ibid.*, July 13, 1807.

89. *Louisiana Gazette*, May 1, 1807.

90. *Ibid.*, May 5, 1807.

91. *Ibid.*, May 8, 1807 (letter of Centurio).

92. *Ibid.*, Sept. 22, 1807 ("Communication" of AN ELECTOR).

93. *Ibid.*, June 21, 1808.

94. *Ibid.*

95. Address dated Feb. 2, 1808, and reprinted in the *Courier*, March 7, 1808.

96. *Ibid.*

97. It is hard to know what the position of the *Telegraphe* was because of the dearth of extant numbers. Months later Thierry accused

Claudius Beleurgey, its editor, of being "one of the most despicable instruments of the miserable Clark" (*Courier*, Dec. 19, 1808). But Thierry's penchant for solo combat raises some doubt. He wanted no allies in debate, preferring to stake out his own positions which he then proceeded to make impregnable to friend and enemy alike.

98. *Moniteur*, March 16/19/26, 1808.

99. *Courier*, March 21, 1808.

100. *Ibid.*, March 27, 1808. Two others were Dominique Bouligny, a planter, and Chevalier La Croix, a justice of the peace. Here again is evidence of the crossing of ethnic lines in political controversy.

101. "Who are the friends and the defenders of Daniel Clark?" he asked some time later. "All the known enemies of the present administration . . . of which in America, Burr is the visible chief. If we expect some divergents at the bar, all, from court-sweeper up to the most distinguished lawyer, re-attach themselves to this visible chief of the Forensic priesthood" (*Courier*, July 22, 1808).

102. *Ibid.*, June 20, 1808.

103. *Ibid.*, June 24, 1808.

104. *Ibid.*, June 29, 1808.

105. *Louisiana Gazette*, July 1, 1808; *Courier*, July 4/6, 1808.

106. Claiborne to Madison, April 5, 1808, *Letter Books*, IV, 169.

107. *Courier*, July 22, 1808.

108. Philip Reibelt tried the same tactic. He also reconjured the specter of Burrism in order to win an appointment (Reibelt to Jefferson, Sept. 7, 1808, Jefferson Papers, LC). For Claiborne's repeated references to Burrites in the territory, see Claiborne to Madison, Jan. 18, Dec. 27, 1808, *Letter Books*, IV, 147, 278; Claiborne to Dearborn, April 21, 1808, *Territorial Papers*, ed. Carter, IX, 784; Claiborne to Jefferson, Sept. 1, 1808, *Letter Books*, IV, 208.

109. Anthony Glass's projected expedition against the Spanish provinces caused some alarm in the summer of 1808 (Claiborne to Carr, Aug. 8, 1808, *Letter Books*, IV, 187-188; Carr to Claiborne, Aug. 15, 1808, Territorial Papers, Orleans Series, National Archives; Claiborne to Madison, Aug. 8, 1808, *Territorial Papers*, ed. Carter, IX, 798-800). Other supposed conspiracies were feared from time to time (Claiborne to Robertson, Aug. 18, 1808, *Letter Books*, IV, 191-192; Claiborne to Cushing, Dec. 29, 1808, *ibid.*, 279-280; Mather to Claiborne, Jan. 8, 1809, *Territorial Papers*, ed. Carter, IX, 817-819). Claiborne had a touch of "conspiracy fever" at this time, a manifestation of his overworked anxiety. He was politely rebuked for it by Col. Cushing, the army commander at Fort Adams (Cushing to Claiborne, Jan. 10, 1809, *ibid.*, 819-820). Cushing believed Claiborne had been deluded by his subordinates (*ibid.*, p. 819n).

110. Claiborne to Madison, Jan. 1, 1809, *Letter Books*, IV, 282-285.

111. Claiborne to Madison, Sept. 7, 1808, *ibid.*, p.212.

112. Claiborne to Dr. Latimore, Oct. 30, 1808, *ibid.*, pp. 234-235.

113. Claiborne to Samuel H. Smith, Dec. 4, 1808, *ibid.*, p. 263.

114. Claiborne To Col. Hopkins, Dec. 8, 1808, *Letter Book*, IV, 265-266.

115. Claiborne to Willaim Kenner, Dec. 22, 1808, *ibid.*, p. 275.

116. The change occurred before the end of November 1808. On Nov. 30, the city council followed the governor's lead and dismissed Bradford as the printer for the municipality (City Council Records, vol. II, no. 1, p. 307, New Orleans Public Library). The opposition press linked Claiborne, Thierry, and Wilkinson as the great triumvirate in the territory (*Orleans Gazette*, Sept. 15, 1809). For Claiborne's own evaluation of the press, see Claiborne to Smith, Nov. 18, 1809, *Letter Books*, V, 13-17.

117. Claiborne to Jefferson, Dec. 8, 1808, *ibid.*, IV, 269.

118. See below, chap. 4, sec. I.

119. Claiborne to Madison, Nov. 10/14, 1808, *Letter Books*, IV, 249-251; Claiborne to Dearborn, Feb. 5, 1809, and to Smith, Feb. 13, 1809, *ibid.*, pp. 316-317; Smith to Claiborne, March 20, 1809, *Territorial Papers*, ed. Carter, IX, 830-831; *Weekly Chronicle* [Natchez], April 5, 1809, p. 2n.

120. Sterrett to Evans, Oct. 28, 1809, Evans Papers, LSU. The troops under Wilkinson's command had departed from the city in June 1809 (Resolutions of the city council, June 10, 1809, *Territorial Papers*, ed. Carter, IX, 844-845).

121. *Courier*, Dec. 21, 1808.

122. Quoted approvingly in Gayarré, *History of Lousiana*, IV, 178.

Chapter 4. Edward Livingston and the New Orleans Batture

1. The "batture" is the sand and silt which lies between the river at its low water point and the levee.

2. The best analysis of the Batture controversy is still William B. Hatcher, *Edward Livingston: Jeffersonian Republican and Jacksonian Democrat* (University City, Louisiana, Louisiana State University Press, 1940), chap. 8. The basic documentary material can be found in U.S. Congress, *American State Papers: Documents, Legislative and Executive of the Congress of the United States* (18 vols., Washington, D.C., 1832-1861), *Public Lands*, II, 1-84. See also Francis P. Burns, "The Graviers and the Faubourg Ste. Marie," *Lousiana Historical Quarterly*, 22 (1939), 385-427.

3. The city responded to Gravier's efforts to enclose the Batture as early as February 1804 (City Council Records, vol. I, bk. 2, pp. 42, 63 in New Orleans Public Library).

4. Judge Prevost delayed the trial of the case until a full complement of three was present on the court (*ibid.* [Dec. 21, 1805], p. 158). During the delay, Prevost permitted the use of Batture soil only for the upkeep of the levee (*ibid.* [Jan. 4, 1806], p. 162; [May 3, 1806], bk. 3, pp. 51-52). This caused considerable annoyance. William Spriggs, George Matthews, and Joshua Lewis were the three judges of the Superior Court at the time the case was decided.

5. There was no question as to the title of the other battures along the river, such as that of Bernard Marigny. For example, see *ibid.* (Dec. 24,

1806), p. 145, where the city contemplated the acquisition of the battures of Villere and Lachaise, apparently anticipating little difficulty.

6. Edward to Margaret B. Livingston, March 30, 1804, Simon Gratz Papers, Historical Society of Pennsylvania.

7. Livingston to [?], May 13, 1804, *ibid.*

8. Court action was commenced by Livingston in behalf of Gravier in October 1805 (City Council Records [Dec. 7, 1805], vol. I, bk. 2, p. 152; Hatcher, *Edward Livingston*, p. 145).

9. Claiborne to Jefferson, May 20, 1807, *Territorial Papers of the United States*, ed. Clarence E. Carter (26 vols., Washington, D.C., Government Printing Office, 1934-1962), IX, 736. There is no certainty about what Livingston actually paid for the property. Livingston said that it cost him $80,000, but the inhabitants of New Orleans believed that he received the property in lieu of fee. See Hatcher, *Edward Livingston*, pp. 144-145.

10. City Council Records (Sept. 23, 1807), vol. II, bk. 1, p. 37. Laminated copies in French and English of these affadavits are in the Louisiana Miscellany, Library of Congress (LC).

11. Claiborne to Jefferson, May 20, 1807, *Territorial Papers*, ed. Carter, IX, 736.

12. The first resolution to this effect was passed on Sept. 16, 1807 (City Council Records, vol. II, bk. 1, p. 35). The official request was made on Dec. 5, 1807 (*ibid.*, p. 82). Documents were forwarded to Washington by action taken on Dec. 12, 1807 (*ibid.*, pp. 84-85). Claiborne and the city had conferred on the desirability of transferring the city's claim to the United States as early as May 25, 1807. As a result of this decision Livingston was confronted by a coalition of municipal, territorial, and national authorities.

13. (Jan. 27, 1808), *ibid.*, p. 124. Claiborne refused to authorize destruction of Livingston's works ([Feb. 6, 1808], *ibid., pp. 141-142*]. The city also feared precipitous action (Feb. 13, 1808), *ibid.*, p. 143, although it did not authorize the use of Batture silt for filler. The city passed ordinances prohibiting further construction on the levee (*Louisiana Gazette*, Feb. 19, 1808).

14. City Council Records (Feb. 6, 1808), vol. II, bk. 1, p. 139.

15. Madison's letter to the U.S. marshal is cited in Livingston v. D'Orgenoy, 7 Cranch (U.S.) 577 (1813), at 578.

16. Jefferson to Gallatin, Gallatin Papers, New York Historical Society.

17. Livingston to Gallatin, Dec. 2, 1807, *ibid.*

18. Hatcher, *Edward Livingston*, pp. 150-151.

19. The *Orleans Gazette*, itself pro-Livingston, admitted that the French majority favored the public's right to the Batture. One "B" scored a telling point in a fabricated debate when, referring to the Mississippi River as "our good old father," he said "that the batture is a part of his inheritance, and consequently that his legitimate issue ought to enjoy his succession, without giving any part of it to the adopted children, who have but lately come into the family" (Oct. 1, 1807). Elizabeth Trist, who often reflected American attitudes on local public ques-

tions, described the demonstrations in mid-September as "Mob Government" (E. Trist to Jefferson, Oct. 27, 1807, Nicholas P. Trist Papers, Southern Historical Collection, University of North Carolina).

20. March 2, 1808, Gallatin Papers, New York Historical Society.

21. Jefferson was not sure of the position of James Brown, then the most influential of the land agents in Orleans. For one thing, the Browns had been named by Wilkinson as having been soft on Burrism. On the Batture question itself, Brown had been one of the attorneys for Gravier in the original law suit against the city (U.S. Cong., *American State Papers: Public Lands,* II, 16). Claiborne would later write that Brown did indeed support Livingston (Claiborne to Jefferson, Sept. 1, 1808, *Official Letter Books of W. C. C. Claiborne, 1801-1816,* ed. Dunbar Rowland [6 vols., Jackson, Miss., 1917], IV, 202). The presence of James Brown on the projected board of land commissioners rendered it suspect in Jefferson's view. That Brown may, in fact, have been sympathetic with the government's claim is suggested by a letter he wrote to Philip Grymes (Nov. 25, 1808, James Brown Papers, LC). Brown's successor as U.S. attorney.

22. Jefferson to Gallatin, Dec. 24, 1807, Jefferson Papers, LC.

23. Gallatin to Jefferson, March 2, 1808, *ibid.;* Daniel Clark to the Mayor and Alderman of New Orleans, Dec. 16/24, 1807, American Documents, New Orleans Public Library.

24. *Orleans Gazette,* Sept. 21, 1807; see also *ibid.,* Sept. 24, Oct. 1, Nov. 16, 1807; Dec. 2, 1808; Sept. 8, 1809.

25. *Courier,* Oct. 14/30 (supplement), Nov. 4 (supplement), 1807. Thierry's penchant for lone advocacy was again revealed in the Batture fight. Thierry staked out his own position on the legal issues and then defended it as one besieged, even refusing to reconcile his forensic posture with any of the other supporters of the public's claim, such as Pierre Derbigny. The result was a rift which the friends of Livingston were quick to exploit. Thierry also fought bitterly with one H. P. Nugent, another ardent champion of the public's cause. See H. P. Nugent, *A Letter to his Excellency Wm. C. C. Claiborne, Govr of the Territ. of Orleans and a Letter to James Brown—A Defence of the Honorable John Rowan and Daniel Clark, Members of Congress Against the Slanders of the Tergiversant Redacteur of the Courier* (New Orleans, 1808).

26. Just as important, of course, was Thierry's position on Burrism. The Burr and Batture issues earned him Claiborne's support for the post.

27. Claiborne to Madison, Oct. 17, 1807, *Letter Books,* IV, 135.

28. *Case laid before counsel for their opinion on the claims to the Batture, situated in front of the suburb St. Mary, August 21, 1807,* reprinted in U.S. Cong., *American State Papers: Public Lands,* II, 28-33, quote at p. 29.

29. This belief was reflected in the newspaper debate. For example, on October 1, 1807, the *Orleans Gazette* printed a piece that was critical of the Superior Court's decision on the Batture. It was charged with ignorance of local laws and usages: "A fair trial of the cause could not be expected from three judges speaking a different language . . . and bred under different laws, usages and religion."

30. The Batture question quickened the hostility toward judges, judge-made law, and lawyers and thereby cultivated the needed sentiment to sustain the repudiation of the common law. The *Courier* voiced these feelings in an article on the Batture on Nov. 4, 1807: "It is certain that a general and well founded belief prevails in New Orleans that a conspiracy of lawyers is formed to rob the city of its property; and that the judges are of a conspiracy, their judgment in the cause of the batture gives strong reason to suspect . . . . Such dextrous lawyers can with ease, Twist law and judges as they please."

31. *Case laid before counsel*, U.S. Cong., *American State Papers: Public Lands*, II, 29.

32. Reprinted *ibid.*, pp. 33-41.

33. This was the date of the secret transfer of Louisiana prior to the formal peace settlement of 1763.

34. U.S. Cong., *American State Papers: Public Lands*, II, 40.

35. Note F, *ibid.*, p. 44.

36. *Examen de la Sentence Rendue Dans La Cause entre Jean Gravier et la Ville de la Nouvelle-Orleans* (New Orleans, 1807), p. 21 (author's translation).

37. *Ibid.*, p. 23. Others also attacked the judges for siding with Livingston. For example, Nugent, *Letter to Claiborne*, p. 14, *et passim*.

38. *Opinion on the Case of the Alluvion Land, or Batture, Near New Orleans*, reprinted in U.S. Cong., *American State Papers: Public Lands*, II, 45-54.

39. *Examen des Droits des Etats Unis et des Pretentions de M. Eduourd Livingston sur la Batture en Face du Faubourg Ste. Marie* (New Orleans, 1808).

40. Derbigny to Jefferson, Nov. 14, 1808, Jefferson Papers, LC.

41. *Refutation Du Memoire en forme de consultation Redige par M. Duponceau au sujet des pretentions des Etats Unis sur la Batture du fauxbourg Ste. Marie* (New Orleans, 1808).

42. *A Review of the Cause of the New Orleans Batture, and of the discussions that have taken place respecting it; containing answers to the late publications of Messrs. Thierry and Derbigny on that subject* (Philadelphia, 1809), reprinted in *American Law Journal*, 4 (1812), 517-562.

43. J. B. S. Thierry, *Reply to Mr. Duponceau* . . . (New Orleans, 1809).

44. Claiborne to Jefferson, Sept. 17, 1808, *Letter Books*, IV, 218.

45. *Examen des Droits* . . . , p. 33.

46. Livingston to Gallatin, Dec. 2, 1807, Gallatin Papers, New York Historical Society.

47. Edward Livingston to Robert R. Livingston, Jan. 28, 1808, Robert R. Livingston Papers, New York Historical Society.

48. Peter Delabigarre was the actual purchaser of two-thirds of the Batture from Jean Gravier, which the heirs of Delabigarre and Livingston then divided after Delabigarre's death. Delabigarre paid the court costs in the litigation of the case between October 1805 and May 1807. See Hatcher, *Edward Livingston*, pp. 144-145.

49. Claiborne to Madison, April 18, 1808, Madison Papers, LC.

50. Gallatin to Jefferson, May 5, 1808, Jefferson Papers, LC.

51. Jefferson to Gallatin, May 6, 1808, *ibid.*

52. U.S. Cong., *American State Papers: Public Lands*, II, 25.

53. Jefferson to Livingston, May 6, 1808, Jefferson Papers, LC.

54. Livingston to Madison, May 6, 1808, in U.S. Cong., *American State Papers: Public Lands*, II, 65.

55. Madison to Jefferson, May 11, 1808, Jefferson Papers, LC.

56. *Ibid.*

57. Jefferson to Madison, May 19, 1808, *ibid.*

58. U.S. Cong., *Statutes at Large*, comp. Richard Peters, vol. II (Boston, Little and Brown, 1845), 445-446; Jefferson later wrote, "on the 27th of November, 1807, I asked the attendance of the heads of Departments to whom the papers received had been previously communicated for their consideration . . . . We took of the whole case such views as the state of our information at that time presented" (U.S. Cong., *American State Papers: Public Lands, II*, 65).

59. Jefferson to Madison, May 19, 1808, Jefferson Papers, LC; Madison to Livingston, May 20, 1808, in U.S. Cong., *American State Papers: Public Lands* , II, 26. Livingston had gone to New York. He returned to Washington, however, and managed to see both the Attorney General and the President, but they remained unmoved.

60. Livingston to Madison, July 13, 1808, *ibid.*

61. Madison to Livingston (undated memorandum in answer to Livingston's letter of July 13), *ibid.*, p. 26.

62. Rodney to Livingston, July 17, 1808, *ibid.*, p. 26.

63. Livingston to Rodney, July 20, 1808, *ibid.*, p. 27.

64. Edward Livingston to Margaret B. Livingston, July 26, 1808, C. J. Ingersoll Papers, Historical Society of Pennsylvania.

65. During the fall months, Livingston made use of the legal opinions sent to him by William Rawle, Edward Tilghman, William Lewis, and Jared Ingersoll—all leading members of the Philadelphia bar. Their short briefs, along with Duponceau's, were posted on the exchange coffee house and read and discussed at length by the public, as was Thierry's *Reply to Duponceau*. Accretions of silt on the Batture for the year 1808 were very considerable (Claiborne to Jefferson, Sept. 17, Oct. 24, Nov. 17, 1808, *Letter Books*, IV, 218, 232-233, 252-253). The city of New Orleans undertook expensive surveys of these accretions because while "imperceptible" accretions favored private rights to alluvions, measurable increases bolstered public title.

66. *Address to the People of the United States on the measures pursued by the Executive with respect to the Batture at New Orleans* (New Orleans, 1808), reprinted in U.S. Cong., *American State Papers: Public Lands*, II, 7-13, quote at p. 7.

67. *Ibid.*, p. 9.

68. *Ibid.*

69. Edward Livingston to Robert R. Livingston, Oct. 24, 1808, Robert R. Livingston Papers, New York Historical Society.

70. Edward Livingston to Robert R. Livingston, Jan. 22, 1809, *ibid.*

71. The piece in the *Courier* was a reprint from a letter to the editor

of the Philadelphia *Aurora* of March 3, 1808: "The expulsion of Edward Livingston and his associate speculators, from the *Batture*, on behalf of the United States, has produced the liveliest emotion of joy and satisfaction at New-Orleans, and throughout the whole country; for a swarm of those locusts from the United States had taken such daring strides, and held themselves up as objects of menace to the Government, and superior to the laws, that for a time, the Government was considered as too imbecile either to assert its own authority or to protect its own laws.

"This affair of the Batture, has however restored confidence to the honest and faithful citizen; and has spread dismay and confusion among 'the choice spirits.' *Livingston, Clark, Watkins and Co.* have found that their efforts to excite commotion, and their rides through all the districts to asperse the Government, and stir up sedition, have at length turned out to their confusion, and to the honor of the General Government. The Legislature have in consequence of this salutary decision of the executive, transmitted their thanks to the President by an express." *Courier*, April 25, 1808.

72. Thierry wrote: "In spite of all the intrigues of the honorable Daniel Clark, the governor is still in place, and, if Louisiana has been affected with some misfortunes, it is meantime evident that we ought to attribute them to Burr, and to the ambitious members of his broken faction, who still remain amongst us. No one, at present questions the paternal interest which governor Claiborne feels for all our citizens. He has not recourse to all those petty tricks which lead to popularity; he has not on all solemn occasions a band of fawning favorites to offer up vows for his health, and to prepare sets of toasts which, being afterwards exhibited in the gazettes, strike the world with astonishment; but he is sincerely attached to whatever interests the country; he is entirely devoted to the prosperity of its citizens, and it is to his earnest solicitations that we shall owe the reinvestiture of the corporation in the possession of the Batture, on the ground of that prescription, which may be considered as immemorial, without the citizens having to dread the injurious consequences which some have wished to deduce therefrom against the right of proprietors bordering on the river to the accessions made to their lands by the alluvions.

"No one is ignorant at this day of all the means which the governor has incessantly employed to obtain the reestablishment of the public in this interesting property; but we do not yet know what our honorable delegate has done on this subject.

"I believe that all the world, as well as myself would be charmed, should he [Clark] design to set forth that which he has done in Congress in this important business." *Courier*, May 16, 1808.

A letter to the editor by one "A.P." in the *Courier* of August 8, 1808, said that Clark's public position was to support the city in the Batture affair, but that privately "he was a strong advocate for Mr. Livingston."

73. H. P. Nugent also connected Burrism and Batturism. In 1811 he wrote, "It has been asserted at the seat of government, that some of our judges were concerned in the Burrite plot, and hence, it is natural to sus-

pect that the project of robbing the banks having been defeated, the Burrites have changed their battery, and have determined to rob the corporation of their lands, by the assistance of their accomplices on the bench" (*H. P. Nugent's Reply to the Calumnies of the Honorable F. X. Martin, One of the Judges of the Superior Court of the Territory of Orleans* [Natchez, 1811], p. 35).

74. This is how Thierry put it: "Always faithfull to his system of destruction, Mr. Livingston does not fear to call on his head all the suspicion of his complicity with Burr, by explaining himself thus: 'Where the destruction of personal liberty is permitted with impunity, the invasion of private property must be a venial crime . . . .' It is very simple that he should speak of the destruction of individual liberty, when there was no alternative left between the momentary destruction of the liberty of some incendiaries and the destruction of public liberty, as is natural enough for him to cry out that private liberty is violated when there is in fact nothing more but that obstacle in his usurping the public property." *Courier*, Dec. 12, 1808.

75. *Courier*, Dec. 21, 1808.

76. Thierry's December editorials were later reprinted as an appendix in his *Reply to Duponceau*. The appendix was called "Refutation of Mr. Livingston's Pamphlet Entitled An Address to the People of the United States."

77. Robert R. Livingston to Edward Livingston, Jan. 19, 1809, Robert R. Livingston Papers, New York Historical Society.

78. Robert R. Livingston to Edward Livingston, April 19, 1809, *ibid.*

79. Edward Livingston to Robert R. Livingston, May 27, 1809, *ibid.*

80. Circular letter of Edward Livingston to members of Congress, June 23, 1809, Miscellaneous Papers, New York Historical Society.

81. Livingston's activities continued to alienate him from the city government. Early in 1809 he helped the saloon-keepers to oppose a municipal tax on taverns. The mayor and the council were thoroughly outraged. Livingston's motive, it seemed to the authorities, was to exhaust the city's resources in needless litigation so that it would be unable to oppose his other "spoilations of public properties" ([Jan. 28, 1809], City Council Records, vol. II, bk. 2, pp. 14-16).

82. Edward Livingston to Robert R. Livingston, Jan. 25, 1810, Robert R. Livingston Papers, New York Historical Society. Apparently, Livingston had stayed in Washington and New York without returning to New Orleans.

83. Edward Livingston to Robert R. Livingston, Feb. 14, 1810, *ibid.*

84. U.S. Cong., *Debates and Proceedings*, 11th Cong., 1st and 2nd sess. (March 1/5/14, 1810), pp. 1469, 1485-86, 1539-58. For earlier debates on the Batture, see *ibid.*, (June 17/20/26, Dec. 7/11/15/18, 1809; Feb. 2/7/28, 1810) pp. 323, 349, 418-419, 701, 707, 739, 744, 1373, 1379, 1468. The debates for this period are not fully reported in the *Debates and Proceedings*. However, from the available evidence it appears that many members feared that a decision on the Batture would serve as a precedent for a disposition of the Yazoo land claim dispute then pending.

85. The bill was later amended to provide for a special commission

to be set up to look into the matter and for a compromise to be worked out between the federal government and Livingston. Agreement was reached in the Senate, but final action was postponed indefinitely on April 21. See *Debates and Proceedings*, 11th Cong., 2nd sess., pp. 1607 (March 21, 1810), 1618 (March 23, 1810), 1694-1699 (March 30, 1810), 1700 (March 31, 1810), 1704-1705 (April 2, 1810), 1858 (April 16, 1810), 1879-1880 (April 17, 1810), 1886 (April 18, 1810), 1935 (April 21, 1810).

86. *Further Observations in Support of the Right of the Public to the Batture of New Orleans or Port of St. Mary* (Washington, D.C., 1809), p. 14.

87. *Speech of Julien Poydras, Esq., the delegate from the territory of Orleans, in support of the right of the public to the batture in front of the suburb St. Mary, Friday, Feb. 2, 1810* (Washington, D.C., 1810), p. 28.

88. *A Defence of the Right of the Public to the Batture of New Orleans* (Washington, D.C., 1809), p. 19; *Speech* (of Feb. 2), p. 27.

89. That the Batture decision was only one manifestation of the oppressions of the legal profession was reflected repeatedly in contemporary publications. See for example, *H. P. Nugent's Reply to the Calumnies*, p. 59, *et passim*.

90. U.S. Cong., *Debates and Proceedings*, 11th Cong., 1st and 2nd sess., (March 14, 1810) p. 1551. Poydras's speech was published in pamphlet form. See *Speech of Julien Poydras, Esq., the delegate from the territory of Orleans, in support of the right of the public to the batture in front of the suburb St. Mary, Wednesday, March 14, 1810* (Washington, D.C., 1810).

91. The distinction between public law and private law is embedded deep in the civil law tradition. Thus, in his chapter on "Legal Categories," John Henry Merryman writes: "It was a kind of negative implication of [the] private law ideology that an entirely different attitude was appropriate in public law matters. There the role of government was not limited to the protection of private rights; on the contrary, the driving consideration was the effectuation of the public interest by state action. . . . In private legal relations the parties were equals and the state the referee. In public legal relations the state was a party, and as representative of the public interest (and successor to the prince), it was a party superior to the private individual" (*The Civil Law Tradition: An Introduction to the Legal Systems of Western Europe and Latin America* [Stanford, Stanford University Press, 1969], p. 101, and chap. 14, *passim*).

Working from within this cast of mind, a man like Poydras could not quite see how a public question such as the Batture could be resolved in an ordinary law court by a private civil suit in disregard and defiance of important public interests. On these points, see also Max Rheinstein, "Common Law and Civil Law: A Comparison," *Pennsylvania Bar Association Quarterly* 12 (1940), 7-19, esp. 13-15.

92. *Speech* (March 14, 1810), pp. 7-8. Apparently, Poydras did not realize that federal circuit courts, when hearing cases on appeal, sat without juries.

93. *Ibid.*, pp. 9-10.

94. The mayor of New Orleans conveyed to Poydras the thanks of the city government "for the firmness, the talent and the zeal" with which he had defended the cause of the Batture in Congress (Message of Oct. 25, 1810, New Orleans Papers, New York Historical Society).

95. Edward Livingston to Robert R. Livingston, April 25, 1810, Robert R. Livingston Papers, New York Historical Society; Livingston v. D'Orgenoy, 1 Martin (O.S.) 87 (1810), and 7 Cranch (U.S.) 577 (1813); Livingston v. Jefferson, 15 Federal Cases (8411) 660 (Va. Cir. 1811).

96. Jefferson to William Wirt and George Hay, May 19, 1810, Jefferson Papers, LC.

97. George Hay to Jefferson, July 15/20, 1810, *ibid.*

98. Jefferson to Wirt and Hay, May 15, 1810, *ibid.*

99. Jefferson to Gallatin, Sept. 27, 1810, in *The Writings of Thomas Jefferson*, ed. Paul L. Ford (10 vols., New York, 1892-1899), IX, 283n.

100. Jefferson to Claiborne, June 11, 1810, Jefferson Papers, LC.

101. Jefferson to Wirt, June 18, 1810, *ibid.*

102. Jefferson to Claiborne, Oct. 16, 1810, *ibid.*

103. See below, n. 118.

104. The text account of Jefferson's efforts to influence Madison's judicial appointments at this time is based upon Albert J. Beveridge, *The Life of John Marshall* (4 vols., Boston, Houghton Mifflin, 1919), IV, 100-116; and Hatcher, *Edward Livingston*, pp. 156-165, supplemented by other materials as noted.

105. Jefferson to Madison, May 25, 1810, in Jefferson, *Writings*, ed. Ford, IX, 276.

106. *Ibid.*, p. 275.

107. Jefferson sent his brief on the Batture to all of the former members of his Cabinet ostensibly for the purpose of getting their advice, but with the thinly veiled threat that they were deeply involved and were possible targets of future litigation. As he explained to Caesar Rodney, "Believing my late associates in the executive would feel an interest in the justification of a conduct in which all concurred and also in the issue of it, I have thought it a duty to consult them as to the grounds to be taken, and to take none against their advice" (*The Writings of Thomas Jefferson*, ed. A. A. Lipscomb and A. E. Bergh [Memorial Ed. 20 vols., Washington, D.C., 1904-1905], XII, 424).

108. The urgency of Jefferson's interest in the Supreme Court appointment was best revealed in his Sept. 27 letter to Gallatin: "What the issue of the case ought to be, no unbiased man can doubt. What it will be, no one can tell. The judge's [Marshall's] inveteracy is profound, and his mind of that gloomy malignity which will never let him forego the opportunity of satiating it on a victim. His decisions, his instructions to a jury, his allowances and disallowances and garblings of evidence, must all be subjects of appeal. I consider that as my only chance of saving my fortune from entire wreck. And to whom is my appeal? From the judge in Burr's case to himself and his associate judges in the case of Marbury v. Madison. Not exactly, however. I observe old Cushing is dead. At length, then, we have a chance of getting a Republican majority in the Supreme judiciary" (Jefferson, *Writings*, ed. Ford, IX, 284n.)

109. Jefferson to Madison, Oct. 15, 1810, *ibid.*, pp. 282-283.

110. Beveridge, *Marshall*, IV, 110.

111. Jefferson to Eppes and Giles, Nov. 12, 1810, Jefferson Papers, LC.

112. *Ibid.*

113. Jefferson to Tyler, May 26, 1810, Jefferson, *Writings*, ed. Ford, IX, 276n.

114. 15 Fed. Cases (8411) 660 (Va. Cir. 1811), at 661, 663; see also Hatcher, *Edward Livingston*, pp. 162-163.

115. 1 Brockenbrough [Marshall's circuit opinions] (1811) 208; 15 Fed. Cases (8411), 664; Hatcher, *Edward Livingston*, pp. 163-164.

116. Tyler to Jefferson, May 17, 1812, *Letters and Times of the Tylers*, by Lyon G. Tyler (3 vols., Richmond, 1884-1896), I, 264.

117. *The Proceedings of the Government of the United States in maintaining the public right to the beach of the Mississippi, adjacent to New Orleans, against the intrusion of Edward Livingston. Prepared for the use of counsel* (New York, 1812); reprinted in U.S. Cong., *American State Papers: Public Lands*, II, 59-83; and in *American Law Journal* 5 (1814), 1-103.

118. See Gallatin's "Memorandum respecting the suit instituted by E. Livingston against T. Jefferson late President and Letters to and from Mr. Jefferson," Gallatin Papers, New York Historical Society (filed among the 1807 papers). Jefferson's position had been thoroughly refuted by Duponceau. Even the *American Law Journal*, in an editorial footnote to a reprint of Duponceau's *Review*, commented critically upon Jefferson's return to Derbigny's position and his failure to answer Duponceau's arguments. Many years later, however, Jefferson's position was supported by Gustavus Schmidt, a leading Louisiana jurist of the mid-nineteenth century in articles published in the *Louisiana Law Journal* (1841-42). (I am grateful to Mr. John H. Tucker, Jr. of Shreveport for bringing this work to my attention.) For further discussion, see below, chap. 7.

119. *An Answer to Mr. Jefferson's Justification of His Conduct in the Case of the New Orleans Batture* (Philadelphia, 1813); reprinted in *American Law Journal* (1814), 113-299. The quote is *ibid.*, p. 289.

120. Beveridge, *Marshall*, IV, 114-115.

121. Claiborne to Jefferson, Dec. 24, 1810, *Territorial Papers*, ed. Carter, IX, 907.

122. These events were reported to Jefferson by James Mather in a letter of November 30, 1810 (Jefferson Papers, LC). Edward Livingston to Dominick A. Hall (District Court judge); J. M. Fortier to Robert Smith (Secretary of State), both Nov. 30, 1810 (Miscellaneous letters, Dept. of State, National Archives). Fortier was about to resign and had notified Smith of his intentions in August. No replacement had been picked by October, however. With Edward Livingston around, the position called for a courageous man: or at least one who was indifferent to law suits.

123. Livingston v. D'Orgenoy, 7 Cranch (U.S.) 577 (1813); Hatcher, *Edward Livingston*, pp. 165-169.

124. "Memoire of Bernard Marigny addressed to his fellow citizens of New Orleans," (from Paris, 1822), trans. Olivia Blanchard, in New Orleans Municipal Papers, Howard-Tilton Memorial Library, Tulane University, pp. 27-28 (in typescript).

125. Jefferson to Monroe, March 27, 1824, Jefferson Papers, LC.

126. In 1811 Livingston failed to win election to the Lousiana constitutional convention. In 1812, his efforts to prevent Claiborne's election as the state's first governor also failed. Favorable federal court judgments with regard to the Batture in 1813 merely inflamed popular sentiment against him. See Edward Livingston to Robert R. Livingston, July 26, Sept. 28, 1811, Simon Gratz Papers, Historical Society of Pennsylvania; and *idem* to *idem*, May 12, June 23, 1812, Robert R. Livingston Papers, New York Historical Society.

Chapter 5. Common Law vs. Civil Law: First Phase

1. Ben R. Miller, *The Louisiana Judiciary* (Baton Rouge, Louisiana State University Press, 1932), 7-11.

2. An Act erecting Louisiana into two territories, and providing for the temporary government thereof, March 26, 1804, U.S. Cong., *Statutes at Large*, comp. Richard Peters (Boston, Little & Brown, 1845), II, 283-289; An Act further providing for the government of the territory of Orleans, March 2, 1805, *ibid.*, 322-323.

3. Orleans Territory, *Acts Passed at the First Session of the Legislative Council* (New Orleans, 1805), pp. 144-209, 388-399.

4. Everett S. Brown, *The Constitutional History of the Louisiana Purchase, 1803-1812* (Berkeley, University of California Press, 1920), University of California Publications in History, vol. X; Dumas Malone, *Jefferson the President: First Term, 1801-1805* (Boston, Little Brown, 1970), chap. 17.

5. Jefferson to Monroe, Nov. 24, 1801, in Jefferson, *The Works of Thomas Jefferson*, ed. Paul L. Ford (12 vols., New York, 1904-05), IX, 317. James Sullivan concluded his important book on real property published in 1801 with a like observation—namely, that uniformity of law was essential to national unity (*History of Land Titles in Massachusetts* [Boston, 1801], pp. 355-356).

6. As he put it some years later in discussing his opposition to the citation of English cases decided after 1760, "It would add the advantage of getting rid of all [of] Mansfield's innovations or civilization of the common law. For however I admit the superiority of the civil over the common law code, as a system of perfect justice, yet an incorporation of the two would be like Nebuchadnezzar's image of metal and clay, a thing without cohesion of parts." Jefferson to John Tyler, June 17, 1812, in *The Writings of Thomas Jefferson*, ed. A. A. Lipscomb and A. E. Bergh (Memorial Ed., 20 vols., Washington, D.C., 1904-1905), XIII, 166.

7. July 11, 1803, in *The Writings of Thomas Jefferson*, ed. P. L. Ford (10 vols., New York, 1892-1899), VIII, 249. Jefferson hoped to make the

rest of the Louisiana purchase into a vase reservation for Indians and possibly for emancipated blacks as well (Merrill Peterson, *Thomas Jefferson and the New Nation* [New York, Oxford University Press, 1970], pp. 771-776; Winthrop D. Jordan, *White over Black: American Attitudes toward the Negro, 1550-1812* [Chapel Hill, University of North Carolina Press, 1968], pp. 564-565).

8. Jefferson to Gallatin, Nov. 9, 1803, Gallatin Papers, New York Historical Society.

9. Jefferson to Breckinridge, Nov. 24, 1803, in Jefferson, *Works*, ed. Ford, X, 51.

10. There is now little doubt that Jefferson authored the original bill which was the basis of the Orleans Government Act of March 1804 and that he used his influence to push it through the Congress. The closest study of the legislative history of the act is James E. Scanlon, "A Sudden Conceit: Jefferson and the Louisiana Government Bill of 1804," *Louisiana History*, 9 (1968), 139-162. Another extensive treatment is in Malone, *Jefferson the President: First Term*, pp. 349-356; see also Peterson, *Thomas Jefferson*, p. 778, and Lowell H. Harrison, *John Breckinridge: Jeffersonian Replublican* (Louisville, Filson Club Publications, 1969), p. 167.

11. Claiborne to Jefferson, Aug. 24, 1803, in Clarence E. Carter, ed., *The Territorial Papers of the United States* (26 vols., Washington, D.C., Government Printing Office, 1934-1962), IX, 21.

12. Judge Prevost of the Superior Court said as much in his charge to the grand jury printed in the *Union*, Nov. 28, 1804. Part of the reason may have been the absence of an entrenched group of barristers committed to the older system of criminal procedure. To take a parallel situation, when the English introduced jury trials in civil cases in Scotland in 1815, most of the early opponents were members of the Scottish bar. As one George Joseph Bell, a professor of Scots law, noted at the time, "It was difficult for the new system . . . to become popular. But it is painful to recollect the opposition with which it had to contend, not from any disinclination among the people . . . but from the disinclination and resistance of the older and more established professional men, unwilling to begin a new course of apprenticeship" ("A Short View of the Difficulties Which Surrounded the Introduction of Trial by Jury in Civil Causes in Scotland and of the Ultimate Success of the Experiment" [1835], in William Adam, *A Practical Treatise and Observations on Trial by Jury in Civil Causes* . . . [Edinburgh, 1836], appendix 2, p. 6).

13. Interesting documentation for this assessment of Spanish criminal justice is Laura L. Porteous, "Torture in Spanish Criminal Procedure in Louisiana, 1771," *Louisiana Historical Quarterly*, 8 (1925), 5-22.

14. "Hints of Evan Jones: Administration of Justice," enclosed in a letter of Daniel Clark to Madison, Oct. 21, 1803, *Territorial Papers*, ed. Carter, IX, 83-84.

15. Claiborne to Madison, Jan. 2, 1804, *Official Letter Books of W. C. C. Claiborne, 1801-1816* ed. Dunbar Rowland (6 vols., Jackson, Miss., 1917), I, 323.

16. *Ibid.*, p. 328. Claiborne's difficulties with respect to the legal question were unique but not atypical. In all of the new American territories the problem of establishing a body of law and some kind of legal system was the most perplexing because of the sheer absence of laws and of experienced and knowledgeable practitioners. On this point see Jack E. Eblen, *The First and Second United States Empires: Governors and Territorial Government, 1784-1912* (Pittsburgh, University of Pittsburgh Press, 1968), pp. 73, 110-112.

17. Feb. 14, 1804, *Territorial Papers*, ed. Carter, IX, 187.

18. Jefferson's policy in regard to such appeals as that of Baudin can be found in his letter to Claiborne, March 18, 1804 (*Letter Books*, II, 118) and in Jefferson to Baudin, May 12, 1804 (*ibid.*, p. 144).

19. Claiborne to Jefferson, May 1, 1804, *Letter Books*, II, 119.

20. Jefferson to Baudin, May 12, 1804, *ibid.*, II, 145.

21. Alliot to Jefferson, April 14, 1804; Jefferson to Alliot, April 27, 1804, in Jefferson Papers, LC. Alliot's appeal, along with a long and detailed descriptive essay on Louisiana entitled "Historical and Political Reflections on Louisiana" appears in James A. Robertson, ed. and trans., *Louisiana under the Rule of Spain, France, and the United States, 1785-1807* (2 vols., Cleveland, 1911; reprint, 1969), pp. 31-232.

22. Edward Livingston to Robert R. Livingston, May 6, 1804, Robert R. Livingston Papers, New York Historical Society.

23. Carleton Hunt, "Life and Services of Edward Livingston," *Proceedings of the Louisiana Bar Association* (1903), p. 24; Orleans Territory, *Acts Passed at the First Session of the Legislative Council of the Territory of Orleans* (New Orleans, 1805), (April 10, 1805), pp. 210-261.

24. Letter to an unknown correspondent, June 2, 1804, Joseph Dubreuil de Villars Papers, Duke University. The language problem also caused confusion in grand jury proceedings. See C. C. Robin, *Voyages dans L'Interieur de la Louisiane . . . pendant les Années 1802, 1803, 1804, 1805, et. 1806*, trans. (and abridged) as *Voyage to Louisiana*, by Stuart O. Landry, Jr. (New Orleans, Pelican Pub. Co., 1966), pp. 180-182. (See *ibid.*, p. 179n, for other complaints about the administration of justice.)

25. *A Letter from Allan B. Magruder of Opelousas . . .* (New Orleans, 1808), p. 20.

26. Claiborne to Madison, June 9, 1804, *Letter Books*, II, 197.

27. Claiborne to Lt. Bowmar, June 27, 1804, *ibid.*, p. 223.

28. Claiborne to Madison, Oct. 29, 1804, *Territorial Papers*, ed. Carter, IX, 317.

29. Claiborne to Madison, Oct. 29, 1804, *ibid.*, p. 317.

30. *The Union*, Nov. 28, 1804.

31. Jefferson had great difficulty in filling positions in the territory. Distance, climate, and disease dissuaded many men from accepting appointment. H. B. Trist and Ephraim Kirby were two of a number of important officials who died of sickness, the first soon after coming to the area, the second en route.

32. Prevost to Madison, Dec. 19, 1804, *Territorial Papers*, ed. Carter, IX, 356.

33. *Louisiana Gazette*, Dec. 21, 1804.
34. *Territorial Papers*, ed. Carter, IX, 356.
35. *The Union*, Nov. 28, 1804.
36. Brown to Jefferson, Jan. 8, 1805, *Territorial Papers*, ed. Carter, IX, 365.
37. Brown to Breckinridge, Jan. 22, 1805, *ibid.*, p. 378.
38. This is precisely what happened in the spring of 1806. See below, chap. 6, sec IV.
39. Brown to Breckinridge, Jan. 22, 1805, *Territorial Papers*, ed. Carter, IX, 378.
40. Claiborne to Madison, Feb. 6, 1805, *ibid.*, p. 390.
41. See below, chap. 6, sec VI.
42. "Remonstrance of the People of Louisiana," in U.S. Cong., *Debates and Proceedings* (42 vols., Washington, D.C., 1834-1856), 8th Cong., 2nd sess., (Dec. 31, 1807) pp. 1597-1608 (appendix).
43. *Ibid.*, pp. 1606-1607.
44. Evan Jones had noted the high acceptability of the largely oral procedures of the commandants, but that applied only to summary process. In fact, all evidence which the commandants submitted for higher adjudication was in written form (see Daniel Clark to Madison, Sept. 8, 1803, *Territorial Papers*, ed. Carter, IX, 39).
45. U.S. Cong., *Debates and Proceedings*, 8th Cong., 2nd sess., p. 1607.
46. Published in the Philadelphia *Aurora*, Dec. 15, 1804.
47. Signed "Serpent d'eau," dated 5th Thermidor, An 12 (July 23, 1804), reprinted in the *Mississippi Herald*, Aug. 7, 1804.
48. *The Union*, Oct. 10, 1804.
49. "A Fellow Citizen," *The Union*, Nov. 10, 1804.
50. "'Common Sense' to the French Inhabitants of Louisiana, September 22, 1804," in M. D. Conway, ed., *The Writings of Thomas Paine* (4 vols., New York, 1894-1896), III, 430-436; reprinted in the *Louisiana Gazette*, Nov. 2, 1804, the *Mississippi Messenger*, Nov. 12, 1804, and other local papers. An answer to Paine by "A Friend of Reason" appeared in the *Union*, Nov. 17, 1804.
51. An extract from the *Intelligencer* was reprinted in the *Orleans Gazette*, Dec. 25, 1804.
52. Claiborne to Madison, Oct. 3, 1804, *Territorial Papers*, ed. Carter, IX, 304.
53. Jefferson to Claiborne, Dec. 2, 1804, *ibid.*, p. 342.
54. John Quincy Adams to John Adams [Nov., 1804], in *The Writings of Johns Quincy Adams*, ed. Worthington C. Ford (7 vols., New York, Macmillan, 1913-1917), III, 81.
55. Dec. 15, 1804, entry in *The Memoirs of John Quincy Adams, 1795-1848*, ed. Charles F. Adams (12 vols., Philadelphia, 1874-1877), I, 321.
56. Dec. 15, 1804, entry in *William Plumer's Memorandum of Proceedings in the United States Senate, 1803-1807*, ed. E. S. Brown (New York, Macmillan, 1923), pp. 222-224.
57. *Reflections on the Cause of the Louisianians Respectfully Sub-*

mitted by their Agents (Washington, 1805), pp. 4, 5, 12. Another pamphlet of unknown authorship appeared at this time and may well have been composed by the memorialists. It was called *Analysis of the Third Article of the Treaty of Cession of Louisiana* (n.n., n.p., n.d.). It called for the immediate incorporation of the inhabitants of Louisiana with the Union in accordance with the agreement between the United States and France.

58. The report of the committee appears in U.S. Cong., *Debates and Proceedings*, 8th Cong., 2nd sess., (Jan. 25, 1804) pp. 1014-19.

59. *Ibid.*, pp. 1017-19.

60. Claiborne to Madison, April 29, 1805, *Territorial Papers*, ed. Carter, IX, 445; Claiborne to Madison, May 4, 1805, *Letter Books*, III, 38.

61. The report was published by the *Orleans Gazette*, June 11, 1805.

62. This was the same James Workman who authored the Crimes Act of 1805 and who was appointed to a parish judgeship in Orleans parish effective May 1, 1805 (*Territorial Papers*, ed. Carter, IX, 598). Details on Workman's career can be found in Charles S. Watson, "A Denunciation on the Stage of Spanish Rule: James Workman's 'Liberty in Louisiana,' " *Louisiana History*, 11 (1970), 245-258.

63. The first English play was performed in New Orleans in 1806. A French theater was already well established, the first French company having arrived in 1791. See Roger P. McCutcheon, "The First English Plays in New Orleans," *American Literature*, 11 (1939-1940), 183-199. *Liberty in Louisiana* was widely performed in the United States, however. See Watson, "A Denunciation on the Stage," p. 251.

64. Several samples of the dialogue convey the general tone. In Act II, in referring to Spanish justice, Sawney M'Gregor, an itinerant Irishman, comments to his companion, Phelin O'Flinn: "Do ye ken that ye are not now in the United States? Na Public trial—na fair and open examination of witnesses; na fixed, impartial laws; na jury—" to which Phelin replies impishly: "An no lawyers, I dare say, to bother the witnesses!"

Toward the end of the play, when Don Bertoldo de la Plata, the Spanish Governor, is accused of violating the powers of his office, the following exchange takes place with the American general in command of the newly arrived troops from Natchez:

"Don Bertoldo: Can your excellency ask me such a question? Do you not know that I am a person of the first rank in this province? That alone is sufficient answer to the calumny of those wretches.

"General: Not so, Señior—Liberty is now in Louisiana. The government which now rules here will not admit your rank as the testimony of your innocence; nor suffer it to shelter you if you have acted wrong. Our laws confer no privilege which justice may refuse to recognize—the humblest are shielded by their protection—the proudest oppressor is not beyond the reach of their avenging power.

"Don Bertoldo: What means all this jargon? I tell you, I insist on having these scoundrels hanged up immediately, for daring to insult Don Bertoldo de la Plata.

"General: I cannot comply with your desire, Señor. No man within the pale of our authority can suffer an ignominious death, until a fair and public trail by those whose own interest is justice shall have indubitably ascertained his guilt. Life would be of mean estimation indeed if held as you would wish—but at a tyrant's mercy" (*Liberty in Louisiana*, Act V, scene 3).

65. H. P. Dart, a noted Louisiana legal scholar, emphasized the continuities in Louisiana legal practice from the French and Spanish to the American period. He argued that Spanish civil law, in particular, was benign, and the inhabitants were loath to accept common law in its place. For his positive evaluation of the administration of justice in Louisiana under the Spanish see "Courts and Law in Colonial Louisiana," *Louisiana Bar Association Reports*, 22 (1921), 17-63; "The Colonial Legal Systems of Arkansas, Louisiana and Texas," *ibid.*, 27 (1926), 43-60; and, "The Legal Institutions of Louisiana," *Louisiana Historical Quarterly*, 2 (1919), 72-103. For a similarly favorable view of the Spanish judicial system in Louisiana, Louis G. Kahle, "The Spanish Colonial Judiciary," *Southwestern Social Science Quarterly*, 32 (1951), 26-37.

66. See above, chap. 2, sec. IV.

67. Claiborne named Derbigny as the author in a letter to Madison, Oct. 22, 1804, *Territorial Papers*, ed. Carter, IX, 312.

68. *Esquisse*, p. 21.

69. *Ibid.*, pp. 22-23.

70. See above, sec. V.

71. *Esquisse*, p. 33.

72. This was a frequent charge during the period, and one not confined to Louisiana. Examples of early nineteenth-century hostility to lawyers in America abound. Two are Thomas Paine's "To the Citizens of Pennsylvania on the Proposal for Calling a Convention," *Mississippi Messenger*, Oct. 29, 1805 [reprinted from the Philadelphia *Aurora*] and "Lawyers," an article defending the profession against "irrational rage" in the *Mississippian*, Aug. 20, 1810 [reprinted from the *Nashville Review*].

73. *Esquisse*, p. 35.

74. Letter of LAELIUS, reprinted in the *Mississippi Messenger*, Nov. 30, 1804. Isaac Briggs named James Workman as the author (Briggs to Jefferson, Feb. 9, 1805, Jefferson Papers, LC).

75. LAELIUS continued, "If ingenuity had been exerted to give opportunity for the corrupt administration of justice, no rules of practise more efficacious for that purpose could have been framed, than those which permit the judge to hear, to examine and decide in private. Such a system offers strong temptation to the unprincipled, and has been generally found to have produced a corrupt Judiciary wherever it has been long established. On the other hand, where the Judge is obliged to act in public he is himself before the severe and vigilant tribunal of public opinion." Since Laelius and James Workman were one and the same, it is not surprising that Spanish procedures should have been singled out for criticism. This, after all, was the thrust of *Liberty in Louisiana*.

76. Claiborne to Madison, Oct. 16, 1804, *Territorial Papers*, ed.

Carter, IX, 352. A similar letter was sent to Jefferson on November 25, 1804 (*ibid.*, p. 338).

77. Proceedings of the Legislative Council, Dec. 4, 1804, reported in the *Mississippi Herald and Natchez Gazette*, Dec. 21, 1804.

78. The council's answer was dated Dec. 7, 1804, and was reprinted in the *National Intelligencer*, Jan. 25, 1805.

79. His speech appeared in the *Orleans Gazette* in installments. Only the conclusion is extant—in the issue of Jan. 26, 1805.

Chapter 6. Common Law vs. Civil Law: Second Phase

1. Claiborne to Jefferson, Jan. 10, 1805, in Clarence E. Carter, ed., *The Territorial Papers of the United States* (26 vols., Washington, D.C., Government Printing Office, 1934-1962), IX, 366.

2. U.S. Congress, *Statutes at Large*, comp. Richard Peters (Boston, Little and Brown, 1845), II, 322.

3. *Ibid.*, I, 550.

4. *Ibid.*, I, 51n; Henry Steele Commager, ed., *Documents of American History* (5th ed., New York, Appleton-Century-Crofts, 1949), pp. 129, 130.

5. The original framers of the Ordinance did not intend to introduce specific laws into the territories to which the Ordinance would be applied, but only general principles of republican government, of which the common law was a major component. It was supposed that the territories would pattern their laws on those of the eastern states, an expectation not easily realized in the Orleans territory. See Jack E. Eblen, *The First and Second United States Empires: Governors and Territorial Government, 1784-1912* (Pittsburgh, University of Pittsburgh Press, 1968), p. 90.

6. Section 5: "*And be it further enacted*, that the second paragraph of the said ordinance which regulates the descent and distribution of estates . . . [is] hereby declared not to extend to, but [is] excluded from all operation within the said Territory of Orleans" (U.S. Cong., *Statutes at Large*, II, 322).

7. Message to the Legislative Council, June 22, 1805, in Dunbar Rowland, ed., *Official Letter Books of W. C. C. Claiborne, 1801-1816* (6 vols., Jackson, Miss., 1917), III, 103.

8. Claiborne to Madison, June 26, 1805, *ibid.*, p. 105.

9. *National Intelligencer*, June 22, 1805.

10. *Louisiana Gazette*, Dec. 21, 1804.

11. *Letter Books*, III, 108.

12. Poydras's speech was reprinted in the *Orleans Gazette*, July 20, 1805, and in the *National Intelligencer*, Sept. 9, 1805.

13. Brown to Breckinridge, Sept. 17, 1805, *Territorial Papers*, ed. Carter, IX, 506.

14. Proceedings of the House of Representatives, *ibid.*, p. 520.

15. Because of the absence of complete records of the debates in the territorial legislature, it is unknown whether or not discussion followed

Delorme's motion. The fact that the House was preoccupied at this time with selecting a list of nominees for the new legislative council—and not primarily with substantive issues concerning territorial administration—gives some indication of how important the deputies considered this subject.

16. William B. Hatcher, *Edward Livingston: Jeffersonian Republican and Jacksonian Democrat* (University City, Louisiana, Louisiana State University Press, 1940), pp. 118-119.

17. It is difficult to document the several judicial efforts to resolve the legal question. There was no system of court reporting during the first years of territorial life. The evidence for these early rulings is based upon accounts written by participants long after the events occurred. Most of the secondary writers have said that November 1804 was the date of the Prevost opinion, but the transcript of proceedings in the territorial House (noted in the text) indicates that these writers are in error. Jeremiah Brown's *Short Letter to a Member of Congress Concerning the Territory of Orleans* (Washington, D.C., 1806) [see below, sec. IX] gives further contemporaneous support for the conclusion that Nov. 12, 1805—not 1804—was the actual date. See also Etienne Mazureau, "George Mathews: President of the Supreme Court of Louisiana," *Louisiana Historical Quarterly*, 4 (1921), 149-188, esp. pp. 173-174. The origin of the erroneous dating of Prevost's original ruling seems to have been Charles H. Hunt's *Life of Edward Livingston* (New York, 1864), pp. 116-117, 121-122. On the Louisiana constitutional safeguard against common law reception, see below, n. 33.

18. *Instructions from the Inhabitants of the Territory of Orleans to Their Representatives in the Legislature* [New Orleans, 1805].

19. *Ibid.*, p. 9.

20. *Ibid.*, pp. 2-3, 7, 8-9, *et passim*.

21. *Ibid.*, p. 4. However, Congress had also, by the spring of 1805, applied the Northwest Ordinance to the territory. The pamphlet overlooked the ambiguity of the statute of March 2. The council was, therefore, unjustly accused of exceeding the vague guidelines of Congress.

22. *Instructions*, p. 5.

23. Periodically, within the common law world itself, there have been efforts to render law more intelligible by reducing it to simple written form. Indeed, the movement to codify common law, in the nineteenth century, was partly inspired by this theme. Many of the arguments attacking common law, whether from civil law or common law writers, were strikingly similar. For an example of the latter see Joseph Hopkinson, *Considerations on the Abolition of the Common Law in the United States* (Philadelphia, 1809), interesting because it reflects the rhetorical debate going on in the common law world at the time the controversy was at its high point in Lower Louisiana.

24. *Instructions*, p. 2.

25. *Letter Books*, III, 274.

26. The proposed legislation in manuscript is in the Territorial Papers, Orleans Series, National Archives. It has been reprinted in Elizabeth G. Brown's "Legal Systems in Conflict: Orleans Territory, 1804-

1812," *American Journal of Legal History*, 1 (1957), 35-75, at pp. 46-48.

27. Claiborne to Madison, May 22, 1806, *Letter Books*, III, 309. The official veto notice of R. Claiborne was sent to the legislature on May 26, 1806 (*ibid.*, p. 313). Richard Claiborne, a relative of the governor and his private secretary, often acted in an official capacity when the regular territorial secretary was absent.

28. Pierre Sauvé tendered his resignation on May 21 and Jean Noël Destréhan on May 24. Both were councilors and both attributed their withdrawal to ill health. Their letters preceded the actual veto, but Claiborne's intentions prior to May 26 were probably known. Colonel Bellechasse seems also to have contemplated resignation but decided against it (*Territorial Papers*, ed. Carter, IX, 641).

29. *Letter Books*, III, 305.

30. May 26, 1806, *ibid.*, p. 309.

31. The House rejected the resolution on May 27 (Claiborne to Madison, May 28, 1806, *ibid.*, p. 319).

32. May 26, 1806, *ibid.*, p. 309.

33. The constitution drawn up in 1811 and adopted as the basic law of the new State of Louisiana specifically barred the wholesale adoption of the common law. Just as statutory law was considered more definitive than a judicial declaration, so constitutional law was more fundamental than statutory law. See Louisiana Constitution (1812), Art. IV, sec. 11.

34. Claiborne to Poydras, May 26, 1806, *Letter Books*, III, 314.

35. The entire manifesto in French and English can be found in the *Territorial Papers*, ed. Carter, IX, 643-657.

36. *Ibid.*, p. 650.

37. *Ibid.*, p. 651.

38. *Ibid.*, pp. 652-653.

39. *Ibid.*, p. 653. For the most part, the fields of private law singled out for emphasis in the manifesto of 1806 have become the landmarks which distinguish the law of Louisiana today from that of her sister states. See Leonard Oppenheim, "Louisiana's Civil Law Heritage: An Address before the Annual Meeting of the Notaries Association of New Orleans," April 10, 1958; and Ferdinand Stone, "The Law with a Difference and How It Came About," in *The Past as Prelude: New Orleans, 1718-1968*, ed. Hodding Carter (New Orleans, Pelican, 1968), pp. 42-70, esp. 68-70.

40. *Territorial Papers*, ed. Carter, IX, 653.

41. John Henry Merryman, *The Civil Law Tradition: An Introduction to the Legal Systems of Western Europe and Latin America* (Stanford, Stanford University Press, 1969), p. 156.

42. *Territorial Papers*, ed. Carter, IX, 653.

43. *Ibid.*, pp. 655, 657.

44. Orleans Territory, *Acts Passed at the First Session of the First Legislature of the Territory of Orleans* (New Orleans, 1807), pp. 214-219; *Orleans Gazette*, July 19, 1806.

45. Jeremiah Brown would later argue (see below, sec. IX) that the use of the term "civil law" was meant to mislead. He wrote, "The ex-

pression *civil law* here may be understood in two very different senses, one as *civil* contradistinguished from *criminal* law, the other as the Roman Code. The reader cannot but smile when I assure him that this duplicity of meaning was actually intended and for the express purpose of deceiving the executive. Unfortunately the trick succeeded" (*A Short Letter to a Member of Congress Concerning the Territory of Orleans* [Washington, 1806], p. 36n. Claiborne was not as simple-minded as Brown seemed to think he was, but his comment is characteristic of the low estimate many Americans had of the governor and the feeling that in his hands the cause of the common law was lost.

46. J[oseph Dubreuil de] Villars, member of the Committee of Instructions, to the Territorial delegate [Daniel Clark], June 5, 1806, in "Notes," Joseph Dubreuil de Villars Papers, Duke University.

47. Fifth Annual Message, Dec. 3, 1805, in James D. Richardson, ed., *A Compilation of the Messages and Papers of the Presidents* (20 vols., Washington, D.C., 1897-1917), I, 385.

48. An Act for Classing the Militia and Assigning to Each Class Its Particular Duties (proposed), in *The Writings of Thomas Jefferson*, ed. P. L. Ford (10 vols., New York, 1892-1899), VIII, 409-412.

49. Merrill Peterson, *Thomas Jefferson and the New Nation* (New York, Oxford University Press, 1970), pp. 833-835; Dumas Malone, *Jefferson the President: Second Term, 1805-1809* (Boston, Little Brown, 1974), pp. 69, 513-516.

50. An outline of the plan entitled "A Bill for the Settlement of a Part of the Territory of Orleans" is in the Jefferson Papers, Library of Congress. "Sketches of parts of a bill for encouraging settlers in the territory of Orleans" and "Notes on the Bill for the defense of Orleans" are in Jefferson, *Writings*, ed. Ford, VIII, 425-427. These are undated, but the editor has placed them with a circular memo from Jefferson to his Cabinet dated Feb. 28, 1806. For a brief account, see E. S. Brown, "Jefferson's Plan for a Military Colony in Orleans Territory," *Mississippi Valley Historical Review*, 8 (1922), 373-376.

51. Jan. 31, 1807, in *The Writings of Thomas Jefferson*, ed. A. A. Lipscomb and A. E. Bergh (Memorial Ed., 20 vols., Washington, D.C., 1904-1905), XI, 145.

52. Ephraim Kirby, one of Jefferson's early appointees to the Orleans territory, writing from Fort Stoddert in Mississippi on his way to New Orleans early in 1804, stressed the military advantages of such a scheme: "A strong American settlement on this River [the Tombigbee in Mississippi territory] will offer an excellent Barrier against the approach of a foreign enemy at the southwestern point of our territories. Upon any emergency succour might be thrown into New Orleans with more ease from this place than any other" (Kirby to Jefferson, April 20, 1804, in Ephraim Kirby Papers, Duke University). At the time of the proposed militia bill for Orleans (1806), Jefferson hoped to provide a similar enactment for Mississippi. In outlining his militia scheme in a circular memorandum to his Cabinet, the President suggested "a similar provision for Tombigby" (Feb. 28, 1806, in Jefferson, *Writings*, ed. Ford, VIII, 425-426).

53. Everett S. Brown, ed., *William Plumer's Memorandum of Proceedings in the United States Senate, 1803-1807* (New York, Macmillan, 1923), p. 474.

54. Jefferson to Gallatin, Jan. 31, 1807, in *Writings*, ed. Lipscomb and Bergh, XI, 145. Mitchell Franklin was the first historian to recognize the relationship between the militia scheme and the legal problem. He emphasized its negative design, however; *viz.*, to "expel" Spanish law rather than to introduce common law (Franklin, "The Place of Thomas Jefferson in the Expulsion of the Spanish Medieval Law from Louisiana," *Tulane Law Review*, 16 (1941-42), 319-338; and "The 18th Brumaire in Louisiana: Talleyrand and the Spanish Medieval Legal System of 1806," *ibid.*, pp. 514-561). Franklin interpreted the enactment of the Digest of 1808 as a victory for Jeffersonian policy—a different position from the one argued in these pages.

55. Paine to Jefferson, Jan. 25, 1805, Jefferson Papers, LC. Paine was very much interested in the disposition of the Louisiana purchase territory. As early as the summer of 1803, even before the actual transfer of sovereignty, he suggested sending "Thousands and tens of thousands in England and Ireland and also in Scotland" to settle there (Paine to Jefferson, Aug. 2, 1803, *ibid.*]. Paine had an abiding hatred for the Louisiana French, because he believed that they were all sympathetic to the *ancien régime* and that, consequently, the territory had become a haven for its supporters. In his "Address to the French Inhabitants of Louisiana"—Paine's reply to the Louisiana Remonstrance of 1804—he reminded the Louisianians that they were not the only people who were meant to live in that area and that the territory had not been purcahsed for their benefit alone (*The Writings of Thomas Paine*, ed. M. D. Conway [4 vols., New York, 1894-1896], III, 430-436). When the Louisiana memorialists—Derbigny, Sauvé, and Destréhan—were in Washington in the winter of 1804-05, Paine warned Jefferson not to make any concessions to them. He even proposed that the very name "Louisiana" be changed, so that the vestiges of French culture and influence could be permanently erased.

56. Jefferson to Dickinson, Jan. 13, 1807, in Jefferson, *Writings*, ed. Ford, IX, 8.

57. Dickinson to Jefferson, Jan. 22, 1807, Jefferson Papers, University of Virginia.

58. Jefferson to Chandler Price, Feb. 28, 1807, Jefferson Papers, LC.

59. Jefferson to Gallatin, Nov. 22, 1807, in *Writings*, ed. Lipscomb and Bergh, XI, 398; also Jefferson to ?R, November 30, 1807, Jefferson Papers, LC.

60. Claiborne to Jefferson, June 22, 1806, *Letter Books*, III, 341. In his letter to John Breckinridge of Sept. 17, 1805 (*Territorial Papers*, ed. Carter, IX, 506), James Brown had written that "the best of all remedies [for the legal chaos] is the one hinted at in your letter—'a plentiful supply of American Emigrants'— . . . Soon would we fill our Legislature with characters devoted to the Union, and firmly attached to their American brethren."

61. *Letter Books*, III, 341.

62. Letters from Jefferson to Dupont de Nemours, Thaddeus Kosciuzko, and John Armstrong, May 2, 1808, Jefferson Papers, LC.

63. Edward Livingston to Robert R. Livingston, Nov. 13, 1806, Robert R. Livingston Papers, New York Historical Society.

64. See Noble E. Cunningham, Jr., *The Jeffersonian Republicans in Power, 1801-1809* (Chapel Hill, University of North Carolina Press, 1963), pp. 258-267.

65. *National Intelligencer,* Aug. 11, 1806.

66. Cunningham, *Jeffersonian Republicans,* p. 264.

67. Several months later in an article entitled "The advantages of Union, with an inquiry into the compatibility of Republican Government with an Extensive Territory"—a piece with obvious if unstated application to the territory of Orleans—the *National Intelligencer* argued that union and a common system of laws were mutually reinforcing. The editorial's implication, clearly reflective of the basic Administration position, was that the adoption of different codes or systems of law in each of the states would weaken the bonds of national unity (*National Intelligencer,* Oct. 6, 1806).

68. Extracts from Thierry's essay were included in a letter by Bellechasse to the *Louisiana Gazette,* April 8, 1808, nearly two years after it was written. See below, chap. 7, sec. IV.

69. Thierry's historical judgment was a bit generous. Americans had a fixed, even dogged, belief that political liberty and common law rights were indissolubly linked. They regarded the Quebec Act of 1774, with its stipulated concessions to the Catholic religion and the French civil law, as a hostile measure designed to intimidate the American colonies rather than as a conciliatory gesture to the French Canadians. American reaction to the Act was made clear in numerous resolutions of the Continental Congress in the fall of 1774: *viz.,* the Suffolk Resolves of Sept. 17, the Declaration and Resolves of Oct. 14, the Association Agreement of Oct. 20, and the Address to the People of Great Britain of Oct. 21 (U.S. Continental Congress, *Journals,* 1774-1789, ed. Worthington C. Ford, [34 vols., Washington, D.C., 1904-1937], I, 34-35, 76, 80, 87-88). The Declaration of Independence itself summarized this attitude when it indicted George III "for abolishing the free System of English Laws in a neighboring Province, establishing therein an Arbitrary government, and enlarging its Boundaries so as to render it at once an example and fit instrument for introducing the same absolute rule into these Colonies" (*Documents,* ed. Commager, p. 101).

The Quebec French were well aware of American hostility to their local institutions and they refused to accept the proferred invitation to oppose British policy in 1774 (Letter to the Inhabitants of Quebec, Oct. 26, 1774, U.S. Cont. Cong., *Journal,* I, 105), or to rise in rebellion and join the American army of liberation sent to Canada in 1776. They viewed American assurances that local liberties were secure with suspicion bordering upon alarm. As one inhabitant of Montreal put it, "Oh! the perfidious, double-faced Congress; let us bless and obey our benevolent Prince whose humanity is consistent, and extends to all Regions; let us abhor all . . . whose Addresses, like their Resolves, are destructive of their own objects" (extract of a letter from Canada, March 24, 1775, in Peter Force, ed., *American Archives*, 4th and 5th Series [9 vols., Washington, D.C., 1837-1853], 4th Ser., II, 231).

The British did attempt to institute the common law in the Proclamation of 1763 which reorganized the province of Quebec. The problems of mixed legal systems, of language barriers, and of popular disaffection—later so familiar in Louisiana—were the result. The Quebec Act, passed a decade later, was a positive response to these problems. Reserving the most popular elements of common law—trial by jury, English criminal law, and habeas corpus—the civil law was allowed to remain in force. For a close analysis of the continuing problems of judicial administration in Canada under the Quebec Act, see Hilda Neatby's *The Administration of Justice under the Quebec Act* (Minneapolis, University of Minnesota Press, 1937). Neatby's more recent *Quebec: The Revolutionary Age, 1760-1791* (Toronto, McClelland and Stewart, 1966) presents a balanced evaluation of the Act and qualifies the extent of its liberal concessions to the French *habitants*.

70. *Orleans Gazette*, Oct. 9, 1806. The *Gazette* referred to the *Telegraphe* articles, but the relevant numbers of that paper are no longer extant.

71. *A Short Letter to a Member of Congress Concerning the Territory of Orleans* (Washington, D.C., 1806). The decision to have the pamphlet published in Washington may have been part of an Administration effort to influence opinion in order to build support for Jefferson's militia scheme. Brown's personal history is obscure.

72. *Ibid.*, p. 13.

73. *Ibid.*, pp. 22-23.

74. Francis R. Aumann, "The Influence of English and Civil Law Principles upon the American Legal System during the Critical Post Revolutionary Period," *University of Cincinnati Law Review*, 12 (1938), 289-317; Anton Hermann Chroust, *The Rise of the Legal Profession in America* (2 vols., Norman, Okla., University of Oklahoma Press, 1965), II, 3-91; Peter Stein, "The Attraction of the Civil Law in Post Revolutionary America," *Virginia Law Review*, 52 (1966), 403-434.

75. The *Instructions from the Inhabitants to Their Representatives* of 1805 is a good example of the widespread hostility toward lawyers in Louisiana in this period. The pamphlet noted that opposition to the Americanization of the courts was partly the result of the fact that this change had caused the number of lawyers to increase. At the time of the cession there had been only three or four attorneys in Lower Louisiana (*Account of Louisiana* [Providence, 1803], p. 51). The *Instructions* reminded the legislators that they were "legislating for a people in their political infancy, agricultural, plain, honest, and laborious; who have hitherto done without a bar, without lawyers, and almost without lawsuits" (*Instructions*, p. 1). Other phrases dotting the work—"artful harranguers," "horrid empire of chicane," "idle pleaders," "the seeds of litigious differences," "retinue of lawyers,"—betray the pervasive animus toward the legal profession which played so distinctive a role in the legal controversies animating the territory.

Another interesting example of this was Julien Poydras's speech to the legislative council on Oct. 1, 1807. This work was reprinted in pamphlet form over the signature of PROBUS in 1808. An answer to Poydras by one MISONOMOS appeared in the *Lousiana Gazette* on Jan. 22, 1808. At this time there was a lively debate in the Orleans legislature over a bill to regulate the practice of law by establishing preliminary examinations and qualifications for attorneys as well as a schedule of fees. From the spare record of debates, it appears that the American faction in the legislature opposed the bill and the French supported it. An American delegate argued that "the tendency of this bill is evidently to bring disgrace upon the bar. Why this deadly animosity against that honorable profession? Are lawyers worse than other men? . . . "—to which one M. Blanque replied, " . . . as the fact cannot be denied that base men have found their way to the bar, it behoves the legislature to purge it of the impurity" (*Lousiana Gazette*, Feb. 23, 1808).

After a visit to the outlying counties in the spring of 1806 Claiborne reported to Madison that the local inhabitants were complaining mostly about the conduct of the lawyers: "They are said to be extravagant in their charges; to encourage litigation; and to speculate on the distresses of their clients" (Claiborne to Madison, June 15, 1806, *Letter Books*, III, 331; also, Claiborne to Jefferson, June 17, 1806, *ibid.*, p. 333).

76. *Short Letter*, p. 11.

77. This was not a terribly original point. The civilians, after all, were the first to charge that the rising volume of litigation was attibutable to the increased number of common lawyers in the territory.

78. Brown said that the list of Spanish legal authorities cited in the vetoed declaratory bill of May 1806 was not a list at all but a haphazard, incoherent, and awkward "burlesque" betraying an effort to give legal sanction only to books in the private libraries of those "few French lawyers" rather than a genuine effort to fashion a legal system.

79. *Short Letter*, p. 18.

80. "It is a matter of public notoriety," wrote Jeremiah Brown, "that our St. Domingo Lycurgus is avowedly copying his new code from that of Bonaparte, to the infinite delight of the whole party by whom he is employed" (*Short Letter*, p. 21). The extent to which the *Code Civil* of Napoleon, promulgated in 1804, served as the substantive basis of the Lousiana Digest of 1808 is still a warmly debated issue. See below, chap. 7, sect. III.

81. *Short Letter*, p. 25.

82. *Ibid.*, p. 26.

83. *Ibid.*, p. 30.

84. *Ibid.*, p. 31.

Chapter 7. The Louisiana Civil Law Digest

1. Claiborne to Madison, Dec. 5, 1806, in *Official Letter Books of W. C. C. Claiborne, 1801-1816*, ed. Dunbar Rowland (6 vols., Jackson, Miss., 1917), IV, 42.

2. Message, Jan. 13, 1807, *ibid.*, p. 92.

3. Official reply of Poydras, Jan. 22, 1807, *ibid.*, pp. 111-112.

4. Claiborne's address appeared in the *Louisiana Gazette* on January 16, 1807. The council's answer appeared in the *Orleans Gazette* on Feb. 5, 1807.

5. There are large gaps in Claiborne's official papers during 1807. Nothing at all appears in the *Letter Books* from April 21 to July 16 and from August 24 to October 17. During February, 1808 the individual books of the forthcoming digest were reported out of committee for legislative consideration. These proceedings were recorded in the *Louisiana Gazette*, but the debates themselves are unrecorded.

6. On the very same day of Claiborne's address to the legislature, Jefferson was writing a long letter to John Dickinson in which he discussed the legal question and the militia scheme in such close juxtaposition that it is clear that the President looked upon these matters as related issues. His letter reveals how sanguine he was, at this time, that the militia scheme would solve the legal problem. "The defence of the country would thus be placed on the spot," he wrote, "and the additional number would entitle the territory to become a state, would make the majority American, and make it an American instead of a French State. This would not sweeten the pill to the French: but in making that acquisition [Louisiana] we had some view to our own good as well as theirs" (Jefferson to Dickinson, Jan. 13, 1807, in *The Writings of Thomas Jefferson*, ed. P. L. Ford (10 vols., New York, 1892-99), IX, 8. Dickinson was not impressed. His reply did not change Jefferson's mind, but it probably dampened his enthusiasm (Dickinson to Jefferson, Jan. 22, 1807, Jefferson Papers, University of Virginia).

7. Orleans Territory, *Acts Passed at the First Session of the Second Legislature of the Territory of Orleans* (New Orleans, 1808), pp. 120-129.

8. *Ibid.*, pp. 128-129; E. B. Dubuisson, "The Codes of Louisiana (Originals Written in French; Errors of Translation)," *Louisiana Bar Association Reports*, 25 (1924), 143-157.

9. Message of April 2, 1808, *Orleans Gazette*, April 2, 1808.

10. Claiborne to Madison, April 5, 1808, *Letter Books*, IV, 168.

11. On this and other points in this chapter I am indebted to Professor Robert A. Pascal of the Louisiana State University School of Law.

12. Orleans Territory, 2nd Legis., 1st sess., *Acts Passed* (1808), pp. 120-121.

13. *Ibid.*, pp. 126-127.

14. Hayes v. Berwick, 2 Martin (O.S.) 138 (1812), at 140.

15. Cottin v. Cottin, 5 Martin (O.S.), 93 (1817), at 94.

16. *Digest of the Civil Laws now in Force in the Territory of Orleans, with alterations and amendments, adapted to its present system of government* (New Orleans, 1808), Prel. Tit., art. 3, pp. 2-3.

17. The redactors wrote, "To say that customs have the force of laws in a country where all laws are written appears to us a contradiction." See "Additions and Amendments to the Civil Code of the State of Louisiana," *Projet* of the Civil Code of 1825, in *Louisiana Legal Archives* (3

vols., Louisiana State Law Institute, Baton Rouge, 1940), I, 1. The Code of 1825 did provide for the partial abrogation of prior law in areas covered by provisions of the revised code (Civil Code, 1825, art. 3521). However, custom was revived by a subsequent court decision (Reynolds v Swain et al., 13 Louisiana Reports [O.S.] 193 [1839]) when the state Supreme Court held that article 3521 of the 1825 code applied only to positive enactments passed before the code's adoption and not to the body of anterior custom.

18. Amos Stoddard, *Sketches, Historical and Descriptive,* of Louisiana (Philadelphia, 1812), pp. 270-271; see also Jeremiah Brown, *A Short Letter to a Member of Congress Concerning the Territory of Orleans* (Washington, 1806), p. 15; [Pierre Derbigny], *Esquisse de la Situation Politique et Civile de la Louisiane, depuis le 30 Novembre, 1803, jusqu'au 1er octobre 1804, par un Louisianais* (New Orleans, 1804), pp. 23, 35. This view, that Spanish law had, by 1800, replaced French law in Louisiana, is evidenced in numerous contemporary sources, some of the most notable of which are presented (and endorsed) in Elizabeth G. Brown's "Law and Government in the Louisiana Purchase: 1803-1804," *Wayne Law Review,* 2 (1956), 169-189, esp. 186-189; see also the important documentary evidence substantiating the resolve of the Spanish government to incorporate Louisiana "into the legal and political system in force in the other Spanish possessions in the Hemisphere" in Rodolfo Batiza, "The Unity of Private Law in Louisiana under Spanish Rule," *Inter-American Law Review,* 4 (1962), 139-156, quote at 150-151. There was, in fact, surprisingly little attachment to French law in Lousiana in the period prior to the enactment of the *Napoleonic Code* (Ferdinand Stone, "The Law with a Difference and How It Came About," in Hodding Carter, ed., *The Past as Prelude: New Orleans, 1718-1968* [New Orleans, Pelican, 1968], pp. 42-70).

19. Miner v. The Bank of Louisiana, 1 Martin (O.S.) 12 (1809); Daublin v. New Orleans, 1 Martin (O.S.) 185 (1809); Caisergues v. Dujarreau, 1 Martin (O.S.) 7 (1809); Magdelaine v. Major, 1 Martin (O.S.) 200 (1809); these cases are briefly analyzed in Brown, "Law and Government in the Louisiana Purchase," pp. 188-189.

20. Beard v. Poydras, 4 Martin (O.S.) 348 (1816); Cottin v. Cottin, 5 Martin (O.S.) 93 (1817).

21. *The Laws of Las Siete Partidas, which are still in Force in the State of Lousiana,* ed. and trans. Louis Moreau Lislet and Henry Carleton (2 vols., New Orleans, 1820), I, xviii-xxii.

22. Dainow, "Moreau Lislet's Notes on Sources of the Louisiana Civil Code of 1808," *Louisiana Law Review,* 19 (1958-59), 43-51, quote at p. 50.

23. Franklin, "An Important Document in the History of American Roman and Civil Law: The de la Vergne Manuscript," *Tulane Law Review,* 33 (1958), 35-42.

24. Pascal, "A Recent Discovery in a Copy of the Digest of the Civil Laws of 1808 with Marginal Source References in Moreau Lislet's Hand," *Lousiana Law Review,* 26 (1965), 25-27.

25. Among others accepting the position that the Digest of 1808 was

based upon French law is Elizabeth G. Brown, "Legal Systems in Conflict: Orleans Territory, 1804-1812," *American Journal of Legal History* 1 (1957), 35-75, esp. pp. 53, 58; also John H. Tucker, Jr., "Tradition and Technique of Codification in the Modern World: The Louisiana Experience," *Louisiana Law Review*, 25 (1965), 698-719, esp. 699n, 715; and Tucker, "Effect on the Civil Law of Lousiana Brought about by the Changes in its Sovereignty," a paper delivered to the Society of Bartolus, Juridical Studies, no. 1.

26. Batiza, "The Louisiana Civil Code of 1808: Its Actual Sources and Present Relevance," *Tulane Law Review*, 46, (1971-72), 4-165.

27. *Ibid.*, p. 9 and n.34.

28. *Ibid.*, p. 28.

29. *Ibid.*, pp. 11-12.

30. *Projet de Code Civil* (1800) 2.2.15 and Louisiana Digest (1808) 2.2.13: "Les attérrissemens et accroissemens qui se forment successivement et imperceptiblement aux fonds riverains d'un fleuve ou d'une rivière, s'appellent alluvion. L'alluvion profite au proprietaire riverain, soit qu'il s'agisse d'un fleuve ou d'une riviere navigable ou non." The Louisiana Digest omitted the Projet's further stipulation that riverfront proprietors keep a footpath alongside the river: "a la charge, dans le premier cas, de laisser le marchepied prescrit par le reglement" (*Projet*, 2.2.15).

31. *Projet* (1800), 2.2.19: "Les îles, îlots, attérrissemens qui se forment dans le lit des fleuves, ou des rivières navigables ou flottables appartiennent a la nation. Il en est de même des îles flottantes."

32. Louisiana Civil Code (1825), art. 512: "Islands and sand bars, which are formed in the beds of navigable rivers or streams, and which are not attached to the bank, belong to the State, if there be no adverse title or prescription."

33. *Projet* [1823] of the Civil Code of 1825, in *Louisiana Legal Archives*, I, 47-48.

34. The 1825 Revision did modify the strict emphasis on private proprietary right to alluvions in the direction of French law by requiring riparian owners "to leave public that portion of the bank which is required by law for the public use"—an addition whose necessity in light of the protracted nature of the Batture dispute was obvious to the redactors of the Revised Louisiana Civil Code. See Louisiana Civil Code (1825), art. 509; *Projet* (1823), *Louisiana Legal Archives*, I, 47-48.

35. Compare the Digest (1808), 2.1.6, with the French *Projet* (1800), 2.1.25.

36. Modern French law holds that the banks of navigable rivers are part of the public domain. See *Amos and Walton's Introduction to French Law* (2nd ed., London, Clarendon, 1963), p. 91; D. M. Aird, *The Civil Laws of France* . . . (London, 1875), p. 74.

37. *Siete Partidas*, Pt. 3, tit. 28, law 6, a provision which remained in force in Louisiana; see *Laws of Las Siete Partidas*, ed. and trans. Moreau Lislet and Carleton, vol. I, p. 337.

38. Morgan v. Livingston, 6 Martin (O.S.), 19 (1819); Municipality No. 2 v. Orleans Cotton Press, 9 Louisiana Reports 436 (1841); A. N.

Yiannopoulos, *Louisiana Practise*, vol. I: *Civil Law of Property: The Law of Things, Real Rights, Real Actions* (St. Paul, Minn., West Publishing Co., 1966), chap. 3, sec. 31, esp. pp. 87, 89. I am indebted to Nina N. Pugh, clerk of the Louisiana Court of Appeals, for guidance on this subject.

39. Batiza, "The Louisiana Civil Code of 1808," appendix B, pp. 36-44; Batiza does note the difficulties caused by the similarity of some codal provisions to diverse sources (*ibid.*, pp. 26-28) but he obviously does not consider that this betrays any serious methodological weakness.

40. John Gravier v. The Mayor, Aldermen, and Inhabitants of the City of New Orleans (1807), U.S. Cong., *American State Papers: Documents, Legislative and Executive of the Congress of the United States* (18 vols., Washington, D.C., 1832-1861): *Public Lands*, II, 24.

41. Using more traditional techniques of textual analysis, Nina N. Pugh concludes that "the matrimonial regimes existing in Louisiana at the time of its purchase by the United States were Spanish in origin and nature" ("The Spanish Community of Gains in 1803: *Sociedad de Gananciales*," *Louisiana Law Review*, 30 (1969), 1-43, quote at p. 1). Batiza, on the other hand, finds that "the Spanish system of community of acquets or gains (*sociedad de ganancias*) that appears in the Code, rather than being opposed to the French system of *communauté*, supplements it" ("Louisiana Civil Code of 1808," p. 29). For a sharp criticism of his method of approach and for Batiza's reply see Robert A. Pascal, "Sources of the Digest of 1808: A Reply to Professor Batiza," and R. Batiza, "Sources of the Civil Code of 1808, Facts and Speculation: A Rejoinder," *Tulane Law Review*, 46 (1971-72), 603-652. Some further support for the Pascal-revisionist school comes from L. A. Darby III and T. J. McDonald, Jr., "A Recent Discovery: Another Copy of Moreau Lislet's Annotations to the Civil Code of 1808," *ibid.*, 47 (1972-73), 1210-13.

42. Batiza, "The Unity of Private Law in Louisiana," *passim*, and "Sources of the Civil Code: A Rejoinder," p.649.

43. Batiza, "The Louisiana Civil Code of 1808," p. 28. Thomas W. Tucker has written that Blackstone's influence on the Digest of 1808 was "pervasive." Specifically, he notes that "Blackstone provided the scheme of Book I, Title 6 of the Louisiana Code and was the immediate source of a number of its articles" ("Sources of Louisiana's Law of Persons: Blackstone, Domat, and the French Codes," *Tulane Law Review*, 44 (1969-1970), 264-295, quotes at pp. 275 and 280n). Batiza, however, has qualified Tucker's assertion and concludes that "the influence of the common law on the Code of 1808 is far more limited" than Tucker suggested ("The Louisiana Civil Code of 1808," p. 10n).

44. As Joseph Dainow has written, "The primary significance of the Civil Code of 1808 was that it constituted the formal recognition and establishment of civil law for the territory. Following the early conflict and the dreaded possibility of an imposed common law system, the fact that the civil law emerged victorious must have been more significant than any concern about whether there was serious difference between

the civil law systems of Spanish and French laws." See Introduction to *Civil Code of Louisiana: Revision of 1870 with Amendments to 1947*, ed. Joseph Dainow (St. Paul, Minn., West Publishing Co., 1947), p. xix. In general, see pp. xvi-xx for some needed perspective on the whole dispute regarding Spanish and French law and the Digest of 1808.

45. *Moniteur de la Louisiane*, March 16, 1926, 1808; *Louisiana Courier*, March 21, 1808 (referred to in *Louisiana Gazette*, April 8, 1808).

46. Bellechasse's letter appeared in the *Louisiana Gazette*, April 8, 1808.

47. In 1806, of course, the *Courier* had not yet appeared and Thierry was dependent upon other New Orleans printers to publish his writings.

48. *Louisiana Courier*, April 4, 1808.

49. Circular form letter of October 4, 1808, *Letter Books*, IV, 220.

50. Claiborne to Madison, Oct. 7, 1808, in *The Territorial Papers of the United States*, ed. Clarence E. Carter (26 vols., Washington, D.C., Government Printing Office, 1934-1962), IX, 802.

51. Message to the legislature, *Orleans Gazette*, April 2, 1808.

52. Claiborne to Judge J. White, Oct. 11, 1808, *Letter Books*, IV, 225. Virtually an identical letter, minus important political observations, was sent to the parish judges on Oct. 22. (*ibid.*, p. 230).

53. *Ibid.*, p. 226.

54. Batiza, "The Louisiana Civil Code of 1808," *passim*; Tucker, "Sources of Louisiana's Law of Persons," *passim*.

55. Thomas Tucker argues, mistakenly I think, that the work of 1808 was a genuine code and not a digest ("Sources of Louisiana's Law of Persons," esp. 293-295).

56. John H. Merryman has emphasized this important ideological and historical role that codes have played in the modern civil law world. See *The Civil Law Tradition: An Introduction to the Legal Systems of Western Europe and Latin America* (Stanford, Stanford University Press, 1969), chap. 5; also, Ferdinand F. Stone, "To Codify or Not to Codify: Derivation of Louisiana Law," Address, *ABA Section of International and Comparative Law Bulletin*, July 1965, p. 16.

57. Jefferson to Claiborne, Dec. 2, 1804, *Territorial Papers*, IX, 342.

58. The common cultural and political background of the American people was a major advantage the United States had in its formative stage as a nation. See Seymour M. Lipset, *The First New Nation: The United States in Historical and Comparative Perspective* (New York, Basic Books, 1963), p. 92, *et passim*. Thus the acceptance of a distinctively different cultural community—as was the case with the people of Lower Louisiana—impaired the relative homogeneity of an emergent American nationality.

59. On the pervasive influence of Blackstone on the legal profession in the late eighteenth and early nineteenth centuries see Julian S. Waterman, "Thomas Jefferson and Blackstone's Commentaries," *Illinois Law Review*, 27 (1933), 629-659; and Perry Miller, *The Life of the Mind in America: From the Revolution to the Civil War* (New York, Harcourt, Brace and World, 1965), pp. 113, 115, 130, 142. Jefferson thought that Blackstone's influence had had a baneful effect on legal education in

America. Writing in 1812, he observed that law students believed they had mastered all when they knew the *Commentaries* and referred to "Blackstone lawyers" as "ephemeral insects of the law" (Jefferson to John Tyler, June 17, 1812, in *The Writings of Thomas Jefferson*, ed. A. A. Lipscomb and A. E. Bergh [Memorial Ed., 20 vols., Washington, D.C., 1904-1905], XIII, 166-167). On Blackstone's datedness, see Roscoe Pound, *The Formative Era of American Law* (Boston, Little Brown, 1938), p. 142. On the obscurity and unavailability of the common law for ready transplantation into Louisiana, see Ferdinand Stone, "The Law with a Difference," p. 57.

60. Batiza, "The Louisiana Civil Code of 1808: Its Actual Sources and Present Relevance," *passim*. There is no doubt that Louisiana law at the time of the cession was a mélange of diverse legal materials. But it is also true that the sense of confusion was much more acute among the Americans than among the local attorneys and officials. New Orleans lawyers had extensive law libraries containing books of Roman, canon, Dutch, French, and Anglo-American as well as Spanish law (Mitchell Franklin, "Libraries of Edward Livingston and of Moreau Lislet," *Tulane Law Review*, 15 [1940-41], 401-414). They worked in French, Spanish, and Latin with facility and were able to cite their sources in these vast bodies of law with apparent ease. They wound their way through the rich but uncodified labyrinth of Spanish law with the help of the legal manuals of Josef Febrero, the eighteenth-century royal notary whose works were well known. On the other hand, the average American attorney coming to Louisiana with two or three volumes of English law was bewildered by what he encountered. Even Edward Livingston was confused, if only at first (see letter to Robert R. Livingston, May 6, 1804, Robert R. Livingston Papers, New York Historical Society). But Livingston was an unusual case. He came better equipped than most and applied himself with his customary diligence to the mastery of what he did not already know. Another example was George Strawbridge, a future Louisiana Supreme Court judge. A graduate of Princeton and a former law student of James Bayard of Delaware, Strawbridge came to New Orleans in 1818 and studied the civil law, "the new civil code" in particular. His knowledge of Spanish gave him some advantage, but even so, he confessed to difficulties beyond the problems of translation. Strawbridge, like Livingston, was devoted to legal studies. Most of his American colleagues at the bar were not, however, and as a result "it was almost as difficult to accustom themselves to the use of the law of Louisiana as to the French language; some of them were men of some eminence with whom it was hard to go back to the ABC learning of the elements and technicalities of a new system; the . . . Judges felt this difficulty and managed as they could" (Autobiography of George Strawbridge, Ledyard Family Papers, Lorenzo State Historic Site, Cazenovia, N.Y., p. 77). For such men the Digest of 1808 was an indispensable guide to local law.

61. In February 1805 a group of New Orleans merchants petitioned the legislative council for the establishment of a commercial court. They complained of the delay of the regular tribunals and the misinformation

of the judges. They wanted special judicial machinery to deal with commerical matters: a panel of merchant arbitrators, an attorney general to represent the public interest in all proceedings, juries selected from the merchant class, special court officers and lawyers, and the enactment of a code of commerce. The merchants resisted the common law because of its deficiency as a body of commerical regulations. Above all, the New Orleans merchants opposed the common law procedure of having commercial disputes decided in ordinary law courts (see Petition of Several Merchants of the City of New Orleans to the Legislative Council, *Orleans Gazette*, Feb. 16, 1805). Commerical law did not become one of the distinctive areas differentiating Louisiana from the rest of the United States because it was not to its economic advantage to do this. A proposed commercial code was rejected in 1824. In fact, until recent years, Louisiana has been quick to adopt uniform commerical laws. (See George A. Pope, "How Real Is the Difference Today between the Law of Louisiana and That of the Other Forty-seven States," *George Washington Law Review*, 17 (1949), 186-198, esp. 193, 196.)

62. The French *Code Noir*, as modified by Spanish practice, remained in force in Louisiana. Portions of it were reenacted in the slavery legislation passed by the territorial legislature on June 7, 1806. See *A General Digest of the Acts of the Legislature of Louisiana . . .* [1804-1827], comp. L. Moreau Lislet (3 vols., New Orleans, 1828), I, 100-119; and for subsequent enactments, *ibid.*, pp. 119-130, II, 383-391. For lucid discussions of the similarities and differences between Louisiana law and that of the rest of the United States, besides the article by Pope ("How Real is the Difference"), see Leonard Oppenheim, "Louisiana's Civil Law Heritage," address to the annual meeting of the Notaries Association of New Orleans, April 10, 1958; and Ferdinand Stone, "The Law with a Difference and How It Came About," esp. pp. 68-69.

63. Mitchell Franklin, "Some Observations on the Influence of French Law on the Early Civil Codes of Louisiana," *Le Droit Civil Francais* (Paris, 1936), pp. 883-845, esp. p. 841.

64. Even after the enactment of the Digest the courts faced a difficult conflict of law problem. For some analysis of early illustrative cases see Brown, "Legal System in Conflict," pp. 60-73. Unfortunately, published Superior Court case reports for the period prior to 1809 do not exist, although there was, apparently, a body of manuscript court records discovered thirty years ago in a WPA Historical Records Survey. From the inventory made at that time it would appear that the administration of justice under the Americans was running more smoothly than contemporaries would have been prepared to admit. Regrettably, these manuscript court records have again disappeared. See Louisiana Historical Records Survey (WPA), Inventory of the State Archives of Louisiana—Series II: The Judiciary, no. 1: *The Superior Court of the Territory of Orleans* (University, Louisiana, 1942).

65. Louisiana Constitution (1812), Art. IV, sec. 11.

66. For a good example of this see Robert A. Pascal, "Of Trusts, Human Dignity, Legal Science, and Taxes: Suggested Principles for a

Louisiana Trust Estates Law," *Louisiana Law Review*, 23 (1963), 639-661, where an effort is made to outline how the common law institution of the trust can be accommodated to Louisiana law without doing violence to basic civil law principles.

67. Merryman, *Civil Law Tradition*, pp. 154-155; Thibaudeau Rinfret, "The Relations between Civil Law and Common Law," in *The Code Napoleon and the Common Law World*, ed. Bernard Schwartz (New York, New York University Press, 1956), pp. 378-388; Arthur T. Vanderbilt, "The Reconciliation of the Civil Law and the Common Law," *ibid.*, pp. 389-400.

68. In the territorial period, the great debate in Louisiana was whether or not Louisiana *ought to be* governed by the civil law. In more recent times this political controversy has evolved into a more academic dispute as to whether or not it *is* civilian. One of the first to challenge the standard view was Charles P. Fenner, who wrote in 1913 that Lousiana jurisprudence "is to a very large extent based . . . upon the common law" ("The Jurisprudence of the Supreme Court of Louisiana," 133 Louisiana Reports [1913]: Gordon Ireland was even more emphatic. Attributing Louisiana's attachment to its civil law heritage to "romantic prejudice," Ireland concluded that "*Louisiana is today a common law state*" ("Louisiana's Legal System Reappraised," *Tulane Law Review*, 11 [1937], 585-598). Four distinguished law professors— H. S. Daggett, J. Dainow, P. M. Hebert, and H. G. McMahon—responded to Ireland ("A Reappraisal Appraised: A Brief for the Civil Law of Louisiana," *ibid.*, 12 [1937], 12-41). They argued that Louisiana was still civilian. This view gained added weight in the 1950's in writings by H. F. Jolowicz ("The Civil Law in Louisiana," *ibid.*, 29 [1955], 491-503 and John H. Tucker, Jr., ("The Code and the Common Law in Louisiana," *ibid.*, 29 [1955], 739-764). Tucker concluded that "in the structure of the code and the processes whereby it has been developed, Louisiana is still civilian." C. Girard Davidson ("Stare Decisis in Louisiana," *ibid.*, 7 [1932], 100-118) took a middle position, arguing that Louisiana has established a unique blend of the two systems, "a jurisprudence which, though fundamentally civilian, has been influenced and molded by observation and contact with surrounding common law, so that a system has resulted *sui generis* in character." Recent scholarship has tended to follow this path—i.e., that Louisiana remains a civil law jurisdiction with substantial transfusions of common law concepts and techniques. Two examples are Leonard Oppenheim, "Louisiana's Civil Law Heritage," Address (New Orleans, 1958), and Albert Tate, Jr., "Techniques of Judicial Interpretation in Louisiana," *Louisiana Law Review*, 22 (1962), 727-755. Tate speaks of a "civilian renaissance" in progress in Louisiana in the past generation.

69. The Charter of the Institute specifies its purposes, including the following: "To make available translation of Civil Law materials and commentaries and to provide by studies and other doctrinal writings, materials for the better understanding of the Civil Law of Louisiana and the philosophy upon which it is based" (*Louisiana Legal Archives*, vol. II, pt. I, pp. xv-xvi). The first project undertaken by the Institute was

dedicated "to the perpetuation of the civil law heritage of Louisiana, of which its people are justly proud" (*ibid.*, p. xvi).

70. "Memoire of Bernard Marigny addressed to his fellow citizens of New Orleans," (Paris, 1822), trans. Olivia Blanchard, in Howard-Tilton Memorial Library, Tulane University. Marigny's reference to Baton Rouge refers to the early agitation by American settlers to remove the state capital from what was thought to be the pernicious influence of the still-dominant French population of New Orleans. Baton Rouge did not become the capital of the state of Louisiana until 1849.

Selected Sources

The sources upon which I have based this study are uneven in strength. In some areas they are rich and abundant; in others, fragmentary and elusive. In this brief essay I should like to describe those which proved to be the most rewarding as well as mention some of the problems that confront the researcher in the legal and political history of Louisiana in this period.

The Jefferson Papers in the Library of Congress are probably the single most valuable collection because of Jefferson's prodigious capacity to maintain active correspondence with a wide assortment of people. Many of Jefferson's letters having to do with public affairs in the Orleans territory have been published in numerous editions of his writings, but equally significant "letters received" deserve more attention than they have had. For example, the letters of Philip Reibelt present sidelights of the Burr conspiracy and its political ramifications in the territory with unique sharpness. Other materials consulted in the Manuscript Division of the Library of Congress were the John Breckinridge Papers, the James Brown Papers, the Burr Conspiracy Letters, the Madison Papers, the George W. Campbell Papers, and the Louisiana Miscellany. The Library's microfilm collection of the Early State Records contains (for the Orleans territory) Executive Department Journals (1803-1809), Governor's Office Letters (1804-1814), a Journal of the Legislative Council (1804-1811), Court Records of the U.S. District Court (?-1812), and Miscellaneous Legislative Records. Unfortunately, these materials promised more than they delivered. The same is true for the Territorial Papers (Orleans Series, 1764-1813) and the Department of State Series (Miscellaneous and Domestic Letters) held by the National Archives.

Of the other major national figures concerned with the American position in the remote southwest probably the most influential, next to the President himself, was Albert Gallatin. This is surprising, since James Madison, as Secretary of State, had primary responsibility for territorial administration. But, while Madison was well informed and always in closest touch with William Claiborne in New Orleans, Jefferson frequently turned to Gallatin for advice and consultation. Some of the most penetrating insights into Administration policy are revealed in notes and letters to and from Gallatin. It was Gallatin, for example, who composed the lengthy manuscript brief on the Batture question which formed the basis of Jefferson's published treatise on that complex subject. It is possible that Jefferson believed that the Treasury secretary's own French background (he was born and educated in Geneva) gave him special insight into the French character of the Louisiana population. Whatever the cause, the Gallatin Papers in the New York Historical Society in New York City proved to be a rich body of material. The Robert R. Livingston Papers, also at the New York Historical Society, are of major importance because they contain the largest group of Edward Livingston letters available to researchers at the present time. In addition, the Van Duzer Miscellaneous Papers contain a number of interesting descriptive letters, several of which are quoted from in the text. The Society holds some thirteen boxes of New Orleans Miscellaneous materials particularly strong for the 1820's, somewhat beyond my period.

A large number of other archives were investigated. These include the Manuscripts and Archives Division of the New York Public Library (containing the Peters Family Letters and some Louisiana Papers); the Historical Society of Pennsylvania in Philadelphia (containing the Peter S. Duponceau Papers, the Gilpin Family Papers, the Simon Gratz Papers, the Josiah Stoddard Johnson Papers, the Logan Collection, the Daniel Parker Papers, and the [James] Wilkinson-[Daniel] Clark File); the American Philosophical Society Library in Philadelphia (containing the Benjamin Vaughan Papers); the William R. Perkins Library, Duke University (containing the Joseph Dubreuil de Villars Papers, The Ephraim Kirby Papers, and the John M. McCalla Papers); the Southern Historical Collection, University of North Carolina in Chapel Hill (containing the Nicholas P. Trist Papers); the New Orleans Public Library (containing the Records of the Conseil de Ville and a manuscript volume entitled "American Documents"); the Department of Archives and Manuscripts of the Louisiana State University Library in Baton Rouge (containing the Henry Wilson Papers, the Henri Remy Papers, the Charles E. A. Gayarré Collection, the Nathaniel Evans Papers, a Claiborne Letter Book, and some James Brown Papers); and, finally, the Howard-Tilton Memorial Library, Tulane University (containing the New Orleans Municipal Papers, 1770-1884, and the John McDonogh Papers).

By far the most important published sources are the two most frequently cited in the text: Dunbar Rowland, ed., *Official Letter Books of W. C. C. Claiborne, 1801-1816* (6 vols., Jackson, Miss., 1917), and Clarence E. Carter, ed., *The Territorial Papers of the United States* (26 vols., Washington, D.C., 1934-1962), vol. IX (Orleans). Used together, these two compendiums of letters, acts, reports, and other public and private documents constitute the two most indispensable collections of printed materials. Two other collections of documentary and other sources are James A. Robertson, ed. and trans., *Louisiana under the Rule of Spain, France, and the United States, 1785-1807 . . .* (2 vols., Cleveland, 1911; reprint, 1969) and B. F. French, comp., *Historical Collections of Louisiana* (5 vols., New York, 1846-1853).

The three best published sources of Jeffersoniana which contain most of Jefferson's expressions of policy and opinion on Louisiana are *The Writings of Thomas Jefferson*, ed. P. L. Ford (10 vols., New York, 1892-1899), *The Works of Thomas Jefferson*, ed. P. L. Ford (Federal Ed., 12 vols., New York, 1904-1905), and *The Writings of Thomas Jefferson*, ed. A. A. Lipscomb and A. E. Bergh (Memorial Ed., 20 vols., Washington, D.C., 1903-1905).

A large portion of the papers of the other key national figures have also been published in multiple-volumed sets: *The Writings of James Madison*, ed. Gaillard Hunt (9 vols., New York, Putnam's Sons, 1900-1910), and *Letters and Other Writings of James Madison* (4 vols., Philadelphia, 1865); *The Writings of James Monroe*, ed. S. M. Hamilton (7 vols., New York, 1898); *The Writings of Albert Gallatin*, ed. Henry Adams (3 vols., Philadelphia, 1879).

Other relevant public documents of considerable importance are *William Plumer's Memorandum of Proceedings in the United States Senate, 1803-1807*, ed. E. S. Brown (New York, Macmillan, 1923); James D. Richardson, comp., *A Compilation of the Messages and Papers of the Presidents, 1789-1897* (10 vols., Washington, D.C., 1896-1899); and U.S. Congress, *Debates and Proceedings in the Congress of the United States, 1789-1824* [Annals of Congress] (Washington, D.C., Gales and Seaton, 1834-1856). On the Batture question a concentrated collection of the principal sources can be found in U.S. Congress, *American State Papers: Documents, Legislative and Executive of the Congress of the United States* (18 vols., Washington, D.C., Gales and Seaton, 1832-1861), *Public Lands*, vol. II. Statutes (both national and territorial), Louisiana court decisions (beginning in 1809), and other government documents relevant to this period and place are available in *The Public Statutes at Large of the United States of America* [1789-1845; 1st-28th Congress] ed. Richard Peters (8 vols., Boston, Little and Brown), vol. II (6th-12th Congress); *A General Digest of the Acts of the Legislatures of the Late Territory of Orleans and of the State of Louisiana,* comp. François Xavier Martin (3 vols., New Orleans, 1816); *Martin's Reports of Cases Argued and Determined in the Supreme Court of the State of Louisiana, 1809-1830,* by François Xavier Martin (10 vols., New Orleans, 1846-1853); and Francis N. Thorpe, comp., *The Federal and State Constitutions, Colonial Charters and Other Organic Laws of the . . . United States of America* (7 vols., Washington, D.C., 1909).

Newspaper sources for early nineteenth-century Louisiana are astonishingly copious. As noted in the text, the territory of Orleans supported a variety of journals reflecting diverse shades of political opinion. Unfortunately, some of the most important papers have had the poorest survival record. Fairly complete runs of the *Louisiana Courier* (*Courrier de la Louisiane*), the *Moniteur de la Louisiane,* and the *Louisiana Gazette* still exist; on the other hand, files of the *Orleans Gazette* are very irregular, and extant copies of the *Union* and the *Telegraphe* are few and far between. A highly worthy project would be the systematic microfilming of all early Louisiana newspapers to protect them from natural hazards and to make them more readily available to students and researchers.

In addition to the assortment of newspapers, Louisiana printers also published a large number of pamphlets. All of the major legal briefs on the Batture question appeared in pamphlet form. Similarly, the Burr conspiracy led to an outpouring of printed opinion. More general legal and political problems were treated in numerous works, the most important being: *Analysis of the Third Article of the Treaty of Cession of Louisiana* (n.n.), [Washington, 1803]; Allan B. Magruder, *Political, Commercial, and Moral Reflections on the late Cession of Louisiana to the United States* (Lexington, 1803); Sylvestris [George Tucker], *Reflections on the Cession of Louisiana to the United States* (Washington, 1803); [Pierre Derbigny], *Esquisse de la Situation Politique et Civile de la Louisiane, depuis le 30 Novembre, 1803, jusqu'au 1er octobre 1804, par un Louisianais* (New Orleans, 1804); *Memorial Presented by the Inhabitants of Louisiana to the Congress of the United States . . .* (Washington, 1804); *Instructions from the Inhabitants of the Territory of Orleans to Their Representatives in the Legislature* (n.n., New Orleans [1805]); *Reflections on the Cause of the Louisianians Respectfully Submitted by Their Agents* (n.n., Washington, 1805); Jeremiah Brown, *A Short Letter to a Member of Congress Concerning the Territory of Orleans* (Washington, 1806); Agrestis [Joseph Alston], *A Short Review of the Late Proceedings at New Orleans: and some remarks upon the bill, for sus-*

pending the privilege of the writ of habeas corpus . . . (South Carolina, 1807); James Workman, *A Letter to the Respectable Citizens, Inhabitants of the County of Orleans Together with Several Letters to Governor Claiborne* (New Orleans, 1807); Edward Livingston, *Faithful Picture of the Political Situation of New Orleans at the Close of the Last and the Beginning of the Present Year—1807* (Boston, 1808); Allan B. Magruder, *A Letter from Allan B. Magruder, Esq. of Opelousas to His Correspondent in the State of Virginia, November 20, 1807* (New Orleans, 1808); and Probus [Julien Poydras], *Adresse au Conseil Legislatif du Territorre d'Orleans* (New Orleans, 1808).

Travelers' reports and other descriptive accounts of Louisiana in the early nineteenth century abound, but they are not always in agreement and must therefore be used with caution. Of the French reporters the most important were Berquin-Duvallon, *Vue de la colonie espagnole du Mississippi, ou des provinces de Louisiane et Floride occidentale . . .* (Paris, 1803); F. M. Perrin du Lac, *Voyage dans les deux Louisianes . . . en 1801, 1802, et 1803* (Paris, 1805); and C. C. Robin, *Voyages dans L'Interieur de la Louisiane . . . Pendant les Annêes 1802, 1803, 1804, 1805 et 1806* (2 vols., Paris, 1807). Visitors from the United States also reported extensively on their journeys, the best of these being Henry M. Brackenridge's *Views of Louisiana together with a journal of a voyage up the Missouri River, in 1811* (Baltimore, 1817) and Christian Schultz, *Travels on an Inland Voyage . . .* (2 vols., New York, 1810). The first intensive English-language description made for the purpose of promoting acceptance of Louisiana statehood was Amos Stoddard's *Sketches, Historical and Descriptive, of Louisiana* (Philadelphia, 1812). Basic factual information compiled by Jacob Wagner, the chief clerk in the State Department, was published as *An Account of Louisiana, laid before Congress by direction of the President of the United States, November 14, 1803 . . .* (Providence, 1803), which, together with the works of William Darby, notably his *Geographical Description of the State of Louisiana* (Philadelphia, 1816), are factual starting points for research into this period of Lousiana history.

Despite this apparent richness of manuscript and published sources, however, there are a number of important gaps in the evidentiary record. Perhaps the most critical of these is the absence of any debates of the Orleans territorial legislature. A journal of proceedings can be pieced together from newpaper accounts, but this is of relatively little value. Fragments in the Joseph Dubreuil de Villars Papers at Duke University reveal intense interest on the part of at least one legislator in civil law maxims, principles, and definitions, but without a journal of debates we cannot tell what kinds of discussions took place in the months prior to the adoption of the civil law digest. Quite possibly such a record was never kept, but without it we cannot successfully reconstruct this vital part of the decision-making process.

Equally troublesome is the thinness in the personal files of James Brown and the almost total absence of papers for Louis Moreau Lislet, the two draftsmen of the Louisiana Digest. The bulk of the papers of another principal, Edward Livingston, remains unavailable to researchers. William Claiborne's papers, while more abundant, have serious gaps in them for the period preceding the adoption of the digest—a period when this central figure thoroughly revised his attitude toward the legal question.

Finally, the most bothersome hole in the evidence is the apparent disappearance of the manuscript court records of the territorial Superior Court. While these papers, as described in an inventory made in the early 1940's (Louisiana Historical Records Survey—Works Projects Administration, *Inventory of the State Archives of Louisiana, Series II: The Judiciary, No. 1: The Superior Court of the Territory of Orleans* [University, Louisiana, 1942]), would probably cast little light upon the politics of the problem of legal "codification" in territorial Louisiana, they could tell us something about the administration of justice in the difficult adjustment period when common law forms were being superimposed upon a civil law base.

Rather than reprint every source in the secondary literature cited in the notes to the text, I should like here to indicate those books and articles of a general character which stimulated and informed this book and which the reader interested in pursuing particular questions would be advised to consult. Still a good starting point for any work in this period is Henry Adams's *History of the United States of America during the Administrations of Jefferson and Madison* (9 vols., New York, 1889-1898). My own interpretation of Jeffersonian policy with respect to Louisiana is closer to Adams in spirit than to the more pro-Jefferson treatments in the two leading works of our time, Dumas Malone's *Jefferson and His Time* (vols. 4 and 5, Little Brown, 1970 and 1974) and Merrill D. Peterson, *Thomas Jefferson and the New Nation* (New York, Oxford University Press, 1970). Irving Brant's *James Madison: Secretary of State* (Indianapolis, Bobbs Merrill, 1953) is similarly focused on the broadest issues of national policy and does not have too much to tell us about Jeffersonian aims and objectives in Lower Louisiana, but it is important to consult because of Madison's key role in the diplomatic maneuverings preceding and following the Louisiana purchase.

The political aspects of the Jefferson presidency are ably treated in Noble E. Cunningham, Jr.'s *The Jeffersonian Republicans in Power, 1801-1809* (Chapel Hill, University of North Carolina Press, 1963), although the book's focus on the Jeffersonian Republican party as the key to national politics is implicity challenged by the work of James S. Young in *The Washington Community, 1800-1828* (New York, Columbia University Press, 1966). The often misunderstood relationship between the Jeffersonians and the courts on the national and state levels is substantially clarified by Richard E. Ellis, *The Jeffersonian Crisis: Courts and Politics in the Young Republic* (New York, Oxford University Press, 1971). The whole history of American territorial growth and the changing political and administrative problems of territorial government are examined in depth by Jack E. Eblen in *The First and Second United States Empires: Governors and Territorial Government, 1784-1912* (Pittsburgh, University of Pittsburgh Press, 1968). Eblen's study puts the problems of government in Lower Louisiana into perspective, even though the area was quite unique. To understand the important role geography has played in shaping the development of Louisiana the reader will profit from Fred B. Kniffen's excellent book, *Louisiana: Its Land and People* (Baton Rouge, Louisiana State University Press, 1968), which shows the relationship between geography and history in many interesting ways. The economic history of the region has been carefully and incisively analyzed in John G. Clark's *New Orleans, 1718-1812: An Economic History* (Baton Rouge, Louisiana State University Press, 1970), the first of a two-volume work. Interesting essays on various themes of New Orleans' colorful history are presented in Hodding Carter, ed., *The Past as Prelude: New Orleans, 1718-1968* (New Orleans, Pelican Publishers, 1968). The constitutional ramifications of the Louisiana Purchase and the related issues arising at the time of Louisiana's statehood were thoroughly examined by Everett S. Brown in *The Constitutional History of the Louisiana Purchase, 1803-1812,* (University of California Publications in History, Berkeley, 1920). Finally, for helpful discussion of the differentiated composition of the Louisiana population in the early nineteenth century and the ethnic antagonisms which existed within it, see Joseph G. Tregle, Jr., "Early New Orleans Society: A Reappraisal," *Journal of Southern History*, 18 (1952), 20-36, and Lewis W. Newton, "Creoles and Anglo-Americans in Old

Louisiana: A Study in Cultural Conflicts," *Southwestern Social Science Quarterly*, 14 (1933), 31-48.

In the field of American legal history there are a number of works that show the kinds of problems legal historians have addressed—works that have established a general framework for further scholarly activity. The most comprehensive of these is Lawrence M. Friedman's *A History of American Law* (New York, Simon and Schuster, 1973), the first real attempt to tell the story of American law and legal institutions from colonial times to the twentieth century. A lively and highly readable book, Friedman's *History* draws from a rich variety of primary sources and recent books and articles and places particular problems—such as that of Louisiana—into the broad context of legal development in general. James Willard Hurst's *The Growth of American Law: The Law Makers* (Boston, Little Brown, 1950) represents a different kind of synthesis and is built around the major institutions of lawmaking as they evolved from the late eighteenth to the twentieth century. A recent collection of scholarly essays will also serve to acquaint the reader with some of the best and most influential writing in the field: *Law in American History*, ed. Donald Fleming and Bernard Bailyn (Perspectives in American History, vol. 5; Boston, Little Brown, 1971). David H. Flaherty's *Essays in the History of Early American Law* (Chapel Hill, University of North Carolina Press, 1969) does the same for the colonial era, a major formative era of American law. Older classics which are still useful and stimulating though somewhat dated in their emphases and concerns are Roscoe Pound's *The Formative Era of American Law* (Boston, Little Brown, 1938) and Charles Warren, *A History of the American Bar* (Boston, Little Brown, 1911). For the English origins of American law there are many excellent works both old and new, but the finest recent volume is S. F. C. Milsom's difficult but rewarding *Historical Foundations of the Common Law* (London, Butterworths, 1969). For the reader interested in comparativist studies the best introduction is René David and John E. C. Brierley, *Major Legal Systems in the World Today: An Introduction to the Comparative Study of Law* (New York, The Free Press, 1968), which shows the Anglo-American common law in relation to a number of other major contemporary legal systems in language which is accessible to the nonlawyer. F. H. Lawson's *A Common Lawyer Looks at the Civil Law* (Ann Arbor, University of Michigan Law School, 1953) is more technical, but it does raise the kinds of questions which practitioners trained in one tradition would confront in the other. A highly lucid and informed study of the contemporary civil law is John H. Merryman's *The Civil Law Tradition: An Introduction to the Legal Systems of Western Europe and Latin America* (Stanford, Stanford University Press, 1969).

The latter books are not primarily historical in orientation, although they all contain much history. In order to reconstruct American common law and Louisiana civil law in the early nineteenth century, therefore, it was necessary to consult contemporaneous works. Although there was no general common law for all America but only the laws and institutions of the individual states, William Blackstone's *Commentaries on the Laws of England* (4 vols., London, 1765-1769) had such pervasive influence in America that it is a good place to begin. James Kent's *Commentaries on American Law* (4 vols., New York, 1826-1830) synthesized "American Law" as of the third decade of the nineteenth century. Kent's work reflected the numerous changes and modifications of Blackstone wrought by statutory and case law since the Revolution. The actual sources of Louisiana civil law and the Digest of 1808 that was drafted to perpetuate that system are still in dispute. But the beginning of an understanding of the substance of Louisiana law in this era can be obtained from two major works of the period: the *Digest of the Civil Laws Now in Force in the Territory of Orleans with Alterations and Amendments Adapted to its Present System of Government* (New Orleans, 1808), plus *The Laws of Las Siete Partidas which are still in force in the State of Louisiana*, trans. and comp. L. Moreau Lislet and Henry Carleton (2 vols., New Orleans, 1820). The *Partidas* are generally recognized to have been the single most important book of private law in Louisiana, though the French *Projet* of 1800 and possibly the *Code Civil* itself were available to the draftsmen of the 1808 Digest.

The periodical literature is very rich, and a number of articles were particularly important in the preparation of this volume. Elizabeth G. Brown's "Law and Government in the Louisiana Purchase: 1803-1804," *Wayne Law Review*, 2 (1956), 169-189, and "Legal Systems in Conflict: Orleans Territory, 1804-1812," *American Journal of Legal History*, 1 (1957), 35-75, focus on the key question of common law versus civil law and delineate some of the principal events having to do with the conflict as it related to problems of government. The most important recent works on the debate over whether the Digest of 1808 was French or Spanish are Rodolfo Batiza, "The Louisiana Civil Code of 1808: Its Actual Sources and Present Relevance," *Tulane Law Review*, 46 (1971-72), 4-165, and Robert A. Pascal, "Sources of the Digest of 1808: A Reply to Professor Batiza," and R. Batiza, "Sources of the Civil Code of 1808, Facts and Speculation: A

Rejoinder," *Tulane Law Review*, 46 (1971-72), 603-652. Mitchell Franklin looked at the issue of Spanish and French law from a political perspective in "The Place of Thomas Jefferson in the Expulsion of Spanish Medieval Law from Louisiana," *Tulane Law Review*, 16 (1941-42), 319-338, and "The 18th Brumaire in Louisiana: Talleyrand and the Spanish Medieval Legal System of 1806," *ibid.*, 514-561.

Some of the best work on the legal institutions of Louisiana before the American period was done by Henry P. Dart: see, in particular, "Courts and Law in Colonial Louisiana," *Louisiana Bar Association Reports*, 22 (1921), 17-63. In his work Dart also emphasized the importance of Spanish law. See, for example, "The Influence of the Ancient Laws of Spain on the Jurisprudence of Louisiana," *Tulane Law Review*, 6 (1931-32), 83-93. There are many works dealing with the development of the Louisiana legal system after 1803. Two places to begin are Samuel B. Groner's "Louisiana Law: Its Development in the First Quarter Century of American Rule," *Louisiana Law Review*, 8 (1947-48), 350-382, and John T. Hood, Jr., "The History and Development of the Louisiana Civil Code," *Tulane Law Review*, 33 (1958-59), 7-20. A very thorough analysis of the numerous sources of modern Louisiana Law is John H. Tucker, Jr.'s, "Source Books of Louisiana Law," *Tulane Law Review*, 6 (1931-32), 280-300; 7 (1932-33), 82-95; 8 (1933-34), 396-405; 9 (1934-35), 244-267. Tucker's "Tradition and Technique of Codification in the Modern World: The Louisiana Experience," *Louisiana Law Review*, 25 (1965), 698-719, examines the relevance of the Louisiana tradition given the uniqueness of its history. Finally, a review of the contemporary relation of Louisiana law to the rest of American law can be found in George A. Pope, "How Real Is the Difference Today between the Law of Louisiana and That of the Other Forty-seven States?" *George Washington Law Review*, 17 (1949), 186-198. Two useful articles that deal with the comparison of civil law and common law are Max Rheinstein's "Some Fundamental Differences in Real Property Ideas of the 'Civil Law' and the Common Law Systems," *University of Chicago Law Review*, 3 (1936), 624-635, and his "Common Law and Civil Law: A Comparison," *Pennsylvania Bar Association Quarterly*, 12 (1940), 7-19. For an analysis of the influence of civil law ideas in the U.S. at the time the two traditions were in conflict in Louisiana, see Peter Stein, "The Attraction of the Civil Law in Post-Revolutionary America," *Virginia Law Review*, 52 (1966), 403-434.

As a final note I need to acknowledge my indebtedness to the two nineteenth-century historians of Louisiana: François Xavier Martin and Charles Etienne Arthur Gayarré. Martin, the distinguished Louisiana jurist and the state's first court reporter, also wrote a one-volume *History of Louisiana from the Earliest Period* (New Orleans, 1827) which remains a reliable, though pedestrian, summary outline of basic factual material. Of greater distinction as a professional work of history is Gayarré's *History of Louisiana* (4 vols., New Orleans, 1885), a much more lively and intensive narrative which contains primary sources not readily available elsewhere. My few references to these two historians do not adequately represent my frequent use of their pioneering books.

Index

Acadians, 7, 8
Adair, John, 51, 52, 56, 57
Adams, John Quincy, 97, 119
Alabama River, 23
Alexander, James, 52, 56, 57
Alliott, Paul, 111
Alluvions: law concerning, 80-81, 86, 87, 161-163; and Batture, 82. *See also* Batture controversy; Civil law
American Revolution, 170
Americans: and yellow fever, 4, 11; in Lower Louisiana, 5, 6, 8, 9-10; and legal question, 11, 168, 170; litigiousness of, 17; and Claiborne, 36, 169; appointments of, 37; divisions among, 43; and Burr conspiracy, 58, 62, 72; rights asserted, 117; need for, 142; population size, 144-145, 147, 181n35; and U.S. policy, 148; prefer Baton Rouge as capital, 240n70
Ancienne population, see Louisianians; Old inhabitants
Appellate review: in civil law and common law, 16. *See also* Civil law; Civil law and common law; Common law
Arpent, 178n12
Assessors, 122
Atakapas, 5
Avoyelles, 8

Batiza, Rodolfo, 161, 163, 164
Baton Rouge, 5, 23, 240n70
Batture, 74, 162, 178n9
Batture controversy, 161; and Burr conspiracy, 78, 90-91; perceptions and interest in, 18, 79, 80, 83-84, 93; politics of, 90; and Congress, 97; *Livingston* v. *Jefferson*, 98-99; concluded, 99; ramifications, 100-101; and legal question, 127, 155-156, 164, 172; J. B. S. Thierry and, 165. *See also* Livingston, Edward
Batture St. Mary: and Livingston, 65, 75-76; and MaCarty, 71; Gravier case, 74, 75; Jefferson's policy on, 76-78; and other alluvions, 84-85; Jefferson's brief on, 95-96
Bastrop lands, 31, 51-52
Battle of New Orleans, 152, 181n36, 187-188n9
Baudin, A., 110-111
Bayou Lafourche, 5, 8
Bayou St. John, 24
Bayou Teche, 5, 8
Beleurguy, Claudius, 165, 166
Bellechasse, Joseph Deville Degoutin, 33; officeholder, 35, 196n121, 226n28; and religious dispute, 45; praised, 62; attacks Thierry, 165, 167
Blacks, 7, 43
Blackstone, Sir William, 170, 235n43, 236-237n59
Bollman, Justus Erick, 52, 55, 56, 63, 64
Boré, Etienne, 28, 35, 36, 62, 196n121
Bradford, James M.: as printer, 38-39, 42, 60, 71, 156; seeks appointment, 38-39; abuses Claiborne, 40; and religious matters, 45, 47; during "reign of terror," 57, 62, 66
Breckinridge, John, 39
Briggs, Isaac, 26-27, 42, 44
Briggs, Joseph, 34
Brown, James: appointed to office, 34; and Bradford, 39; alleged Burrite, 56; in treason trials, 58; and legal question, 114-115, 131-132, 141, 154-155; on Claiborne, 122; characterized, 152; and habeas corpus, 201n34; newspaper subscriber, 206n86; on Batture, 210n21; on militia scheme, 228n60
Brown, Jeremiah, 149-153
Brown, John, 39
Brown, Samuel, 56
Burr, Aaron, 51, 53, 55, 64; trial of, 53, 59, 63, 65
Burr conspiracy, 90; purposes, 51-52, 54; political impact, 53, 55, 58, 61-62, 63, 66, 69-70, 72, 166; and "Mexican Association," 55-56, 58-59; and "reign of terror," 56, 57, 64, 72; cipher letters, 55; and Wilkinson, 59-60, 65; from national view, 72; and local tensions, 72-73; and legal question, 73, 155, 167; Clark-Wilkinson dispute, 90; and

Batture, 90-91; as "conspiracy," 198n2; and Louisianians, 201n29. *See also* Wilkinson, James

Cantarelle, Michael, 36
Carondelet Canal, 24
Casa Calvo, Marquis de, 42, 43, 46
Case law, 16
Cause, 14
Chase, Philander, 47
Chase, Samuel, 120
Chew & Relf, 62, 64, 68
Civil law, 115, 137, 138; in Lower Louisiana, 11, 79, 155, 157, 171-172, 174, 232-233n17; and equity, 16; establishment of, 49, 114, 116, 131, 132, 147, 151-152, 153, 155, 156; and Batture, 80; proponents, 135-136; defended, 137-141; and code, 140, 141; and Claiborne, 146, 154, 157, 167-168; Digest (1808) and, 157-158; differences within, 164; attacked, 166; meaning, 181-182n43, 215n91, 226-227n45; in Quebec, 229-230n69; accepted, 167. *See also* Common law
Civil law and common law: differences, 12-16; contrasts and conflicts between in Louisiana, 17, 18-19, 49-50, 106, 117, 121, 129, 131, 135-136, 138-139, 147, 149-150, 152, 164, 172, 235-236n44, 239n68; and Batture, 80, 83, 94-95, 100-101; transition between, 127; Jefferson on, 218n6. *See also* Civil law; Common law
Claiborne, Richard, 226n27
Claiborne, William C. C.: early career, 25; characterized and criticized, 26, 27, 28, 37, 42, 43-44, 121-122, 131, 204n63, 226-227n45; problems as governor, 26; and ethnic conflict, 27-28; wants limited self-government, 28-29; defenses of 30-31, 37, 60, 68-69, 77, 91, 124-125, 146-147, 148, 166; and Remonstrance, 32; political position, 32-33, 38, 47-50, 60, 62, 63, 73, 122, 125; appointments policy, 33-36, 47-48, 62, 70-71; accuses Livingston, 35; address by, 36-37; press relations, 40-41, 42, 43-44, 70; opposes party spirit, 41; on religious questions, 46, 47; on legal question, 49, 50, 108, 109-110, 113, 114, 115-116, 124, 128, 129-130, 136-137, 140, 141, 145-146, 154, 155-157, 167-168; and Americans, 49, 169; and Burr problems, 53-55, 57-58, 64, 71, 72; and Louisianians, 62, 63, 65, 70, 168-169; and Jefferson, 71; and Batture and Livingston, 76, 77, 89; powers, 105; and militia scheme, 145; assessed, 169; personal factors, 197n131
Clark, Daniel: political position, 9, 32 38, 49, 61, 64; identified and characterized, 31-32, 42, 191n41; as officeholder, 35, 36, 71; and Burr plot, 54, 55, 62, 63-64, 65-66, 67, 72, 100, 165; controversy surrounding, 64, 66-69, 91, 165, 166; other activities, 204-205n72, 213n72
Code Civil (Fr.) *see* Napoleonic Code
Code Noir, 7, 171, 238n62
Codes and codification, 16, 150; need for, 114, 116, 129, 140, 141, 152; of Spanish law, 136; of Louisiana law, 146, 154, 156; and Louisiana Digest, 157-158, 164; meaning of, 169-170; of common law, 225n23; of commerce, 237-238n61
Commandants, 116, 135, 149; continued, 105, 192n49; popularity of, 109, 133, 134; procedures of, 221n44
Commentaries on the Laws of England, 170. *See also* Blackstone, Sir William
Common law, 112, 115; favored, 11, 107, 121, 123-124, 170, 224n5, 229-230n69; and Batture, 80, 94; opposed and criticized, 93, 130-131, 132, 134, 136, 150, 151, 167, 168, 171, 226-227n45, 237-238n61; guarantees, 106; introduction and problems, 106, 113, 114, 115, 118, 119, 122, 124, 129-130, 135-136, 139-140, 142, 145, 147, 153, 154, 157, 166; in Northwest Ordinance, 128; and Louisiana, 138, 166, 171, 172; characterized, 140, 148, 151, 173; in U.S., 147; uncodified, 170; defined, 182n44; codification of, 225n23; in Quebec, 229-230n69; influence disputed, 235n43. *See also* Civil law; Civil law and common law
Common lawyers, 17. *See also* Lawyers and judges
Community property system, 12
Company of the West, 8
Congress, U.S.: and government of Lower Louisiana, 29, 30, 48, 105, 106-107, 108, 120, 128, 136, 137, 138; memorialized, 30; supported, 117, 134; and militia scheme, 142, 145
Consideration, 14
Constitution (La.), 132, 171
Constitution (U.S.), 138, 171

Corpus Juris Civilis, 112
County courts, 106, 133, 134
Courrier de la Louisiane, see *Louisiana Courier*
Court of commerce, 237-238n61
Court of pleas, 105, 121, 125
Courts: in common law, 15, 16; established, 105, 124, 125; confusion in, 110-111, 112; criticized, 113, 116, 117, 121-123; and Louisiana Digest, 158; French attitude, 168
Creoles, 7-8, 9, 10, 179n24. *See also* Louisianians, Old inhabitants
Crimes act, 121
Criminal law, 127. *See also* Civil law; Common law; Spanish law
Cushing, William, 97
Custom, 158, 232-233n17
Custom of Paris, *see* French law

Dainow, Joseph, 160, 235n44
Daveiss, Joseph H., 53, 198-199n3
Davis, Samuel, 64, 68
Dayton, Jonathan, 55
De La Vergne manuscript, 160, 161, 162
De Sedella, Antonia, 45-46
Delabigarre, Peter, 34
Delorme, Hazure, 132, 135
Derbigny, Pierre, 137, 151; in politics, 35, 37, 118, 121, 123, 196n121; and Batture, 77, 79-81, 82, 83, 87; on civil law, 127
Destréhan, Jean Noël, 35, 118, 196n121, 226n28
Dickerson, Mahlon, 34
Dickinson, John, 144, 232n6
Digest of the Civil Laws . . . (1808): contents, 14, 156, 161-163; and Claiborne, 50, 132, 146, 167, 169; in political and historical context, 73, 101, 165, 169, 170, 171, 173-174, 235-236n44; James Brown and, 114; and legislature, 154, 155-156, 157-158; purposes, 157-158, 159-160, 237n60; sources of, 160-164, 169. *See also* Codes and codification
District Court (U.S.), 152
Doctrine, 172. *See also* Civil law and common law
Domat, Jean, 163
Dorcier, Eugene, 36
D'Orgenois, Le Breton, 35, 76, 95
Dow, Robert, 36
Dower, 12
Dubreuil de Villars, Joseph, 29, 112, 196n121
Dubuys, Gaspar, 36
Dunbar, William, 108
Duncan, Abner, 58, 62
Duponceau, Peter S.: supports Livingston, 79, 90, 91, 100; on Batture, 80, 83, 84, 87

Encyclopedia, 77
English (language): community, 9; official use, 10; and appointments, 15; newspapers, 38; need for, 123; and Louisiana Digest, 156, 159, 161. *See also* Americans
English law, 161. *See also* Common law
English Turn, 9
Eppes, John Wyles, 97
Equity, 16
Esquisse de la Situation Politique . . . , 37, 121-123, 127
Eustis, William, 182n45
Evidence, 16

Family Councils, 15
Faubourg St. Mary, 10, 64, 74, 94, 181n37
Febrero, Josef, 237n60
Federalist party, 34, 193n78
Feme Covert, 12
Fidei Commissum, 14
Florida, 23. *See also* West Florida
Forced heirship, 4, 13
Fort Petites Coquilles, 23
Fort Plaquemines, 24
Fort St. John, 24
Fort San Carlos, 23
Fortier, J. M., Jr., 62, 99
Franklin, Mitchell, 160
Free people of color, 7
French (inhabitants): attitudes to Americans, 4, 11; in Lower Louisiana, 6, 7-8, 10; and the Spanish, 28; on legislative council, 48; during Burr conspiracy, 58; and America, 144; oppose courts, 168; size, 181nn34, 35. *See also* Louisianians; Old inhabitants
French (language): and appointments, 35; newspapers, 38; problems, 116-117; opposed, 131; and Louisiana Digest, 156, 159, 161
French Canadians, 229-230n69
French law, 112, 132; and Batture case, 80, 81, 82, 83, 84, 86, 87, 96, 99, 161-163, 234nn34, 36; superseded by Spanish, 158-160, 164; as source of Digest, 160, 161, 164; little attachment to, 233n18. *See also* Civil law; Spanish law
French Revolution, 170
Future interests, 14

Gallatin, Albert, 76, 78, 99, 187n3
German Coast, 8
Germans, 6, 8-9
Giles, William B., 97, 201n34
Glass, Anthony, 207n109
Governors (territorial), 30, 49-50, 188n16, 197nn128, 130
Governor's Court, *see* Courts
Graham, John, 61, 62, 64
Granger, Gideon, 39-40, 97
Gravier, Bertrand, 74, 75, 82
Gravier, Jean, 74, 75-76
Gravier v. *New Orleans*, 74, 80, 93, 101
Griffin, Cyrus, 96, 97, 98
Guardian of Freedom, 38
Guardianship, 15
Gurley, John, 10, 58, 62, 167, 196n121

Habeas corpus: provided for, 106, 126, 138; desired, 107, 136, 185n70, 229-230n69; suspension, 201n34. *See also* Common law; Jury trials
Hall, Dominick A., 34
Hatcher, William B., 77
Hobart, John H., 195n114
House of Representatives (Orleans), 42, 48, 63, 131-132, 133
Hulin-Villamil dispute, 42-43

Illegitimacy, 13
Ingersoll, Jared, 212n65
Inheritance, 13
Instructions from the Inhabitants . . . , 133-135, 154
Irish, 9

Jackson, Andrew, 51, 54
Jefferson, Thomas: on Louisiana in general, 6, 23, 24, 108, 118-119, 170, 173-174, 178n9, 182n45, 186n2; and militia scheme, 24, 142-145, 152, 232n6; on appointments, 33-36, 37, 96-98, 193n74, 196n121; opposes Federalists, 34; on Claiborne, 38, 44-45; and Burr conspiracy, 52, 53, 59-60, 198-199n3; and Livingston and Batture, 76-78, 81, 85, 87, 88, 90, 95-96, 99, 100; on John Marshall, 96, 97, 98-99, 216n108; on common law, judiciary, and legal questions, 100-101, 107, 110-111, 116, 146, 202-203n41, 216n108, 218n6, 236-237n59; as "dupe," 166; and Cabinet, 216n107
Jefferson Administration, 18, 72, 146-147
Jeffersonian Republicans, 34
Jesuits, 74

Jones, Evan, 9, 38, 61; and appointment to office, 34, 35-36, 196n121; on Louisiana, 108, 109
Judicial administration, 108, 129; problems, 108, 109-110, 113, 120; confusion and criticism, 109-111, 116-117, 121-123, 133-134, 135, 238n64; necessity of, 125; reforms favored, 154; problems elsewhere, 220n16; under Spanish, 222-223n64
Jury trials, 124, 126; in common law, 16; attitudes toward, 17, 107, 113, 134, 135, 136, 185n70, 222n64; introduced, 105, 106, 108, 110, 138; in Scotland, 219n12; in Quebec, 229-230n69. *See also* Common law; Habeas corpus
Justices of the peace, 106, 109

Kenner, William, 35, 36
Kent, James, 99, 183-184n54
Kerr, Lewis: political position, 43, 61, 72, 201n30; and Burr conspiracy, 56, 58-59, 62, 69
Kirby, Ephraim, 34, 220n31, 227n52

Lafayette, Marquis de, 34
Lake Pontchartrain, 23
Land commissioners, 78
Language problem, 112, 116-117, 118, 122, 123, 131, 152
Lanterne Magique, 66
Laussat, Pierre Clement de, 28, 105
Law, *see* Civil law; Civil law and common law; Common law; Louisiana law
Law and legal tradition, 11
Law merchant, 171
Laws in force: preserved, 105, 106, 126, 128, 136, 138; undefined, 106, 125; and Superior Court, 132; preferred, 133-134
Laws of the Indies, 110
Lawyers and judges, 136; allegedly pro-Burr, 68, 202n37, 203n42, 207n101; attitudes toward, 17, 82-83, 101, 134, 149, 150, 168, 211n30, 230-231n75, 231n77, 231n78; proliferation of, 123; and opposition to common law, 151; and criminal law, 219n12; legal knowledge of, 237n60
Legislative council, 30; established, 29, 105; early work, 36, 41-42, 47, 106; and legal question, 114, 131, 137-141, 149, 154, 155; and Claiborne, 62, 115, 125-126; appointments to, 33-36; French domination, 48

Legislature (Orleans): and legal question, 49, 132, 136-137, 140, 141, 151-152, 156, 157-158, 164; on Burr conspiracy, 58; change in, 130; opposition to Claiborne, 136-137
Lesion, 15
Levees, 3, 5
Lewis, Joshua, 208n4
Lewis, Micajah G., 44
Lewis, William, 212n65
Liberty in Louisiana, 120-121
Lincoln, Levi, 97
Livingston, Edward, 151; political position, 9, 31, 38, 61, 76, 100, 123, 218n126; and Batture, 18, 65, 75-76, 77, 81-82, 84, 99, 209n9; other activities, 32, 42, 214n81; and Burr conspiracy, 56, 57, 59, 60, 62, 68, 77; trips to Washington, 85-89, 91-93; Jefferson and Madison and, 88, 89-90, 92, 99; criticized, 91; and legal question, 100, 111-112, 114, 146, 237n60
Livingston, John, 90
Livingston, Robert R., 23, 91-92
Livingston v. *Jefferson*, 95, 98-99
Louisiana: in relation to America, 50, 80, 166, 229n67, 236n58, 237-238n61; District of, 105; information sought, 108; compared to thirteen colonies, 118; and Batture controversy, 155-156; laws in force in, 159-160, 171-172, 239n68; ethnic divisions, 180n32; under French, 190n33. *See also* Lower Louisiana; Orleans Territory; Upper Louisiana
Louisiana Bank, 91
Louisiana Courier, 38, 67, 68, 79
Louisiana Digest, see *Digest of the Civil Laws*
Louisiana Gazette, 39, 66-67, 69
Louisiana law, 7, 12, 162-163, 223n65, 237n60
Louisiana memorialists, 118-120
Louisiana Purchase and cession, 23, 26, 29-30, 105, 120; and southwestern separatism, 52; celebrated, 71; opponents of, 182n45; purposes, 218-219n7
Louisiana Remonstrance, 17, 61; preparation and purposes, 30, 32, 127, 190-191n38; grievances, 32, 116-117; and Claiborne, 32, 33, 191n45; failure of, 119
Louisiana State Law Institute, 172
Louisiana treaty, 30. *See also* Louisiana Purchase and cession
Louisianians: attitudes toward Americans, 11, 18, 45-46; uncertain allegiance of, 24, 25, 143; reaction to cession, 26-27; and first organic law, 29-30, 31; as Americans, 126; loyalty of, 166; attitude toward legal change, 14, 17, 18, 109, 110-111, 119, 133, 148, 166, 171-172; attached to civil law, 134, 138-139, 150, 169, 170, 173-174; during Burr conspiracy, 58, 60, 63, 73; and Claiborne, 65, 168-169; and U.S., 69, 144; and Batture controversy, 93; and self-government, 118, 119, 142, 190-191n38; criticized and defended, 118, 143, 165-166, 181n39, 228n55.
See also Old inhabitants
Lower Louisiana: described, 3, 5; population in, 6-11; and statehood, 6, 125; French culture in, 8; ethnic conflict in, 9, 10, 11, 27-28, 135, 180n31, 189n22, 195-196n114, 207n100; legal clash and confusion, 11, 12, 17, 18-19, 113, 116, 154; vulnerability of, 23-24, 72, 90, 143, 144, 145, 152; in relation to U.S., 25, 50, 72, 119, 123-124, 138-139, 143-144, 146-147, 148, 151, 152-153, 156, 170, 173-174, 182n45, 232n6; governor of, 26; government established, 29; and Burr conspiracy, 53; Jefferson and, 107-108; militia scheme, 144-145; and Quebec compared, 148; Protestants in, 195-196nn114, 115, 116; lawyers in, 230-231n75, 231nn77, 78. *See also* Louisiana; Orleans Territory
Lyon, James, 38, 40

MaCarty, John B., 62, 71, 76, 79, 196n121
Madison, James: and Louisiana, 23, 108, 186n2; on Claiborne, 44; and Batture, 76, 77, 86-87, 88; judicial appointments, 96-97
Magruder, Allan B., 113
Marbury v. *Madison*, 216n108
Marigny, Bernard, 100, 172-173, 208n5
Marriage regime, 12, 139, 235n41
Marshall, John, 53, 59, 63, 98-99
Mather, James, 36, 60, 62, 203n51
Mathews, George, 132, 208n4
Mead, Cowles, 54, 204n61
Mexican Association, 55-56, 58-59, 60, 67
Militia scheme: proposed, 24, 142-145, 152, 227n52, 230n71; and Burr conspiracy, 52; and legal question, 11f,

147, 148, 155, 232n6
Mississippi Delta, 5
Mississippi River: settlements, 3, 4; roadway along, 5; and human fertility, 6; Americans along, 9, 10; gunboats on, 24, 188n10; as dump, 178n9
Mississippi Territory, 23, 52, 57, 107, 108, 227n52
Moniteur de la Louisiane, 38, 68
Monroe, James, 23, 35
Moreau Lislet, Louis, 82-83, 88, 141, 155, 159-160, 161; Batture argument, 82-83; jurisconsult, 141, 155; characterized, 152; on Louisiana law, 159-160
Morgan, Benjamin, 33, 35, 62, 114
Mowry, John, 69

Nacogdoches, 46
Napoleonic Code, 152, 156, 160, 161, 163. See also *Digest of the Civil Laws*
Natchez, 5, 39
Natchitoches, 5, 46, 180n30
National Intelligencer, 118, 146-147, 165, 166
New Iberia, 9
New Orleans: descriptive, 3, 4, 5, 178n9; population, 4, 6, 7, 9, 10-11; ethnic divisions in, 10, 11, 27-28, 240n70; Batture and, 18, 76, 78, 82, 83, 99; strategic weakness of, 23-24, 53, 152; newspapers in, 38, 39; Protestant church established, 47; and Burr conspiracy, 52, 53, 55, 56, 57; ropewalk in, 64; fire in, 205n78; theater in, 222n63
Newspapers and the press: and Claiborne, 37, 40-41, 42; in New Orleans, 38, 194n94; and political controversies, 66-69, 79, 165
Northwest Ordinance, 128, 129, 136, 137, 151, 224n5
Notaries, 15

Obligations (legal), 139
Ogden, Peter, 52, 55, 56, 57
"Old Code," 157
Old inhabitants: as group, 8, 9, 18, 37, 172; loyalty of, 58, 62, 67, 70, 201n29; and Claiborne, 62, 63; on legal questions, 101, 106, 115, 127, 128-129, 135, 164, 168; desire statehood, 118. *See also* Louisianians
Opelousas, 5
O'Reilly, Alexander, 45, 159
Orleans Gazette: as political organ, 38, 39, 42, 148-149; on religious questions, 45, 47; anti-Wilkinson, 66; pro-Livingston, 79; supports common law, 156
Orleans Territory, 26; government established, 29, 48, 49-50, 105, 108, 128, 190n28; slaves embargoed, 30; political activity in, 34, 118-120; press in, 39-40; ethnic-religious tensions in, 45-46, 47, 65, 168; Burr conspiracy and, 53, 60, 61-62, 69-70, 72; vulnerability of, 63; Batture controversy and, 74, 93, 95; statehood question, 119, 120, 145; legal question in, 127, 138, 139, 144-145, 146-149, 155, 156, 157; in relation to U.S., 146-147, 149, 152-153; appointments to, 220n31. *See also* Louisiana; Lower Louisiana
Ouachita River, 5, 9, 31, 51-52

Paine, Thomas, 118, 143-144, 228n55
Partible inheritance, 4
Partidas, see *Siete Partidas*
Pascal, Robert A., 160
Pearl River, 23, 24
Pintard, John, 108
Pledge, 15
Plumer, William, 119, 143
Poindexter, George, 93, 94
Pointe Coupée, 8
Politics and parties: absence of, 11; nature of, 34, 44, 180n31, 195n100; factionalism, 37, 38; attitudes toward, 41, 47, 201n36; and legal question, 165, 167; Federalists nonexistent, 193n78; and Burr conspiracy, 198-199n3
Pollock, George, 36, 114
Poydras, Julian: American defender, 9,; as officeholder, 33, 35, 36, 37, 71, 196n121; praised, 62, 216n94; and Batture controversy, 82, 83, 84, 93-95, 97, 101, 215n91; and legal question, 126, 130-131, 155
Practice act (1805), 100, 112
Pradel, Jean, 74
Precedent, 172. *See also* Civil law and common law
President, U.S., 146-147. *See also* Jefferson, Thomas
Prevost, John B., 34, 42, 122; on judicial administration, 113-114; on laws in force, 132, 135, 137, 151
Private law, 140
Procureurs, 112
Projet (of *Code Civil*), 156, 161-162, 163, 164. *See also* Codes and codification

Property, 13-14, 18, 139. *See also* Batture controversy
Protestant Episcopal Church, 42

Quebec, 148, 229-230n69
Quincy, Josiah, 182n45

Randolph, John, 59, 65, 119, 120
Rapides, 180n30
Rawle, William, 212n65
Real property, 183-184n54
Recopilacion de Indias, 158
Red River, 5, 9
Reibelt, Philip, 202n37
"Reign of terror," *see* Burr conspiracy; Wilkinson, James
Religious dispute, 45-46
Renard, André, 74
Revised Civil Code (1825), 157, 158, 162, 234n34
Rigolets, 23
Riparian law, 75, 161-163. *See also* Alluvions
Rodney, Caesar, 76, 77, 88
Roman, John, 35
Roman law, 124, 138; and alluvions, 83, 86, 87; in Louisiana, 132, 158, 160, 161, 163
Ross, George, 60

Sabine River, 46, 52
Saint Domingue, 8
Santo Domingo, 7
Sauvé, Pierre, 35, 118, 196n121, 226n28
Scots, 9
Sheffey, Daniel, 92
Ship Island, 23-24
Siete Partidas, 82, 158, 159, 162, 163. *See also* Spanish law
Slaves and slavery, 6, 7, 30, 31, 171, 190n33, 191n45
Smith, Samuel H., 146
Spain, 9, 18, 24-25, 46, 52
Spanish law, 111, 112, 122, 123, 148, 166, 170; and Batture case, 75, 81, 82, 83, 84, 95, 96; and alluvions, 86, 87, 161, 162, 163; system criticized and caricatured, 108-109, 121, 222-223n64; attempted establishment of, 116, 130, 135, 136, 140, 145; in force in Louisiana, 124, 132, 158-160; restoration desired, 127; and Louisiana Digest, 160, 161, 164; and French law, 164; positive evaluation of, 223n65. *See also* Civil law; French law
Sprigg, William, 56, 208n4
Sterrett, James, 37, 43-44, 56, 60
Stoddard, Amos, 158
Story, Joseph, 97, 99
Strawbridge, George, 237n60
Substitutions, 14
Successions, 139
Superior Court: functions and practice, 42, 125, 134, 135, 151; and Batture, 74, 75, 79, 99, 101, 163, 208n4; established by Congress, 105, 113; on laws in force, 132, 137, 140; on Louisiana Digest, 158-159; appointments to, 216n108. *See also* Courts
Swartwout, Samuel, 52, 55, 56-57, 63

Telegraphe, 38, 45, 148
Terre aux Boeufs, 9
Thierry, J. B. S., 172; as public printer, 40, 71; on various persons, 67, 68, 147-148, 165, 206n97, 210n25; on Batture, 79, 82, 83, 84, 87, 90-91, 101; attacked, 165; on Burrism and legal question, 167
Thirteen colonies, 148
Tilghman, Edward, 212n65
Tombigbee River, 23
Trist, Elizabeth, 209-210n19
Trist, H. B., 220n31
Trusts, 238-239n66
Tulane Law Review, 161
Tutors, 15
Tyler, John, 96, 98-99

Uniformity of law, 116, 123-124, 125
Union, 38, 40, 41, 71
United States, 12, 25, 76. *See also* Congress, U.S.; Jefferson, Thomas; Louisiana; Lower Louisiana; Orleans Territory
Upper Louisiana, 24

Vermillion River, 5, 8

Walsh, Patrick, 45-46
Warranties, 15
Watkins, John: officeholder, 33, 35, 36, 60, 63, 114; in politics, 56, 59, 61, 62, 72
West Florida, 23, 186n2, 187n3
Wickham, John, 98
Wilkinson, James: role in Louisiana, 24, 25-26, 52, 62; and ethnic conflicts, 27, 28; and appointments, 34; and Burr conspiracy, 51, 52, 54-55, 56; "reign of terror," 56-57, 77, 91; praised and condemned, 58, 59-60, 65; and Clark, 62, 66, 67, 100, 165; defends Louisianians, 67

Wolcott, Alexander, 97
Workman, James: political position, 43, 61, 72, 123; and Burr conspiracy, 56, 57, 58-59, 60, 69; and legal question, 120, 124, 127
Worthington, Thomas, 143
Wykoff, William, 35, 36

Yazoo lands, 214n84
Yellow fever, 4, 11, 181n40

Bei Fragen zur Produktsicherheit wenden Sie sich bitte an:
If you have any questions regarding product safety,
please contact:

Walter de Gruyter GmbH
Genthiner Straße 13
10785 Berlin
productsafety@degruyterbrill.com